Daniel Hobohm

Investors in Private Equity Funds

GABLER RESEARCH

Daniel Hobohm

Investors in Private Equity Funds

Theory, Preferences and Performances

With a Foreword by Prof. Dietmar Harhoff, Ph.D.

GABLER

RESEARCH

Bibliographic information published by the Deutsche Nationalbibliothek
The Deutsche Nationalbibliothek lists this publication in the Deutsche Nationalbibliografie; detailed bibliographic data are available in the Internet at http://dnb.d-nb.de.

Dissertation Ludwig-Maximilians-Universität München, 2009

1st Edition 2010

Editorial Office: Ute Wrasmann | Jutta Hinrichsen

Gabler is part of the specialist publishing group Springer Science+Business Media.
www.gabler.de

Cover design: KünkelLopka Medienentwicklung, Heidelberg
Printed on acid-free paper
Printed in Germany

ISBN 978-3-8349-2183-3

Foreword

As the world emerges from one of the biggest financial crises in history, the list of causative factors for the global bubble that preceded it becomes clear. A lack of transparency in the investment markets, a rush to illiquid assets and a glorification of aggressive investment strategies are some of those factors. If we can learn anything from the crisis, it definitely includes that many of the largest and most important investors knew too little about how to deal with investments outside the classic, public stock markets.

Indeed, investments in illiquid Private Equity (PE) and Venture Capital (VC) funds have played a significant role in many seemingly low-risk, high-return investment strategies, even though investors in these funds had few guidelines from academics or regulators on how to treat this asset class.

This is unfortunate, not only because these funds play a crucial role in the financing of non-public companies – e.g. the essential financing of many innovative start-up firms or the capital investments in so many non-public medium-sized companies. The lack of analysis is also regrettable, since economically important investors, e.g. pension funds or insurances, seek to diversify their investments. But only few studies have empirically analyzed how investors choose and invest in PE and VC funds. Daniel Hobohm helps to fill this research gap with his doctoral thesis.

For investors, funds and academics, three overarching questions arise naturally. First, what preferences do investors have when choosing funds? Second, what returns do they achieve with their investments? Third, do the various types of investors differ in their preferences and returns when investing in different types of funds? In his study, Daniel Hobohm relies on an extensive database of past investments in funds. He can therefore tackle these important questions empirically, using data from more than a decade and for several global regions.

His results show, for example, that different types of investors, e.g., pension funds vs. insurances, are characterized by distinct investment preferences.

He also finds that there is a very high degree of home bias and asks whether endowments have adjusted their fund allocations differently following external shocks. When analyzing investment returns, he challenges the notion that endowments have always been the best PE fund investors and questions the usefulness of external advisors in the fund selection process. Finally, in an innovative investigation, his results suggest that physical proximity between fund investors and VC funds is much more important for picking good funds than has been shown in prior research.

Daniel Hobohm's results will spur a range of discussions on fund investing, fund raising and on how to study this important asset class. His study helps to understand this asset class much better, and he creates pointers for all stakeholders dealing with PE, VC and investing in general. This book is therefore warmly recommended to practitioners and academic researchers alike.

Prof. Dietmar Harhoff, Ph.D.

Preface

'To end the work designed, a pair of hands needs but a thousand minds.'*

Indeed, it is hard to pay tribute to all who have helped me. Foremost, I would like to thank Prof. Harhoff, whose passion for empirical research, trust in my abilities and fantastic support motivated me throughout the years. Similarly, Prof. Rudolph always proved a great source for ideas and help. In addition, Prof. Lerner and Prof. Kerr offered many valuable comments.

Of my fellow doctoral students, I thank in particular Markus Ampenberger & Philip Mayrhofer. During our extended research experiences abroad, both advanced their own research, but still found time to read, review & criticize my work. In addition, many students in various seminars & classes asked all those tricky questions that turn a research idea into a thesis – thank you!

There is also an uncountable number of people in my life who have helped me indirectly. I owe so much to so many professors, teachers, their supporting staff, but also to my family, my godparents and friends. It would be nearly impossible to name them all. Most significantly, they instilled in me the curiosity to ask questions and to pursue an answer. Without this desire a doctoral thesis would have been nearly impossible.

I am also indebted to the Studienstiftung des Deutschen Volkes for supporting my financially and for their fantastic doctoral seminars.

Finally, I dedicate this work to all who have raised me and who have given me a home: My parents. And Elisabeth, as well as Inge & Mike, Brigitte and Lucia & Roger.

Daniel Hobohm

*Johann Wolfgang von Goethe, and translator Philip Wayne, may forgive me for humbly adapting their words: "To end the greatest work designed, A thousand hands need but one mind." – Faust II, translated version published by Penguin Classics, London, 1959.

Contents

List of Figures

List of Tables

List of Abbreviations

CA	Cambridge Associates
CalPERS	California Public Employees' Retirement System
CEO	Chief Executive Officer
DB Pension Plan	Defined Benefit Pension Plan
DC Pension Plan	Defined Contribution Pension Plan
DD	Due Diligence
EUR	Euro
EVC	Early Venture Capital Fund
EVCA	European Venture Capital Association
GLM	Generalized Linear Model
GP	General Partner
IMF	International Monetary Fund

Continued on next page

IPO	Initial Public Offering
IRR	Internal Rate of Return
Log-L.	Log-Likelihood
LP	Limited Partner
LSW	Lerner, Schoar, and Wongsunwai (2007b)
LVC	Late Venture Capital Fund
MLE	Maximum Likelihood Estimator
MLogit	Multinomial Logit
Opp.	Opportunity Funds
OLS	Ordinary Least Squares
PA theory	Principal-Agent Theory
PE	Private Equity
PE FoF	Private Equity Fund-of-Funds
PME	Public Market Equivalent
PP Fund	Public Pension Fund
PPP	Purchasing Power Parity
PreQin	Private Equity Intelligence

Continued on next page

Q-Q	Quantile-Quantile
ROW	Rest of the World
SPF	Sovereign Pension Fund
SWF	Sovereign Wealth Fund
USD	US Dollar
VC	Venture Capital
VE	Venture Economics
bn	billion
mn	million
e.g.	exempli gratia (Latin: 'for example')
i.e.	id est (Latin: 'that is')
vs.	versus (Latin: 'against')

Chapter 1

Introduction

1.1 Investments in Private Equity Funds

Little is known about the heterogeneity in investment strategies and success across different investor types. Since investor types, e.g. endowments, insurances or asset managers, differ in their economic role, one may expect them to differ in the way they participate in international investment markets. As investment intermediaries for their clients, they may also be differentially subject to information asymmetries. Shleifer and Vishny (1997) argue that such information asymmetries create limits to arbitrage, which in turn affects portfolio strategies and success from investing. Other differences that could affect investment choices are country-specific legislation, organizational structure, and investment objectives.

A limited body of literature documents such heterogeneity.[1] There is also anecdotal evidence that some investors, for instance endowments, are institutionally less restricted in their investment possibilities than others.[2] Other factors for investor heterogeneity that have been cited are internal incentives for employees of investor types, inadequate human resource management and

---

[1] See Gompers and Metrick (2001) as an example: They document that institutional investors prefer stocks with greater market capitalization and liquidity. Other papers link institutional stock purchases to the trading volume (Barber and Odean (2006)), herding (Lakonishok et al. (1992)) and investment styles (Froot and Teo (2004)).

[2] See Swensen (2000) for this argument.

investment objectives that extend beyond pure return-generation.[3]

However, empirical work is limited by difficulties of obtaining comparable data for different investor types. For example, some investors trade often and quickly in public stock. Those activities therefore leave little lasting record of their specific investment decision. Investments in private equity (PE) funds, however, differ in this respect. PE funds usually acquire large parts, often the entire shareholdings, of companies. The target firms are either already 'non-public', i.e. their shares are not publicly traded, or the PE fund acquires such a significant shareholding to turn the firm non-public, and therefore private. Those activities require a long time horizon. Naturally, then, investments in those PE funds are therefore long-term and illiquid. Hence, once an investor commits to invest in a fund, this decision remains lasting evidence of the investors decision. For this reason, a study of investor differences should be particularly fruitful in the PE industry.

While PE is a fascinating test-bed to examine differences in investor decisions, it is also an important and growing asset class in its own right. With its relatively high expected return and low correlation to other asset classes, PE can play a significant part in the portfolio allocation of diversifying investors. Average yearly returns, measured usually as the internal rate of return (IRR), are usually estimated to be at least 10%,[4] and empirical studies suggest that investors should allocate between 5% and 10% of their portfolio to PE.[5] However, the variance of returns on the level of the individual PE fund is generally quite high and investors in PE funds do face the possibility of either enjoying very high returns, but also a total loss of investment.[6] Hence, investors are very interested in how to select promising funds that, at the same time, offer a risk-profile that fits the overall strategy of the specific investor type.

PE is also an important asset class for policy-makers and researchers of innovation. Venture capital (VC) funds are an important subgroup of PE in gen-

[3]See Lerner et al. (2007b).

[4]See Gompers and Lerner (2001), Jones and Rhodes-Kropf (2003), Ljungqvist and Richardson (2003a) and Kaplan and Schoar (2005).

[5]See von Braun and Harhoff (2004).

[6]See Weidig and Mathonet (2004). The risk and return of PE fund investments differ according to fund type, but also the method of investment: Naturally, investments in fund-of-funds are less risky than direct investments in PE funds.

eral. In contrast to buyout funds, who invest in established and larger firms, VC funds usually invest in young, often very innovative companies before they have significant alternative financing sources. Therefore, their role in nurturing new industries, and with them economies, is often highlighted.[7] However, there has been scant research so far on how those VC funds fundraise their own financial resources, and if their ultimate investors differ in their approach of investing in VC funds. Under the presumption that VC funds play an essential role in the growth of many technology-driven start-up firms, the question of differences across investors in VC funds gains particular significance.

For such reasons, this research focuses on the overarching question of how different investor types invest in PE funds. In this context, the investors are also known as limited partners (LPs), the fund managers as general partners (GPs).[8] However, to further specify this general question, theoretical arguments are developed first. The relationship between the investor and the PE fund can be characterized, from a theoretical viewpoint, as that of a principal and its agent. The investor thus employs the PE fund to invest in companies on its behalf. Based on this principal-agent theory, the investment decision can be matched to the general allocation process of investors. In doing so, it becomes clear the investor faces two more specific problems: How to define a PE investment strategy that fits his risk-profile, and subsequently how to select promising funds. These problems form the framework of the research and therefore define the two major research questions:

1. How do investor types differ in their preferences for private equity fund types?
2. How do investor types differ in their performance when investing in private equity funds?

In principle, the questions can be approached either by directly examining investor types, for instance through surveys, or by analyzing past, realized investment behavior. The approach in this research is primarily based on the latter strategy: I investigate up to 17,345 investment observations by 1,864 LPs in 2,444 PE funds.

[7]See, for example, Kortum and Lerner (1998) and Kortum and Lerner (2000).
[8]Generally, the term GP is often used interchangeably with (PE) fund. I, too, use this terms instead.

1.2 Related Research

This section reviews the related academic literature on PE and VC. Aim of the section is therefore to better place this research in the context of prior work and hence to underline its motivation. While there is a whole range of different themes related to this asset class, I identify four general motives: 1) Research on the macroeconomic impact of PE and VC, 2) papers on the interaction between a PE fund and its portfolio companies, 3) publications on the performance of PE funds and 4) contributions on the interaction between LPs and PE funds.

I. Macroeconomic impact. This research field is often divided by research on either VC funds or buyout (PE) funds. An important publication on the economic impact of VC funds was presented by Kortum and Lerner (1998) and Kortum and Lerner (2000). In general, this research comes to the conclusion that there is a significant relationship between the number of patents filed by firms and the support they receive through invested VC firms. In a similar vein, Frommann and Dahmann (2003) highlight the potential of VC-funded firms to create jobs and support the growth of funded firms, while Romain and van Pottelsberghe (2004) point to a positive impact of VC on the knowledge transfer between universities and firms. The research on the innovative activities is also recently mirrored for PE, and not just VC, by Lerner et al. (2008). They also find increased patenting activities by PE-financed firms, and also a higher quality of patenting, measured in patenting originality and generality. However, Davis et al. (2008) find only limited support for the notion that firms acquired by buyout firms also create more jobs than similar comparison firms. Job creation is generally lower for established, newly acquired firms and potential job growth in some segments is generally more than offset by larger job destruction through the shedding of business subsidiaries or through cost-cutting exercises.

II. The Fund-Firm relationship. This broad field can be divided into a number of different subgroups. The **selection of target companies** is one important area of research and also one of the oldest. Representative of many of those studies, Tyebjee and Bruno (1984), MacMillan et al. (1985), Riquelme and Rickards (1992), Fried and Hisrich (1994), Franke et al. (2004) or Franke et al. (2006) are particularly noteworthy. Many of these studies use direct survey-based methods to identify criteria. However, they are mostly restricted to VC investments in younger firms. Ljungqvist and Richardson (2003b) analyze also the investment behavior of non-VC funds, while Lossen (2006) takes the important step to also analyze the value of diversification on the GP level. Basis of this analysis is that the investment decision, naturally, is not just driven by the prospects of the individual firm, but also the risk-profile of the GP's portfolio. Lerner (1994) and Meuleman and Wright (2006) complement this idea by analyzing how PE firms also co-operate by syndicating deals, depending on the competitive landscape. Gompers (1996), in contrast, looks at the timing behavior of fund managers and argues that younger PE firms sell, for reasons of reputation, company shareholdings earlier than more established, older funds. Younger PE firms also more strongly underprice firms at initial public offering (IPO) in the hope of a more positive, reputationally valuable post-IPO performance.

Another area within the topic of fund-firm relations is the topic of **legal and financial control**. Staging of investments, as well as legal control rights (e.g. convertible notes) are key levers to influence the management of portfolio companies. Groundbreaking publications on this topic are Gompers (1995), as well as Neher (1999). Their arguments are partly based on agency-conflicts between the PE fund manager and the portfolio firm. This agency-problem also forms the basis for Kaplan and Stromberg (2001, and 2004). Kaplan and Stromberg (2003) look, in a large empirical analysis, at the contracts between VC firms and the companies in light of financial contracting theory. In a more general perspective, Lerner (1995) looks at the oversight of portfolio firms through representation in the board of those firms. VC firms more intensely control and monitor their portfolio companies at sensitive times of the firm, e.g. a change of the executive officer.

A third area in the fund-firm relationship is the role of advice and interaction directly with the **management team**. MacMillan et al. (1989), Sapienza and Timmons (1989) and Sapienza (1992) are papers that deal with the question if and when VC investors can add value to their shareholdings. The support by VC investors is, generally, valuable at all stages of the investment. However, it is usually most effective if non-conflictive and therefore supportive. This is to say that the VC manager can aid through experience, contacts and financial expertise. Because of those findings, young firms themselves have an important incentive to prefer established firms with good reputations. In a more recent research, Kaplan et al. (2007) look at what CEO characteristics matter most for the performance of the newly acquired firm. Interestingly, the results suggest that performance of the firms is highest if the PE firm installs, post acquisition, a 'strong' CEO that does not shy away from conflicts.

III. Performance of Private Equity. There is a range of publications on the overall performance of PE and VC funds. In principle, most studies find an outperformance of the PE asset class vis-à-vis public equity markets. Gompers and Lerner (2001), Jones and Rhodes-Kropf (2003), Ljungqvist and Richardson (2003a) and Kaplan and Schoar (2005) deserve special mention here. However, there are also critical voices. In particular, when also considering the issues of risk-adjustment and selection bias, this outperformance probably appears less significant: See Kaserer and Diller (2004) for an adjustment of European PE returns to arrive at a so-called 'public-market-equivalent' estimation and Cochrane (2005) for a correction of returns for survivorship bias. Moreover, there are some specific issues related to portfolio firm valuation and reporting standards, which prompt industry associations to try to establish standards, see EVCA (2006b) for valuation guidelines and EVCA (2006a) for reporting guidelines which also describe the intricacies of return measures such as internal rate of return (IRR). Gompers and Lerner (2000) and Diller and Kaserer (2008) also underscore the dependance of PE returns on the inflow of funds into the industry. Finally, Weidig and Mathonet (2004) and von Braun and Harhoff (2004) deal with the overall riskiness of the asset class for investors.

IV. The LP – GP relationship. The academic contributions on this topic can be further divided into research on the contracts between funds and their investors, determinants of fundraising and on the investments and performance of LPs that invested in PE funds.

An early significant work on the **contractual** relations between funds and their investors was presented by Sahlman (1990), followed by Gompers and Lerner (1996) and Gompers and Lerner (1999). Those are chiefly empiric works on a range of contracts, with a special focus on the economic relationship based on covenants, management fee and carry. Covitz and Liang (2002) also highlight the role of preferred returns. A, perhaps surprising, result of all these studies is that the economic relation between LP and GP is fairly standardized. Only in times of high demand, or for very few, outstanding, funds, the economic relation is sometimes bent in favor of the fund. The implications thereof are discussed in more detail in chapter 2.

A separate group of publications is concerned with the determinants of **successful fundraising**. Gompers and Lerner (1998) focus on industry-specific and funds-specific factors. Kaplan and Schoar (2005) established that there is a statistically significant link between the performance of one fund and its follow-on fund. This fact is likely used by investors as a signal of future performance. Hege et al. (2003) examine performance differences between the USA and Europe and come to the conclusion that parts of this can be explained by different use of contractual stipulations and covenants. In a more detailed empiric approach, Tausend (2005) investigates the actual 'hard' criteria used predominantly by fund-of-funds when screening and selecting funds. In this work, the composition and experience of the management team of VC funds are identified as the key criteria.

The third group in this topic is concerned more directly with the **investments by LPs in PE funds**. Because they are discussed in more detail in chapter 2, I only briefly discuss them here. The first is by Mayer et al. (2005) and deals with the sources of VC funds in different countries. More specifically, these authors look at Germany, Israel, Japan and the UK to establish if the investor composition, by investor type, differs for VC funds. They then aim to link those results to (historic) differences of the institutional investor landscape in the examined countries. The second important publication was published by Lerner, Schoar, and Wongsunwai (2007b), who analyzed 4618 investments of 352 US investors in 838 US PE funds. They document large heterogeneity in the performance of investor types. As had been hypothesized, endowments were particularly successful at picking funds and were also better at deciding whether to reinvest in a follow-on fund. The authors therefore conclude that investor types differ systematically in their investment strategies, and in particular in their sophistication when assessing funds.

Which research field is developed least? The literature review shows that somewhat less is known about the (I) macroeconomic impact of PE than about the (II) relationship between PE funds and their firms and the (III) performance of private equity as an asset class. Within the area of (IV) LP – GP relationships, most contributions deal with the contracts and fundraising. However, of all fields, comparably least is known about the **performance and preferences of different LP types**. Differences between LPs in various countries, or the drivers of investment success by LPs, are thus far largely unexplored. This particular research area is thus relatively young and it is this area that the research presented here fits into. To a significant degree, the research void is likely due to the unavailability of data. Yet, the dramatic growth and development of this asset class over the last decade and across the globe make this research question, from the point of view of the investors in PE funds, a particularly pressing one. With few comparative data-points on how other investor types are performing and what their preferences are, PE investors would likely welcome any increased transparency in this segment. Likewise, regulators and external observers concerned with the activities of often tax-exempt, economically important investor classes such as pension funds, insurances or endowments would welcome increased awareness of the activities of such institutions. Last, given the presumed macroeconomic significance of VC funds, policy-makers will welcome the research into their investors differ and in what way. The research presented here extends the current academic landscape in a number of significant dimensions: First, it expands the knowledge on LP preferences, as well as our understanding of structural and LP-specific characteristics that impact the LP investment decision. Second, it analyzes not just US LP performance, but also global investments and across a larger time-period than before. Third, it explores a number of additional hypotheses that could explain the investment decision by LPs, and performances therefrom. It does so by analyzing a thus far academically unpublished dataset on global LP investments from 1991 until 2005.

1.3 Aim and Structure

Aim of the research is to analyze differences across investor types in their preferences for PE funds and their performances from investments in those funds. The emphasis is on analyzing past investment decisions, based on a dataset of investments. However, this research question is novel: For either research question, preferences or performances, there are only very few existing publications and none based on theoretical considerations. Therefore, this research is a combination of *theoretical, explorative* and *quantitative, confirmatory research methods*.

The research encompasses essentially the entirety of global investor and PE fund types. This generally means a focus on differences between specific investor types on the one hand, and differences between fund types on the other hand. This means I rarely endeavor to differentiate between investors within an investor class or funds within a fund type. I also focus on the time-period 1991 to 2005. Fund investments before or after those years are not considered. The confirmatory, empirical research part is necessarily restricted by the breadth of the data. This data does not contain funds with only one investor, e.g. so-called captive or corporate PE funds.

Chapter 2 offers an introduction to the PE asset class and a discussion thereof in light of principal-agent (PA) theory. Aim of the chapter is to develop a generic LP fund investment theory with two leading hypotheses regarding the investment behavior of LPs. After discussing the historic development of the asset class, the chapter therefore reviews the principles of PA-theory in light of the PE industry. I argue that because the contracts of the investors and the funds are very standardized, a) risk-sharing and b) fund-selection challenges are of particular significance. Those are reflected in the fund investment process employed by large investors and can be empirically analyzed by looking at the a) executed investments in PE funds and b) the returns generated by those funds. The separation of fund preference and selection of funds thus forms the basis of the research.

Aim of **chapter 3** is the generation of the key empiric research hypotheses in elaboration of the results of the previous chapter. Therefore, first, different investor types are presented and their potential investment differences are discussed. Those lead to preliminary results that are the impetus for the ensuing investor interviews. The interviews help generate specific hypotheses on LP preference and LP investment performance. The results also prompt me to develop additional theoretical arguments on fund preference and selection. The chapter thus concludes with the list of key hypotheses.

To test those hypotheses, I employ a large dataset on LP investments in PE funds. **Chapter 4** therefore describes the source, preparation and characteristics of this dataset. In total, I base my analyses on up to 17,345 investment observations by 1,864 LPs in 2,444 PE funds. This is one of the largest, if not the largest, dataset analyzed for this research question. Moreover, I describe the chief econometric methods and statistical instruments used in the quantitative parts of the research.

The preferences of LPs are analyzed in **chapter 5**. The basis for this chapter lies in the previously generated hypotheses. In this empirical, quantitative chapter I first turn to the general *fund preferences*: Do certain investor types have stable preferences for specific fund types? Subsequently, I examine if LPs are subject to *home bias*, i.e. if they invest significantly more often on the home continent than would be expected. In the final section of this chapter, I then test the hypothesis that endowments, who are reputed to be among the most flexible and sophisticated investors, adjust their *overall portfolio strategy* more quickly and flexibly than other LPs.

While preferences formed the basis of the previous chapter, **chapter 6** then focuses on the performance generated by the selected PE funds. Based on the stated hypotheses, I first present average *investment returns* by LP type, both in the US and globally. These are then tested for robustness in multivariate analyses. This empiric, quantitative chapter then examines if endowments, who enjoyed particular investment success in VC funds, achieved those returns by particular *risk-taking*. Following this inquiry, the chapter then highlights the role and impact of the use of *external advisors* in the success from PE fund investments. Finally, the chapter uses the historically defined locations of public pension funds as a natural experiment to investigate what role the *geographic proximity* to successful VC funds plays in the successful selection thereof. While public pension funds are a specific fund types, the results are likely applicable to most 'average' LPs interested in the question of whether to open representative offices near active hubs of start-up activity and hence close to VC funds.

In **chapter 7** the main empiric results are summarized and discussed. This work then concludes the research with an outlook onto future research questions and opportunities.

Chapter 2

Theory of Fund Investments

This chapter aims to place the asset class private equity in the framework of principal-agent theory. Section 2.1 develops a generic theory of fund investments. Key corollaries of this theory are that investors must take special care to a) choose funds in accordance with their risk-sharing preferences, and b) then to select funds out of a group of possible alternatives. In section 2.2, existing empirical research is examined in light of this proposition, before the chapter is concluded in section 2.3.

2.1 Risk-Sharing and Selection

The private equity (PE) and venture capital (VC) industry has experienced dramatic increases in size over the last decades.[1] From early VC funds in the 1950s, the industry has grown to be of significant importance for both the entrepreneurial, private, as well as public markets. For instance, even before the boom this millennium, from 1980 to 1995, the industry grew from under \$ 5 bn to over \$ 175 bn annual investment volume – a compounded annual growth rate of more than 25%.[2] In 2006, this number was surpassed in Europe alone.[3]

Two changes facilitated this growth. First, in 1979 the potential investor

[1] For an overview of the PE industry, see Gompers and Lerner (1999).
[2] See Fenn et al. (1995).
[3] See http://www.evca.com. Date of access: February 13, 2008.

base changed: An amendment to the 'prudent man' rule permitted large institutional investors, in particular pension funds, to invest in PE funds. Before that, those investors were restricted from making investments in illiquid and high-risk assets such as VC funds. Prior to the amendment, therefore, only less risk-averse and unregulated investors were permitted to contribute to the asset class. The share of pension funds and similar large institutional investors has since grown significantly. For instance, the European Venture Capital Association (EVCA) records that more than 37% of commitments to PE funds stem from pension funds and insurance.[4] In the US, with its large pension funds, this share is likely higher: In 1998, Gompers and Lerner (1998) estimated that more than 40% of VC funding between 1993 and 1997 stemmed from pension funds.

The second contributing change was the rise of the limited partnership structure to govern the relations between the investors (now also Limited Partners, LPs) and the VC/PE funds (now also General Partners, GPs). While in 1980 this structure accounted for 40% of VC pools, by 1992 80% of VC assets were governed in this structure.[5] Today, it is essentially the standard for most VC/PE investment structures.

The limited partnership exchanges one principal-agent (PA) relation with another. In the absence of GPs, institutional investors would have to invest directly in portfolio companies. However, because investors have neither the time nor expertise to overcome the various due diligence and monitoring challenges associated with investments in growing or struggling companies, this task is left to the GPs. In this setting, the LP assumes the role of the principal employing the GP as an agent. However, this introduces its own problems of *hidden action*, *moral hazard* and *adverse selection* common with PA-relations. In parts, these issues are solved through the LP-GP contract, in particular the payoff-stipulations. Gompers and Lerner (1996) identified a 2%/20% contract as most common in the industry: A management fee of about 2% and a 20% profit-sharing, or 'carry' regulation. In addition, there can be 'preferred return' regulations, which limit the GP's participation in the carry unless the returns meet a minimum 'hurdle' rate. Also, instead of actively monitoring the GP, contractual covenants can be included that frame the fund's activities.

[4] See http://www.evca.com. Date of access: February 15, 2008.

[5] See Gompers and Lerner (1999).

Based on the limited deviations from these fairly standardized contracts, Gompers and Lerner (1996), Gompers and Lerner (1999) and Covitz and Liang (2002) established that in times of high demand for specific PE funds, or the industry as a whole, the archetypal 2%/20% rule can be bent in favor of the GP. Similarly, because changes to covenants and the introduction of preferred returns are costly, they are mostly only observed when the benefits thereof clearly outweigh the costs. The off-shot is that contracts are altered less often than one may expect. Another conclusion of this research is that the contracts hold essentially no signaling value for the LP.

A question that has attracted much less scrutiny, however, is what *standardized contracts* mean for the LPs. While one may argue that moral hazard problems are addressed with the economic stipulations, we know from PA-considerations in other settings[6] that the contract between the principal and the agent can also serve to

1. signal the quality of the agent and

2. balance the risk-aversion preferences between principal and agent.

Neither of these two properties, however, are appropriately addressed under standardized contracts. This puzzle is exasperated by the fact that different types of investors act as LPs. Thus, to the extent that these LPs, e.g. pension funds, insurances, endowments, investment corporations, to name but a few, are again only agents to their *own* clientele and fulfill specialized economic functions, the question remains how LPs overcome adverse selection problems and see their individual risk-sharing preferences served.

This leads me to theorize the following:

LP-specific adverse selection and risk-sharing problems are solved through differential GP-selection.

Specifically, *differential GP selection* is further specified:

- **Adverse selection** problems are solved through extensive due diligence of agents in the selection process, while

[6] See Eisenhardt (1989) for a review.

- **Risk-sharing** preferences are expressed by investing in funds that match the intended risk-profile.

Before discussing the practical implications of these assumptions, it pays to compare them to the previous assumptions of Gompers and Lerner (1996) and Gompers and Lerner (1999), who looked at the LP – GP contracts empirically. In fact, the assumption of risk-sharing preferences is in breach with their previous models. While the theory proposed here spells out that LPs, as principals, are differentially risk-averse, Gompers and Lerner (1996) believe the opposite: Because "investors in venture funds are primarily large institutions, such as pension funds and insurance companies, investor risk neutrality is reasonable.", while risk aversion of the VC manager "may result from...lack of investment portfolio diversification."[7] Under these assumptions of LP risk neutrality, risk-sharing in contracts would indeed be irrelevant. However, there are at least three reasons why this assumption may be invalid:

1. First, as agents to their own clients, the investors that act as LPs may be subject to direct or indirect investment objectives or organizational differences, especially with regard to the amount of risk-taking.[8]

2. Second, the investment decision is, in reality, not taken by the institution, but by the individual decision maker within the LP. Therefore, if his incentives are set to avoid risk-taking, then he will be interested in sharing some of his own risk with that of the investment target, the GP. This view is also mirrored by Covitz and Liang (2002): "Limited partners (e.g., an investment manager at a large public pension fund) may be very risk-averse if their own compensation contracts limit their upside potential from investments."[9]

3. Third, not even large institutions are necessarily fully diversified in PE. In fact, practically, it is exceedingly difficult to be truly diversified in

[7] Gompers and Lerner (1999), page 33 (Appendix to their work). The same authors also assume "that one investor and one venture capitalist negotiate over the terms of the compensation." and with "equal bargaining power." However, this assumption is not necessarily valid considering the multitude of LPs in both VC and PE funds.

[8] See also Shleifer and Vishny (1997) for an argument that information asymmetries between investors and intermediaries may impact investment strategies and hence returns.

[9] Covitz and Liang (2002), page 6. Brackets part of the original quotation.

> PE. Notwithstanding the fact that probably no LP, not even the largest, has access to all funds worldwide and thus could easily formulate a diversification strategy, classical risk and correlation measures as found in portfolio theory do not exist for PE funds.

Therefore, my assumption of potential, differential levels of risk-aversion of LP types seems more justified than risk-neutrality for all LP types.

As it turns out, there are two major decision points in the asset allocation process of LPs where risk-preferences and adverse selection issues are addressed – see also figure 2.1.[10] Risk-sharing and other preferences are considered primarily at the stage of defining the overall **investment strategy**. At this stage, LPs will weigh their portfolio of potential PE fund types according to their own criteria.[11] There are a number of publications that estimate the risk and return from different fund types; based on various datasets. Based on these results, one should expect more risk-averse investors to prefer historically less volatile buyout funds over VC funds.[12] It is also at this stage where some investors may try to alter the overall strategy in anticipation of the future market trends for a specific fund type. Overall, therefore, the universe of potential funds is narrowed down at this stage.

Adverse selection problems are most important, however, at the second stage when selecting individual funds.[13] It is here where, in the process of extensive and costly due diligence, funds are selected. Figure 2.1 illustrates

---

[10]Broadly speaking, when allocating their assets, investors are guided by a trade-off between return, risk and liquidity, see Steiner and Bruns (2000), page 568f. See also Rudolph (2001) and Rudolph (2003). Other criteria can also be inflation sensitivity or differential tax treatments; see Rudolph (2003). For a more thorough review see also Tausend (2005), pages 45 – 52.

[11]Based on historic values, von Braun and Harhoff (2004) calculate an optimal portfolio distribution for a large, fully diversified investor of US-VC 25%-60%, US-buyout 26%-45%, EU-VC 0%-10% and EU-buyout 13%-24%.

[12]For instance, see von Braun and Harhoff (2004), Weidig and Mathonet (2004) and Cochrane (2005).

[13]A number of publications highlight key factors in the selection of funds. There is a positive relationship between reputation and the returns of previous funds and the ease and usually also size of raising a follow-on fund – see Gompers and Lerner (1998), Hege et al. (2003) and also Kaplan and Schoar (2005). However, a narrow focus of the fund on a specific industry has not been shown empirically to have a significant effect on the fund performance, see Manyem (2002). When looking at specific criteria in the due diligence process, the study by Christian Tausend (2005) is particularly noteworthy. For a summary, see Tausend (2005), page 110 and pages 173–176.

these decision points in a simplified version.

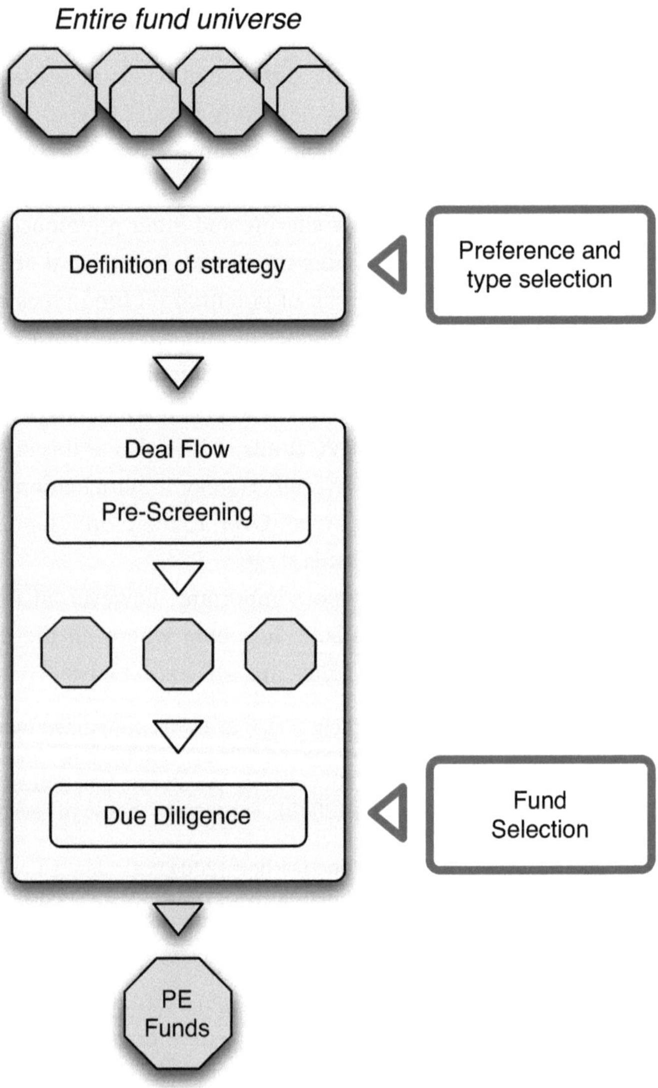

Figure 2.1: PE Allocation Process. Adapted: Tausend (2005, p. 48).

In summary, two groups of hypotheses emerge as a consequence of the generic LP investment theory.

1. **LP preferences**, e.g. risk preferences, are expressed primarily in the process of defining the overall investment strategy. It is also at this stage where flexible LPs that try to anticipate market developments may wish to adjust their portfolio weighting.

2. **LP performances**, i.e. all LPs will struggle with adverse selection and therefore more sophisticated investors should be able to select, on average, better performing funds than others.

2.2 Empirical Evidence

As the literature review showed, there are few papers on the relationship between LPs and GPs. In fact, there are only two significant publications that compare investments by different LP types in PE funds. Neither of the two develop a theory based on principal-agent theory or more generally the asset allocation of investors, but their results still offer important pointers.

The paper by Mayer, Schoors, and Yafeh (2005) examines **LP preferences** and compositions in funds. Specifically, they examined the investor composition in VC funds across different countries: Germany, Japan, Israel and the UK. Aim was to examine if the LP composition – not the returns of the LPs – differed in VC funds and if those differences could be linked to country-specific characteristics. In total, 508 VC funds were analyzed. Those were classified along a number of criteria, e.g. stage, industry or regional focus. Unfortunately, the number of LPs, or the number of their investments in those funds, is not reported; instead, the LP composition is reported in percent on a fund type level. The research is organized along two chief dimensions: Differences across LP types, and differences across countries.

In terms of differences across LP types, they find that "Financial institution (bank, pension fund and insurance company) backed funds are focused on late-stage investments."[14] Banks in particular seem to invest more in later stage VC funds. In contrast, corporate investors and individuals focus more on

[14]Mayer et al. (2005), page 602. Brackets part of the original quotation.

early stage VC funds. Interestingly, banks and governmental investors seem to also invest more often in domestically active VC funds. Insurances, corporations and individuals also invest in funds that are active globally.

With respect to differences across countries, the authors had hypothesized significant differences in the funding and activities of VC funds: Germany and Japan as so-called bank-oriented economies, the UK with a more market-based economy and Israel with its many high-tech corporations were hypothesized to differ in several regards. However, the authors could not find any significant differences.

The paper is an indication that institution-specific, but not country-specific, variation matters in terms of LP composition in VC funds. This would corroborate the theory stated in this research, which does not necessarily reflect country-specifics. The finding on home bias for banks in particular is also noteworthy. Unfortunately, however, the research only focuses on VC funds and not other types of PE funds. Moreover, it is unclear just how many LPs are examined, and what time-period. Still, in light of the theory stated in this research, the empirical results would motivate a further inquiry in the direction of LP preferences.

With regard to differences in fund selection ability and **LP performance**, Lerner, Schoar, and Wongsunwai (2007b) are particularly important. They present evidence that LP types differ dramatically in fund selection sophistication. The authors were able to analyze 352 LPs and their investments in 838 funds from 1991 to 1998.[15] In their analysis, they focus in particular on the returns, internal rate of returns (IRRs), that the funds achieved that were selected by different types of LPs. Their results are startling. Funds that were selected by endowments achieved IRRs nearly 21% – in absolute terms – higher than the average: This means that while the average IRR in the GP sample for that period was 23.7%, funds selected by endowments achieved IRRs of 44.3%. In relative terms this means that endowments picked funds

[15]The authors were able to compute mean statistics for 4,618 investments in this period, even though could only include 2,755 investment observations in most of their multivariate analysis.

that were nearly twice as successful, on a yearly basis.

These results were driven in particular by successes from early VC investments, where endowments picked funds with average IRRs of 95.4%, public endowments like university endowments even funds with 106.4% average IRR.[16] Banks, in contrast, picked funds that only achieved, on average, IRRs of 4.3% and corporate pension funds also underperformed. In addition, the authors show that LPs also differ in their re-investment patterns, i.e. to invest in follow-on funds. They find that follow-on funds that were chosen by endowments achieved significantly higher mean IRRs per fund than when other investors took the same decision, while banks again were the worst re-investors. In a set of additional tests, experience proved important, while neither access, nor excessive risk-taking can account for endowments superior performance. The authors conclude that "LPs differ in their ability to evaluate the quality of funds and to invest based on this information, that is, in their level of sophistication."[17]

While very telling, the research does leave room for questions. The analyzed dataset only covers a period during which VC funds vastly outperformed buyout funds (for instance, early-stage VC achieved even IRRs of 68.9% on average and, at the same time, buyout funds achieved only IRRs of 3.2% on average in their sample). The authors make limited note of this in their analysis, but figure 2.2, which shows benchmark performances published by Cambridge Associates, highlights this important point.[18] The authors present mean return measures, but it is not widely discussed how much of the success is driven by simply investing more often in VC funds during that time, not by better choosing VC funds than other LPs. And even though the authors include fund fixed effects in their multivariate analysis, they do not present the coefficients by fund type. It thus remains unclear how the individual fund types impacted the estimated LP returns. So while overall funds selected by endowments did outperform those selected by other LPs, it remains unclear if this successful fund selection was due to general preference for VC funds, or

[16] In fact, the authors write that the results are mainly driven by private universities, not public universities.

[17] Lerner et al. (2007b), page 733.

[18] Cambridge Associates publishes yearly performance benchmarks for the US PE industry. http://www.cambridgeassociates.com .

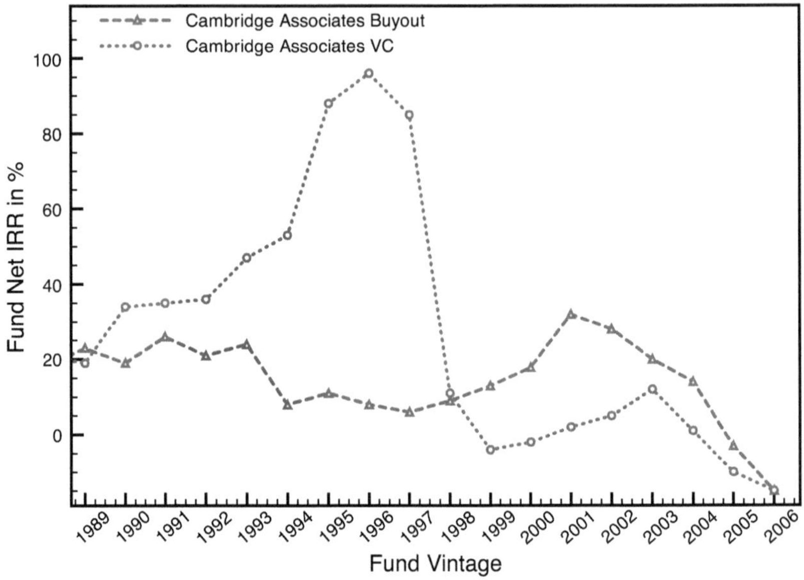

Figure 2.2: Returns of PE Funds in % of IRR and by Vintage

the sophistication to overweigh those funds and then to pick the best among those.

2.3 Conclusion

In conclusion, this chapter argued first that because economic contractual agreements with GPs are very standardized, they offer no signaling, nor risk-sharing mechanism for the LP. Therefore, under the LP investment theory described here, when investing in PE funds, LPs define a PE allocation strategy that suits their individual risk preference. Moreover, they expend large amounts of time and resources to carefully select funds. Since both steps reflect individual preference and expertise, differences in investment strategies and success can be expected. The empirical evidence thus far shows that there are LP-specific differences in preferences for VC funds, or LP composition therein. Banks and governmental investors also invested more often in domestically active funds. However, country-specific differences were insignificant. Similarly, there are large differences in returns, on a fund level, for different (US) LP types. Hence, the ability to select funds differs from LP type to LP type. However, with regard to the two groups of hypotheses, i.e. on LP fund preferences and if LPs differ in their fund selection ability, it also becomes clear that a dataset is required that a) also looks at non-VC funds in many more countries and b) that covers a longer time-horizon. The ability to pick promising funds should then be measured within a fund type, after controlling for additional factors. To develop more concise hypotheses that link investment choices to *specific* LP types, the next section reviews LPs, presents the results from interviews and introduces additional theoretical considerations.

Chapter 3

Limited Partners

This chapter develops the research hypotheses for the empirical, quantitative analysis. Section 3.1 therefore discusses the major investor types that invest in PE funds. Section 3.2 presents preliminary results that formed the basis for the explorative interviews with a number of industry practitioners. The interviews are found in section 3.3.1. Before summarizing the hypotheses, section 3.3.2 takes a few key notions of the interviews and develops specific hypotheses. Section 3.3.3 then states the hypotheses and concludes the chapter.

3.1 Different Types of LPs

The EVCA defines an LP simply as: "An investor in a limited partnership (i.e. private equity fund)."[1] To gain a sense of the relative importance of these groups, figure 3.1 presents the share of (European) PE funds by each LP type over the last 20 years. However, for graphical purposes, I group investors into four broad groups:[2] 1. Institutional investors – including pension funds and insurances, 2. Investment corporations – including asset managers, banks, fund-of-funds (FoFs), 3. Foundations and family offices – including private and university endowments, as well as family offices of rich families, and 4. Government agencies – including sovereign wealth funds, sovereign pension

[1]See the online glossary under http://www.evca.com. Brackets are part of the original quotation. Date of access: December 5, 2007.

[2]EVCA knows 10 separate LP type groups.

funds and political investment agencies. Classic institutional investors in Europe and investment corporations contribute comparable funds to PE, followed by government agencies and foundations and family offices.[3] In the following,

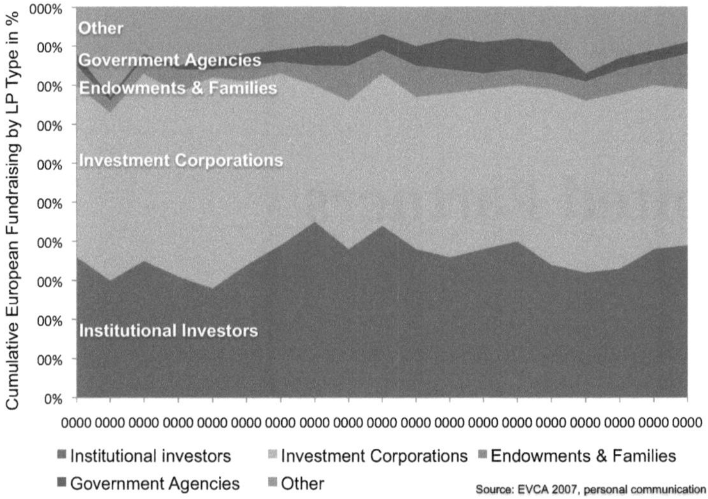

Figure 3.1: PE Fundraising by Investor Type

I describe the major LP types by function, size and role in the PE markets. In total, I describe nine major types that will also form the basis for the empirical investigation in future chapters.

Pension funds and insurances

Pension funds and insurances are often grouped under the umbrella term 'Institutional Investors'. Davis and Steil (2001) defines them as '(...) specialized financial institutions that manage savings collectively on behalf of small investors toward a specific objective in terms of acceptable risk, return maximation, and maturity claims."[4] Institutional investors thus entail different types of **pension funds**, e.g. public and corporate pension funds, as well as different

[3]The data for recent years can be found under http://www.evca.com. The data on the years before were sent to me in a personal communication.

[4]Davis and Steil (2001, p.12).

types of **insurances**.[5] They are among the largest investors worldwide, with globally managed assets reaching USD 50 trillion; and, as table 3.1 shows, with heterogeneous international distribution. Most of the largest investors are found in Anglo-Saxon countries. In fact, the importance of institutional investors has increased significantly over the last decades. Household savings are now more and more directed towards these investors to the extent that in some countries they challenge banks as the largest holders of household savings.[6] To understand how institutional investors differ in their investments, "The nature of the liabilities is the key."[7] The liability is the obligation of an institutional investor vis-à-vis the client, that is, for instance, providing retirement funding in the case of a pension fund.

[5]Mutual funds are also often included as they are specialized vehicles for a specific investment purpose.

[6]For example, the Bank for International Settlements estimates that in 2003 total world assets of commercial banks amounted to USD 49 trillion, whereas institutional investors claimed USD 47 trillion of assets under management. See CGFS (2007).

[7]Davis and Steil (2001, p. 55).

Financial Assets of Institutional Investors

Values in $ bn

Country	Insurers	Pension Funds	Mutual Funds	Total Assets	GDP[1]	% of GDP	% of largest 300 pension funds[2]
Australia	241	566	700	1507	754	199 %	
Canada	391	550	491	1432	1269	112 %	4.7 %
Euro Area[3]	4665	1149	4308	10164	9304	109 %	
Belgium	212	14	118	344	393	87 %	
France	1614	32	1363	3008	2231	134 %	
Germany	1573	238	297	2152	2897	74 %	1.9 %
Italy	528	29	451	1007	1852	54 %	
Luxembourg	53	na	1636	1689	40	4162 %	
Netherlands	407	749	126	1282	663	193 %	5.9 %
Spain	278	87	317	682	1225	55 %	
Japan	3243	997	470	4710	4367	107 %	21.0 %
Singapore	52	80	311	443	132	335 %	
Switzerland	227	338	117	681	377	180 %	1.6 %
UK	1979	1487	547	4014	2373	169 %	7.5 %
USA	5601	7306	8905	21811	13244	164 %	44.7 %
Total	16399	12472	15849	44762	31823	140 %	$ 8400 bn

Source: Committee on the Global Financial System *Institutional investors, global savings and asset allocation* CGFS Papers, Bank for international settlements, 27, February 2007.

[1]International Monetary Fund, World Economic Outlook Database. Date of access: April 4, 2007

[2]Watson Wyatt, The world's 300 largest pension funds, http://www.watsonwyatt.com. Date of access: December 3, 2007

[3]Including only the European countries as shown

Table 3.1: Financial Assets of Institutional Investors

Pension funds act as investment fiduciaries for the contributing employers. One can distinguish between defined contribution (DC) or a defined benefit (DB) plans. Generally speaking, corporate pension funds are more often of the former type, public pension funds more often of the latter type. A DB pension fund promises a specific cash benefit to the client upon retirement, usually dependent on years of total contribution and salary. Many older or public schemes are of that type. DB plans also often enjoy preferential tax-treatment over DC plans.[8] In contrast, the benefits from DC pension plans vary with the investment success of the fund managers.

The investment objectives of either fund type varies. In order to meet their liabilities, DB funds employ an investing strategy to match their clients expected claims by emphasizing bonds or inflation-secured assets in the investment portfolios. DC funds, in contrast invest more freely in assets that also include equities or alternative assets. It should also be noted that public pension funds are politically created bodies and often impressive in size as they serve a large public constituency.[9] Usually, the boards of these funds are dominated by political appointees or union members who have little understanding of investing and may even follow a political agenda when deciding on key investment strategies.[10]

Insurances differ more widely in their liabilities. For instance, life insurers offer life assurances or financial help in times of mishap, while property-casualty insurances protect against property damages or liability losses. In most cases, the insured claim is a defined nominal sum, and an insurer is thus comparable to a DB pension fund in terms of its liability. However, many life insurances

[8]See http://www.irs.gov/retirement/index.html for more information

[9]Some are among the very largest investors in the world, such as the California Public Employees' Retirement Scheme, CalPERS.

[10]For example, only six of the 13 board members of CalPERS are elected, the others are political appointees. Of the six elected members, three are elected by unions and similar stakeholders, only three are elected freely. Some may argue that political appointees may, for instance, favor investments in local industries or in companies with significant number of employees – and not necessarily in the, from a financial point of view, most promising investment targets. This political dilemma may even be aggravated by the fact that the pensions of the contributing employees, used for the investments, are ultimately guaranteed by the state which will make up for any shortfall if the fund underperforms strongly.

also offer important retirement benefits. For this reason, life insurances often have a significant variable wealth accumulating part that permits insurances to act more like DC pension plans.

The Bank for International Settlements records important international differences in the percentage of equities and bonds institutional investors hold. Anglo-Saxon institutional investors, including pension funds, hold more than 40% of their assets in relatively risky equities, while, for instance, in continental Europe, institutional investors allocate less than 20% of their portfolio to equities and instead tend to favor bonds.[11] These allocations are largely correlated to the type of DB or DC pension system prevalent in the countries. Similarly, surveys show that there are large differences in the percentage institutional investors allocate to PE. As figure 3.1 shows, Anglo-Saxon investors allocate a significantly higher share of their assets to PE than investors elsewhere.

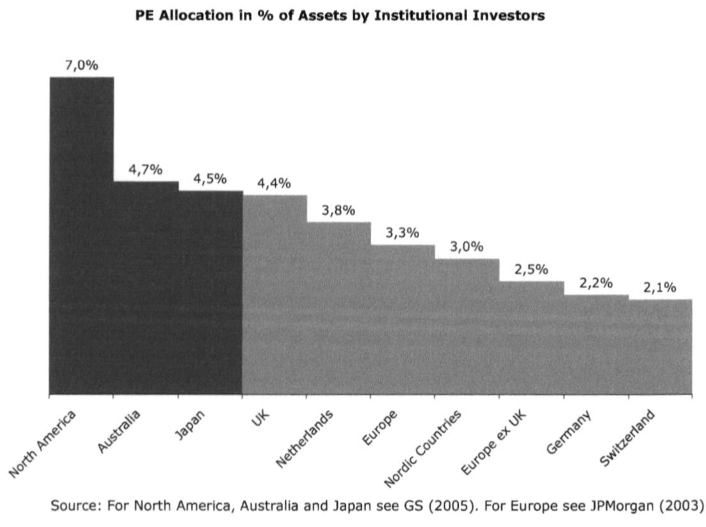

Figure 3.2: PE Allocation by Institutional Investors

Investment corporations

Investment corporations engage in the business of investment management and investment advisory to generate returns for their shareholders. Often, in-

[11] See CGFS (2007).

vestment corporations are seen as institutional investors and both terms are used with little distinction. Here, the differentiation is made that whereas institutional investors also manage investments, they do so in order to fulfill a specific saving function, for example to meet pension liabilities.[12] In contrast, investment corporations, while often investing on behalf of institutional investors, are responsible, generally, towards their shareholders, usually on a quarterly basis.

Investment corporations can include asset managers, hedge funds and similar investment companies. London's International Financial Services estimates that the global assets under management, including also banks, exceed $ 61 trillion.[13] Backed by global share price advances, these numbers have risen steadily over the past years and indeed nearly doubled since 2002. About 48 % is managed by US institutions, followed by Japan with 11 % and the UK with 7 %. Table 3.2 lists the largest asset managers in the world.[14] They professionally manage securities and assets primarily for their clients, but also *own* funds via proprietary trading vehicles. In doing so, investment corporations employ the same principles of asset allocation as others. However, a study by Froot and Teo (2004) suggests that the investments fall into a few well-defined styles.[15]

As LPs, investment corporations benefit from their experience in investing in other asset classes, including similarly illiquid real estate. They may benefit also from economies of scope as they can also generate revenues from advisory services or underwriting debt.

[12]Sometimes, institutional investors are also simply termed 'tax-exempt' organizations, as opposed to investment corporations that have to pay (higher) taxes on their investment returns. However, tax-laws differ widely from country to country and from investor type to investor type.

[13]See IFSL (2007).

[14]One should differentiate when citing these numbers. between whose assets are managed and who manages them: Institutional investors, for instance, often entrust investment corporations with their finances, yet both count these assets as 'theirs'. In the UK, about 78 % of total funds under management originate from institutional investors, the rest is split fairly evenly between retail funds, private clients and alternative funds such as hedge funds. In contrast, when viewed as assets by type of manager, only 36 % of the total UK assets are actually managed by institutional investors directly, 26 % by asset / fund managers, 17 % by retail banks and 13 % by investment banks.

[15]See also Gompers and Metrick (2001) who report a preference for stocks with higher market capitalization, high liquidity, have a higher book-to-market ratios and realized lower returns in the year before.

The World's Largest Asset Managers

Values in $ bn of assets. Ranking as of Dec. 31, 2005

Rank	Manager	Country	Assets
1	UBS	Switzerland	$ 2016
2	Barclays Global Investors	UK	$ 1513
3	Allianz Group	Germany	$ 1493
4	State Street Global	USA	$ 1441
5	Fidelity Group	USA	$ 1421
6	AXA Group	France	$ 1260
7	Capital Group	USA	$ 1165
8	Credit Suisse	Switzerland	$ 1128
9	Deutsche Bank	Germany	$ 1026
10	Vanguard Group	USA	$ 957

Watson Wyatt, The world's 300 largest pension funds, http://www.watsonwyatt.com. Date of access: December 5, 2007

Table 3.2: The World's Largest Asset Managers

Banks

Economies of scope are also particularly important for banks. As lenders to companies, they have contacts to many firms and sometimes also opt to be shareholder in companies, i.e. to undertake a direct PE investment. In the USA, three legal arrangements permit banks and bank holding companies to invest in PE. Firstly, the Small Business Act of 1958 allowed banks to set up subsidiaries for this purpose, 'Small Business Investment Corporations'. In 1956, the provision was followed by the Bank Holding Company Act which permitted banks to be shareholders in companies as long as the position did not exceed 5 % of voting rights and 25 % of total equity. In 1999, the Gramm-Leach-Bliley Act ruled that banks could set up financial holding companies to invest directly in companies. This regulation allows a ten-year holding period for direct investments and a fifteen-year holding period in PE funds. In addition, by investing in a PE fund, they may hope to generate additional revenues by providing loans for levered buyouts.[16] For these reasons, Lerner et al. (2007b) believe that many banks may even prefer investing in less promis-

[16] See Allen (1993) and Allen and Gale (2000).

ing PE funds if in turn the fund relies on the bank for the required investment banking services. Many investment corporations also founded their own PE fund, including Goldman Sachs, SVG Capital (which founded the first Permira funds but is also a FoF) and Investor AB (which is a large asset manager and which also founded the large EQT funds).

Endowments

Endowments, or foundations, are considerably smaller, on average, than other investor types. Foundations are usually philanthropic organizations that either financially support other organizations, or directly engage in philanthropic activities while relying on their financial endowment.[17] Some foundations manage more than one endowment. For instance, Harvard University manages 10,800 separate endowments with a total of more than $ 25 bn.[18] Most of the large foundations are based on private endowments, as in the case of, for instance, the Bill and Melinda Gates foundation or the large US university endowments. For a list of the largest, see table 3.3. In the US, a foundation is usually also a tax-exempt entity. In order to qualify for this status, it has to fulfill a number of legal requirements.[19] One important constraint in the US is the so-called 5% pay-out rule for private foundations, whereby foundations need to use 5% of their endowment to fund their activities to retain the tax-favorable status. Therefore, foundations look to generate income, net of all fees, of at least 5% per year to at least maintain the endowment asset base.[20]

As LPs, private university endowments are considered to be among the most sophisticated PE investors, in particular VC investors. Much of this reputation is due to the successful foundations of well-known Harvard and Yale University. Some accredit this to the increased flexibility that independent

[17] Hence, technically, the foundation is the investor that manages the financial endowment. But the terms are often used interchangeably.

[18] See http://www.hno.harvard.edu/guide/finance/index.html. Date of access: January 11, 2008.

[19] In the USA, the United States Internal Revenue Code, provision 501 (c) lists those legal entities that are considered exempt from Federal income taxes.

[20] Because of the 5% pay-out rule for foundations to maintain favorable Federal tax regulations, a governmental subsidy is much more valuable than it may seem at first sight. For example, a $50 million subsidy is as valuable as a $1 bn endowment that can be invested and from which 5% income is generated.

The World's Largest Foundations

Values in bn of currency

Rank	Name	Country	$	Local
1	Bill und Melinda Gates Foundation	USA	$33.1	$33.1
2	The Wellcome Trust	UK	$25.6	£12.6
3	The Ford Foundation	USA	$11.6	$11.6
4	Church Commissioners for England	UK	$9.6	£4.8
5	J. Paul Getty Trust	USA	$9.6	$9.6
6	Robert Wood Johnson Foundation	USA	$9.3	$9.3
7	William & Flora Hewlett Foundation	USA	$8.5	$8.5
8	Lilly Endowment Inc.	USA	$8.3	$8.3
9	W. K. Kellogg Foundation	USA	$7.8	$7.8
10	Robert Bosch Foundation	Germany	$7.1	€5.1

Sources: For US data, see The Foundation Center, http://foundationcenter.org. For UK data see CharitiesDirect, http://www.charitiesdirect.com/CharitiesTop500UK.asp. For other data see wikipedia, http://en.wikipedia.org/wiki/List of wealthiest foundations. Date of access: January 12, 2008.

Table 3.3: The World's Largest Foundations

(university) endowments enjoy, which in turn permit them to exploit investment opportunities that others, in particular large institutional investors, do not consider.[21] Similarly, Lerner et al. (2007b) argue that this sophistication resulted in significant outperformance of these LPs. However, it should be noted that most foundations are in fact too small to maintain their own investment team. Instead, they mostly rely on external advisors or FoFs.[22]

The list of largest foundations is dominated by US and UK private foundations, with the Bill and Melinda Gates Foundation ranking first – with more

[21] Endowments "on the cutting edge choose from a broader opportunity set. [...] By considering alternatives outside the mainstream, investors increase the likelihood of discovering the next big winner well before it becomes the next big bust. By evaluating managers without the requisite institutional characteristics, investors might uncover a highly motivated, attractive group of partners. Operating on the periphery of standard institutional norms increases opportunities for success." Swensen (2000), page 335.

[22] For example, The Investment Fund for Foundations (TIFF), is an investment organization founded by a network of foundations in 1991 and which, though a series of different investment vehicles, manages the endowments of more than a hundred foundations. TIFF essentially operates a FoF business founded by and specifically for foundations. See http://www.tiff.org/.

than $ 20 bn.[23] Only one non-US, non-UK foundation, the Robert Bosch Foundation in Germany, makes it to the top ten, with an estimated $ 7.1 bn (€5.1 bn).[24] However, the ranking excludes universities.[25] They are commonly not included in the list, even though some, like Harvard University, Yale University and Stanford University, control cumulative assets of endowments that would put them in the top five of global foundations (with more than $ 25 bn, $ 15 bn and $ 14 bn, respectively).[26]

Family Offices

Compared to foundations, many family offices are of similar size. However, unlike the mostly philanthropic foundations, they are created to further the wealth of individuals. According to some estimates, there are about 2,500 active family offices across Europe, possibly 11,000 in the US, each with assets more than $ 100 million and sometimes more than $ 10 bn. Around 20 new family offices are estimated to be established each month across Europe.[27] With these numbers, a conservative estimate would be a global asset base in family offices of $ 2700 bn.[28]

---

[23]See for US data, The Foundation Center, http://foundationcenter.org. For UK data see CharitiesDirect, http://www.charitiesdirect.com/CharitiesTop500UK.asp. Date of access: January 12, 2008. For other data see wikipedia, http://en.wikipedia.org/wiki/List of wealthiest foundations. Date of access: December 7, 2007

[24]Although, by some legal ingenuity to minimize taxes, the ownership of Swedish home furniture maker IKEA is controlled by the Stichting Ingka Foundation with an estimated net worth of $ 36 bn. This would make this foundation the largest in the world. See The Economist, May 11, 2006: *Flat-pack accounting*.

[25]See also http://www.charitiesdirect.com/CharitiesTop500UK.asp for more information. Date of access: January 12, 2008.

[26]See http://en.wikipedia.org/. University foundations also differ somewhat as they usually receive additional state funding or similarly beneficial tax allowances that other foundations do not necessarily receive. Date of access: January 12, 2008.

[27]See The Guardian, April 17, 2006: *Super rich*. An interesting database is also found at http://the-family-office.org/, which lists 936 US, 627 European and 146 other global family offices. Date of access: January 12, 2008.

[28]This is the result of a simple estimate. If there are indeed more than 13,500 family offices worldwide, and if they, on average, control assets of $ 200 million each, then all family offices together hold $ 2700 bn in assets.

Government Agencies

While all investor types described so far are largely located in developed countries, the governments of many emerging countries have also come to control very large funds. In principle, one can distinguish between **sovereign wealth funds** (SWF) and **sovereign pension funds** (SPF). In addition, government agencies also entail smaller, **special purpose agencies**. The total asset base of SPFs is estimated at $ 4.3 trillion, dominated by the US Social Security trust funds and the Japanese Government Pension Fund, together with a total of $ 3.5 trillion alone. Others include the Australian Age Pension fund and the Canadian Pension Plan.

The size of SWFs can only be approximated. The IMF believes that Asian countries hold more than $ 3 trillion in foreign exchange reserves, thanks to their large current account surpluses. China's reserves alone exceed $ 1 trillion.[29] Most of these are re-invested in foreign government bonds, but some are already managed by investment corporations. By some estimates, the Chinese State Foreign Exchange Investment Corporation and that of Central Huijin together control about $ 300 bn for investment.

While China leads the group of foreign exchange-funded SWFs, commodity-funded SWFs are headed by the Abu Dhabi Investment Authority. These have been investors for longer, but their volume has increased strongly in recent years with rising oil prices. SWFs, not counting China's passively invested foreign-exchange reserves, currently manage assets of probably more than $ 2.5 trillion, more than the entire hedge fund industry, and may grow to $ 12 trillion by 2015.[30] In comparison, the current estimate for the world's entire public pension fund universe, and the largest 300 pension, funds are estimated to currently account for $ 8 to $ 9 trillion.[31] The cumulative size of the focused, special-purpose agencies, i.e. non-SPFs or non-SWFs, has not been published. For a listing of the largest funds, see table 3.4. As investors, SPFs behave essentially like very large public pension funds. For example, the world's single largest pension fund is an SPF, the Japanese Government Pen-

[29]See IMF (2007), page 73.

[30]See Financial Times, August 21, 2007: *China moves from gatherer to hunter.*

[31]For data on international pension funds, see http://www.watsonwyatt.com, date of access: December 12, 2007.

Financial Assets of the Largest Sovereign Funds		
Values in $ bn		
Country	Fund Name	Assets
	Sovereign Wealth Funds	
Utd. Arab Emirates	Abu Dhabi Investment Authority	$857
Singapore	Govt. of Singapore Invest. Corp.	$330
Saudi Arabia	Various Funds	$276 - 300[1]
China	State FX Investment Corp.	$300
Singapore	Temasek Holdings	$100
Kuwait	Kuwait Investment Authority	$70 - 250[1]
Australia	Australian Future Fund	$40
USA	Permanent Fund Corporation	$35
Russia	Oil Stabilization Fund	$32 - 89[1]
Norway	Govt. Pension Fund of Norway	$300
	Sovereign Pension Funds	
USA	Social Security trust funds	$1900
Japan	Government Pension Investments	$1623[2]
Australia	Age Pension	$237
Canada	Canadian Pension Plan	$110
France	Fonds de réserve pour les retraites	$43
Sweden	Premium Pension System	$38
Switzerland	AVS	$36
Canada	Régie des Rentes du Québec	$32
New Zealand	New Zealand Super Annuation Scheme	$10

Source: Financial Times, *State Pension Funds Spread Wings* published September 3rd, 2007

[1]International Monetary Fund, *Global Financial Stability Report*, 2006

[2]Watson Wyatt, *The world's 300 largest pension funds*, www.watsonwyatt.com, date of access: December 12, 2007.

Table 3.4: Financial Assets of Sovereign Funds

sion Fund with an estimated $ 1.6 bn assets under management.[32] However, this fund is an exception in size, most SPFs are smaller than $ 500 mn in assets.[33] SWFs, in contrast, are a somewhat mysterious group of investors. Their volumes, as well as their activities, have been watched by many with subtle

[32]See Financial Times, September 3, 2007: *State pension funds spread wings.*

[33]See http://www.watsonwyatt.com, date of access: December 12, 2007.

fear.[34] It remains in most cases opaque to outsiders how large these funds are, who controls them and what their agenda is.[35] Apart from SPFs and SWFs there is also limited number of smaller funds, often set up with a specific political purpose. For example, the Belgian Investment Company for Developing Countries was set up by the Belgian government to invest primarily in funds active in Africa.

With regard to PE funds, the IMF notes that "Middle Eastern sovereign wealth funds, which recycle some of the petrodollar profits from high oil profits, are also believed to have invested in private equity funds."[36] This is mirrored also for Asian SWFs. For example, Singaporean Temasek already maintains a PE fund investment branch and has invested in several VC and buyout funds in the past. This is significant also because much larger China plans to design its funds after Temasek.[37] China's funds already made headlines when it purchased roughly 10 %, at $ 3 bn in the management company that manages the Blackstone PE funds.[38] Carlyle, one of the largest PE firms worldwide, also expressed interest in fundraising from government agencies.[39]

---

[34]See Süddeutsche Zeitung, July 7: *Angst vor der Staats-Heuschrecke.*

[35]One significant exception is the Government Pension Fund of Norway, formerly known as the Government Petroleum Fund. As the name and indeed the name change suggests, this fund is by function an SPF, but receives its inflows primarily from the sale of Norwegian oil, which makes it essentially also an SWF. It is therefore usually included in discussions of both SWFs and SPFs. When it was designed, very transparent, very simple investment guidances were established that are even considered standard-setting by many. See Financial Times, August 31, 2007: *Norway sets standards in investing world.* The Government Petroleum Fund and was set up in 1967 and currently holds an internationally diversified portfolio of between 3000 and 4000 public companies. Information on the fund can be obtained via the managing Norges Bank http://www.norges-bank.no , including a list of current investments.

[36]IMF (2007), page 12.

[37]See The Economist, July 26, 2007: *Keep your T-bonds, we take the bank.* What is also interesting, Temasek, for instance, is both LP, public investor and PE fund at the same time.

[38]Disappointingly for China, the management company had a spectacular IPO but then lost nearly 30 % in value briefly after. Strictly speaking, this investment did not make China an LP, but only a shareholder of a company that receives part of the carry, or return, from the Blackstone funds. Still, it highlights China's interest in investing in PE funds.

[39]See Handelsblatt, August 22, 2007: *Carlyle will Staatsfonds anzapfen.*

Fund of funds

A fund of funds (FoFs) is "a fund that invests in a portfolio of private equity funds."[40] FoFs point to their proprietary selection process to identify new funds and often boast their investment access to prestigious funds. Because FoFs do not employ their own finances, investors regard them only as intermediaries. However, when investing in PE funds, FoFs also assume limited partnership, like any other LP. Including FoFs in an analysis is particularly valuable because any outside investor faces the choice of either relying on their own in-house PE fund selection, or to outsource that activity to a FoF - but at an additional layer of fees and the caveat of potential principal-agent issues. Therefore, an analysis of FoFs should help identifying if and how FoFs really offer a specialized product that merits the additional cost.

FoFs have become significant players in the PE industry. For example, in Europe, about 18.2 % of raised funds stem from FoFs and this share has risen steadily in the past year, while others have declined in relative contribution.[41] However, as Christian Tausend points out,[42] the decline of other investors is possibly not due to a reduced interest in PE by them, but instead their decision to invest in FoFs rather than try it alone.

External advicers to LPs

In addition to LPs, another PE market participant deserves mention. External advicers, or gatekeepers, advice investors on their PE fund investments in return for an advisory fee. They are therefore somewhat in competition to FoFs, as they usually also maintain a large database on funds, offer selection services and may even consult on the monitoring post investment. However, the actual investment decision remains with the original investor.[43]

---

[40] www.candela-capital.com/glossary.htm. Date of access: January 24, 2008.

[41] The EVCA publishes fundraising data annually. See http://www.evca.com.

[42] See Tausend (2005), page 23.

[43] Indeed, some advicers enjoy standard-setting reputation in the industry. Massachusetts-based Cambridge Associates, for example, is so respected in the industry that they regularly publish industry-performance metrics that are widely used and quoted, see https://www.cambridgeassociates.com.

3.2 Preliminary Results

The theoretical discussion in section 2 highlighted two principal groups of hypotheses, one concerning risk-preference, the other fund selection. After reviewing principal characteristics of the four major groups LPs, differences by LP types emerge.

First, the **economic function** and the liability towards their clients places large institutional investors into the group that is presumably most risk-averse and least sophisticated. One would therefore expect these LPs to prefer reputed, supposedly less risky buyout funds. Investment corporations like asset managers would be expected to take a more balanced approach, while small investors, endowments and family offices would be expected to be most likely to also invest in VC funds. For banks, economies of scope – lending for buyouts and IPO-underwriting – has been speculated to impact their investments. Government agencies will be expected to support their own nascent industry through VC funds, while simultaneously investing in large, reputed buyout funds abroad.

Second, in terms of **sophistication**, endowments and investment corporations should have the highest expertise and experience to invest in PE funds. Within their preferred fund type, therefore, one would expect these LPs to outperform their peers. With their more passive and reserved approach to other asset classes, one should further expect institutional investors to only invest with large, well-established firms, where sophistication in selecting funds matters less. With little to no experience, government agencies should be expected to underperform other LPs.

Third, the review highlighted also some **additional factors**. First, there are large differences in size, location and reputation among LP types. The significance of these should be further examined also in the interviews. Second, investment objectives beyond pure return-generation seem likely important for banks (especially as underwriters to buyout leveraged loans), government agencies (potential political investment objectives) and public pension funds (with political appointees on the investment decision boards). Finally, presumably unsophisticated LPs like pension funds are most likely to utilize external advisors.

3.3 Hypotheses

3.3.1 Interviews

Methods

The previous section generated results that formed the basis for further exploration. Focused interviews are a commonly used and effective method to gather further information on these results. The aim of the focused interview can be summarized as follows: 1. discovery, 2. measurement, 3. interpretation and 4. fine-tuning of statistical interaction.[44] The interviews should be partly structured, in this case based on results from the extensive literature review, without too much emphasis on a rigid structure. In this way, the interviewer is able to respond to new topics in the interview itself and incorporate these results in his assessment.[45]

The use of open interviews is particularly apt in this case. The execution of the focused interviews was based on the criteria outlined by Merton and Kendall.[46] In addition to validating previous results, the interviews were expected to also generate some fully unexpected results concerning the preferences and investments of specific LP types.

This kind of interviewing, while having particular advantages, also has pit-falls. First, the interviewer must be flexible and possess a sufficiently high initial level of knowledge. Therefore, the interviews were only conducted by the researcher. Second, compared to standardized interviews, open interviews require a higher level of preparation and post-interview consolidation. Third, the interviewer himself may in fact influence the interviewed person, especially when leading an open and interactive discussion. I therefore tried to avoid any leading or guiding questions.[47]

Sample

32 experts at 22 institutions were interviewed between spring 2007 and spring

[44]See Atteslander and Kopp (1995), pages 157 – 160.

[45]See Atteslander (2000), page 142.

[46]See in summary Merton and Kendall (1993), pages 171 – 172, and in detail pages 172 – 186.

[47]See also Atteslander and Kopp (1995), page 154.

Interviewee Type	No. of Firms	No. of People
Insurance	1	2
Public Pension Fund	1	1
Investment. Corp.	2	3
Fund of Funds	2	5
Bank	1	1
Endowment	2	2
Family Office	1	2
Government Agency	1	2
Small GP	3	4
Large GP	2	2
Advisor	2	4
Industry Experts	4	4
Total	**22**	**32**

Table 3.5: List of Interview Partners

2008. I selected interviewees from a broad spectrum of LP types; GPs were interviewed because they had had contact with different LP types in their fundraising. About half were met in person, the other by phone-interview; about two-thirds were available for more than 45 minutes. Table 3.5 gives an overview of the interview-partners. The interview-partners are all decision-makers in their respective organizations. They all participated actively as they confirmed that this topic was of high relevance to their field. The initial partners were approached via personal contacts or via friends. In addition, interview-partners were asked to name additional interviewees. Also, some were approached directly at VC and PE industry conferences. The selection of partners was therefore non-random. However, this is not problematic since the novelty of the question necessitates an open approach in which existing ideas can be tested, but also *new* ones be generated.

Results and Topics

The following sections are typical, selected quotes from interviews. The answers are representative snippets selected to illustrate major results. It should be noted, however, that many interviews yielded similar results, while some were not very fruitful. The following therefore represents a selection. They are organized as I. General comments, II. Preference, III. Sophistication and IV. Additional interview comments. In section 3.3.3, I summarize some of these notions as hypotheses for the empiric research.

I. General: How do LP types differ?

In the beginning, I asked this very open question to get a reply to build on.

Experienced GP: *"LPs differ in two major dimensions: risk and location... I mean, different LPs simply have a different preference for risky funds... when we started fundraising for an Eastern Europe fund, we knew there was no point approaching large pension funds, we went for endowments and family offices instead... In terms of location, it also matters that some investors simply don't want to or can invest elsewhere. This has also to do with fund structures and costs of looking at funds abroad."*

FoF: *"Yes, in principle, what we do can be replicated by anyone. But the real difference then comes from the people, from the experience. They have networks, they are good at assessing managers, knowing regional differences. It is important to see regional differences, even France is different from Germany, not to mention India... [We] do not use a mathematical, quantitative approach. I think if we did this, we would overdo it. You see, I think it would give you a false sense of what is important. Having said that, though, the people at [a different FoF] probably do this. They have very sophisticated methods.... "*

LP Advisor: *"[Our] clients are mostly German institutional investors that seek to start or launch a PE investment process / portfolio. They rarely have a track record in PE. Usually, they are insurances, even though there have also been banks... We [...] take the investor by the hand and manage their investments, but we react to the investors' needs. For instance, we have an overview of many funds out there, we can compile a cash flow schedule as we have a good idea what and how they want to invest.... [We] say that if you want to invest more than 100 M Euro, you really should take a Key Account approach, with a gatekeeper helping you."*

These examples confirm the principal hypotheses. First, LP types differ in their preference for new or risky funds. Second, they highlight the relevance of experience and sophistication. Third, sophistication is divided between selection of funds and definition of strategy. As the comments show, the first step is to define an overall strategy, while fund selection is a separate issue – both require market knowledge and experience. Fourth, location and knowledge of regional markets is important.

II. Preference

In this section, I asked a number of questions on the perceived risk-preference and the choice of PE funds.

Insurance: *"I told my team that we only invest in funds that have a long track-record and were a top-quarter fund before... Everything else is just too risky."*

FoF: *"Look, everyone knows that the university endowments made that much money in the 90's because they always invest more often in VC funds, they can afford to, but they are also close and it is their purpose, right?... But those times are over. Actually, it was the risk-averse pension funds that made much more money recently, because they always go for the big buyout funds with track-record. And those did really well in recent years."*

Advisor: *"Our [large, institutional] clients just want PE exposure but at limited risk. So their natural idea was to invest in notable PE Fund-of-Funds, to reduce risk as much of possible... Even though that comes at high costs."*

First-time GP: *"Yes, fundraising was very hard. I found it hard, but eventually I did find a small number of LPs who were willing to finance me... My LPs are special. My underlying NAV keeps growing, but I return no cash, as I do buy-and-build. That is fine with my LPs. On the contrary, they like it as they are not interested in getting money back immediately. They are more interested in multiples, not IRRs... They have effectively given me permanent capital."*

Family office: *"We are pretty return-driven... But we seek long-standing, trust-*

based relations. [Our firm] does invest in first-time funds and in fact looks for them, if they seem to offer the option for long-term, follow-up fund investments. [Our firm] considers itself to be sophisticated to spot these.... In principle, we like buyout funds, no VC, but it is hard to establish those relations with the big buyout funds." From their webpage: "As a 5th generation family business, [the firm] understands long-term thinking.... [The firm] is constantly looking for the right mix of established top quartile funds and innovative new strategies, teams and opportunities."

Government PE firm: *"We have no time-horizon, whatsoever. When we think this is a good firm, we can invest and keep as long as we want... We can invest in everything, but we like firms that are just growing in exciting markets who keep growing... Our single shareholder, our government, lets us do anything we want, except for a few sensitive industries, like oil, telecommunications and the like.*

These comments underscore that LP types differ in their risk-preference when investing in PE funds. While generally all LPs are return-maximizing, differences do exist. First, insurances and pension funds are much more risk-averse than smaller investors, in particular endowments. This is underlined with relatively defensive, risk-limiting heuristics of only investing in top-quarter, established funds. Second, some suspect that university endowments have a certain liking, but also the time-horizon, to support their local VC industry. Third, family offices, and perhaps other small LPs too, seem to also consider the option of choosing a few, very select funds with which they maintain very close relations. A surprising result here is that the interviewed family office did not have a preference for VC funds, but rather buyout funds. Fourth, government agencies seem to be the least sensitive to risk in the short run.

Size

First-time GP: *"If you are a small LP with little access to funds, then you are happy to stay with a fund that is successful but that reinvests the money before it returns it.... If you are big and have access to many funds, then you are less interested in the specific funds. You need to employ your money and are interested in getting it back quickly, so you can re-employ it."*

Family office: *"We look for control, and long-standing relations. So we actually focus our investments in a few funds. 50% of the money is invested to be the very largest shareholder in some funds, like 90% [shareholding] or so, about 50% are invested in a range of funds."*

FoF: *"Size matters for the big ones. I mean, it is hard to invest and you spend time. So if you are a very large LP, you prefer writing big tickets for big funds... In VC, the odds are against you anyway, I ask all the time if it makes sense to invest in VC funds... So if they have the choice of investing many small amounts in many small risky VC funds, or several bigger investments in safer buyout funds, they go for the buyout funds."*

US public pension fund: *"We don't have many people, really, not like CalPERS. It is basically me and a partner, then we have eight people or so who also do other things but they can help us. So we focus on a few good funds that we look at."*

Like location, size is an important control variable. First, LPs differ in their staff numbers, which in turn affects their ability to select funds. It seems unlikely that as the overall size of an LP grows, the PE fund staff grows in proportion. As a result, large LPs have less time per fund investment to conduct due diligence. Second, this also impacts the general preference for funds: Large LPs prefer large funds.

Regional distance / Home Bias

Advisor: *"Well, it is mostly a hear-about market. A US investor may travel Europe solidly for three months, meets up with several people through connections, and invests in the fund he heard most often in the end. Not very sophisticated... In Germany, [there is] not yet very much [a market for advisors] at all. In the US and UK there seems to be a good market. Also, there are Placement Agents acting on behalf of Funds, something that hardly at all exists in Germany. In this respect the German market is really behind."*

Fund-raising fund: *"We had a good fund here in the US. But when we were recently raising for a new one in Eastern Europe, we knew we didn't even have to* *ask the pension funds, they just would not invest abroad like this."*

FoF: *"We have offices in London and in Boston. In Asia? No, but it may be a good idea. Have someone on the ground... For Asia, we are learning, quite frankly... [What about Blackstone who basically have a global fund?] Yes, they basically diversify for us by investing for us. That is a strange situation, they already allocate about 20 per cent of their money in Asia. But to understand Blackstone, of course, we also need to understand Asia."*

LPs seem to differ in experience and exposure to regional PE markets. For instance, non-US LPs are likely less experienced, and the PE market less developed. Location is also emphasized as an important factor to understand 'regionally' operating funds. Therefore, LPs that do not have an international presence are likely to be more subject to home bias. These would include the smaller LPs, like endowments or family offices, but also the public pension funds who are usually located near or in their state capital.

III. Sophistication

In this section, I asked about the ability of investors to screen and assess funds.

Advisor: *"Endowments. I have been to Harvard and others. I am not surprised that they do much better than everyone else. They just have so much institutional knowledge in there... We have a scoring system that is one of the best, certainly better than that of the investor and at least at par of that of FoFs... In total, we ask about 100 to 120 questions per fund and about 160 questions for FoFs; more, as we also assess their risk management, their dealing with currencies, for instance, or underdiversification by just going for the best funds that all do the same.... Most, in particular the large investors, simply do not have the time and expertise to do this."*

University endowment: *"Well, we have a pretty big endowment and have always tried to invest smart. But in PE Harvard and MIT are obviously in a different league. So we just hired someone from MIT... who is trying to set up a structure like they have."*

Experienced GP: *"In my experience, PE is predictably cyclical, we have boom and bust. The large investors, however, rarely adjust their allocations, while some of the smaller, smarter LPs know pretty well when to go for this type or this type or when not to invest at all."*

Experienced GP: *"Large LPs are subject to similar biases as public equity investors: Home Bias, Industry Bias, Category Bias etc. They all often go for the same big funds. This is different for smaller LPs, more sophisticated ones that are also able to change their strategy."*

FoF: *"We follow a clearly defined strategy. However, I am then responsible for the fund selection... Well, due diligence for new funds really takes a long time, several months... If you are an investor already for a follow-on fund, you have months to decide. For the rest, they only have a one month fund raising period. So if you then start DD, then it is too late. You have to look out if and when someone is slowly finishing a fund, usually when about 60 to 80 per cent of capital is drawn down and then you start looking for it."*

These comments highlight how LP types differ in their ability to define strategy and in their selection skills. First, university endowments, in particular Harvard University endowment, are singled out again as particularly sophisticated investors. Second, large LPs are thought of as only slowly responding to market changes, while smaller LPs react more quickly to market changes. Third, large LPs are also expected to be more subject to home bias and to prefer buyout funds. Fourth, everyone underlines the difficulties of conducting a thorough due diligence, but the comments suggest that LPs differ in the quality of their due diligence. Fifth, timing is also important. It seems that smart investors already screen the market even before a new fund is fundraising.

Proximity

Investment corporation with own GP: *"We are a global firm, really. We have people everywhere. So we understand what our GP is doing."*

FoF: *"Quite frankly, it pays to be door-to-door with your GP. I know some here* *that I meet for lunch, I can talk to them all the time. I think for VC funds that is really important. You just have to know what is going on."*

Like for preference, the role of location has also been mentioned in connection with the ability to choose good funds. However, when mentioned, location was more understood as close proximity to the funds, not as differences in geographic regions.

IV. Additional comments

In this section, I present two additional themes that emerged during the literature review and the interviews: Investment objectives and the role of other LPs as a signal to other investing LPs.

Investment objectives

Family office: *"We have no 'higher agenda' of investing, no philanthropy or so. We look for returns... However, the family has some other subsidiaries that invest directly in firms that are active renewables etc. This, in parts, I think is also because they 'like' these industries, not just for return-reasons."*

Advisor: *"Banks often have all sort of side-conditions. They may look for additional MA Advisory Fees, Debt underwriting fees etc."*

US public pension fund: *"Before I got to the team [as CEO] several years, I think there had been some cases where basically we invested because someone sort of suggested it. But really, this has stopped. We have a fiduciary role and we take it very seriously."*

Investment corporation: *"Additional objectives? No, we don't have any, and I don't think anyone else has them, they could not afford to."*

FoF for endowments: *"No, we don't have any additional objectives, we are here to manage money and make money. But endowments that invest directly may have them."*

Government Agency: *"I love working here. It is the only place that lets me invest into pretty much anything I want. We only have one major limiting objective: Our investments must not harm the local economies. So we would never invest in natural resources in Congo or credit card firms in Africa. Otherwise we are free.... But I told you, we are staying clear of oil and telecommunications."*

The results on investment objectives are mixed. First, banks are singled out as being subject to investment objectives. Second, public pension funds, presumed by others (e.g. Lerner et al. (2007b)) to be subject to objectives, may have changed in this respect. Third, endowments were linked to have an objective to invest in VC funds, in turn, then invest in their university spin-offs. Fourth, the interviewed government agency claims to have hardly any objectives, except to avoid two key industries in their home country.

Role of other LPs

Finally, some LPs highlighted a recurring theme that I had initially not considered: The behavior of other LPs, especially their reinvestments.

Publicly listed FoF: *"I think the investor composition is a fairly important sign. Firstly, most investors do stay on, and if many drop out at once, it would be a serious sign that something went wrong. When you are invested, you learn so much about the fund and then you wonder, as a new investor, why some left. I even think that some investors act as signals to others in the sense that if, for instance, Harvard is an investor, then the others very quickly join, with little due diligence. I am sure a small LP could do a fairly good job by just looking where we or say [another FoF] is invested and then invest as well, little DD needed."*

Public pension fund: *"I do look for other LPs. But of course we still do lots of DD. We have to, really, it's our fiduciary responsibility."*

Investment corporation with own GP: *"Well, we are not directly involved in our GP, they do their own things. But we know them very well and I think it helped them fundraise even in harder times because other investors knew we would stay with the fund."*

These comments highlight three important issues. First, LPs learn about the quality of a fund while they are invested. Second, because this is the case, new LPs will take into account of others' re-investments. Third, some reputed LPs give particularly strong signals.

In conclusion, the interviews highlighted important points with regard to preference and investment expertise. Those will be summarized and stated clearly in section 3.3.3.

3.3.2 Additional Arguments

In this section I discuss five arguments that are only partly, or indirectly, based on comments from the interviews. I discuss them here and summarize them as hypotheses in section 3.3.3. The first four will also be tested in this research, while the fifth, *size bias*, cannot be tested given the data-structure. Still, it might be an interesting hypothesis for future research.

I. Strategy-Adjustment. Endowments are accredited with pursuing new and novel asset classes.[48] It is likely that also within PE, endowments may take a different portfolio approach than other LPs. Hence, GP preference will not just be a function of the LPs general preference, but also the LPs' different perception of future market trends and risk-factors of GP types that in turn affect adjustments of portfolios. Delineating those two effects, general preference and allocation adjustments, will be difficult without 'looking inside' the LP. However, some external shock that is unrelated to a specific LP preference, i.e. a systemic shock, should show if LPs differ in their responses thereto.

One such shock should be the financial environment post the VC-bubble and 9-11 2001: While the future of VC funds at the time may have looked largely uncertain, LPs probably re-assessed their weighting to different fund types within the PE asset class, notably buyout funds. Did endowments do the same as everybody else? Or did they more quickly and strongly adjust their overall portfolios?

[48] See Lerner et al. (2007a) and Lerner et al. (2007b) for this argument; also Swensen (2000), page 335.

I hypothesize that endowments, more than any other LP, more quickly adjusted their overall portfolio allocations. In contrast, large LPs, in particular pension funds, should have invested more in specific fund types, in particular large buyout funds and possibly have caused a new, buyout-, bubble. Small, 'flexible' LPs, in contrast, should have likely embraced also other PE fund types. This hypothesis is also discussed again in some detail in section 5.2, together with the specific methodology of testing it.

II. Risk-Taking. It could be argued that investors with longer time horizons can take greater risks in investing in PE funds. Especially for VC funds, this could be a worthy strategy: In good years, some very successful VC funds return a multiple of invested equity to the LPs. Yet in bad years, even the worst VC funds can 'only' lose their equity once. LPs with a long time horizon could benefit from this most.

Of the LP universe, it is likely that endowments, as financial guardians with a long time horizon, should be able to afford such risk-taking more than most other LPs. Therefore, one should expect the return of those LPs, especially for VC funds, to contain both some 'home runs' and some 'real dogs', i.e. very well and very poorly performing funds.[49]

III. External Advisors. PE is an opaque market with unclear information on investment targets. In section 3.1 I described that external advisors are important market participants. They advice LPs on the potential fund universe, the fund selection and also on the overall portfolio of the LP. However, they also incur additional fees. Therefore, for them to survive in a market place, one would expect them to provide additional value to the LP. Moreover, this additional value is likely greatest for the least sophisticated LPs.

I therefore hypothesize that LPs with external advisors achieve higher returns than comparable LPs without external advisors. In addition, LPs should

[49] Of course, this behavior well be closely linked to the incentive structure for employees. If an employee is paid for and assessed on solely the annual performance, he or she may have a different investment preference than someone whose performance is assessed over a longer time-horizon. Thus, the hypothesis does not solely rest on the time-horizon of the LP, but also on contractual limitations and factors such as frequency of employee turnover. See 2007b for this argument.

differ by the probability of employing costly advisors; large, 'unsophisticated' LPs should be more likely to employ advisors.

IV. LP Proximity. Proximity of the LP to the funds emerged as a theme for selection ability. This point merits more in-depth discussion: In an efficient market, with perfect information flows, one would not expect location to matter for investors, except for additional factors such as taxation or regulation. Hence, if information on investment targets is easily dispersed, personal interaction or physical proximity should not matter much.

It can be argued, however, that private equity is *not* an efficient market in this respect. The market for fund investments is not public, the information on funds is predominantly generated by the fund and the investor (i.e. there are few additional information sources) and the investment decision is always a certain 'bet' on those, yet unknown, future targets of the GP. Hence, the LP is really faced with an investment decision in 'people' – fund managers – as well as the future development of some 'target-industry', without even knowing the actual assets. I argue that since VC funds are more focused on an industry, and arguably more dependent on the specific skill set of the fund manager, such factors should matter most for this fund type. Hence, LPs will likely assess geographically close VC funds more diligently and invest in them with greater confidence than in funds located farther away. This also means, however, that LPs might forego potentially lucrative opportunities elsewhere, if they instead gain greater subjective confidence for funds in their physical proximity.

I therefore argue that close geographic proximity to VC funds should have an important impact on the LP decision: Fund returns achieved by the LP should be closely correlated the funds found in local proximity. This should be expressed both in the returns achieved from those funds, as well as the probability of actually investing in local funds.

V. Size Bias. In my discussions, interviewees stated that the actual size of the LP, linked also to the size of the investment team, should be highly correlated to the size of the fund. Some argued that large LPs, who have to invest large amounts of money and who feel 'sufficiently' diversified, will have a natural preference to conduct good diligence on a select few GPs, rather than conduct less thorough diligence on many smaller funds. In essence, because the number of individuals working at an investor does not scale with the asset size of the investor, relatively fewer people are responsible for larger sums per person and hence only have time to consider a limited number of investments of increasing size. I call this the *constrained-attention hypothesis*.

I would also argue that there are two more arguments. One is based on a result derived from principal-agent theory – I call it the *GP-compensation hypothesis* – the other is based on GP fundraising – the *LP-screening hypothesis*. While they are three separate arguments, they all still lead to the same prediction: The size of LP and GP should be highly correlated.

GP-compensation hypothesis. As was discussed previously, contractual relations, especially with regard to the economic compensation of the GP, have been found to be very standardized. A theoretical result by Golec (1992) on empirical ramifications of the Principal-Agent relationships in the mutual fund industry can be used here to see the implications thereof.[50] In his work, Golec argues that mutual fund managers operate under a contract with a base 'management fee' on the assets under management, and a 'profit-sharing' fee based on the outperformance of the fund. In many ways, the general fee structure is thus similar to that of a PE manager. Ultimately, the activities of the agent are determined by his fee structure. Golec derives the following fee structure:[51]

$$E(\phi) = [\beta_p k_b + (\beta_p - \beta_x)k_i]A\bar{M} + [k_b + k_i]AI \tag{3.1}$$

where $E(\phi)$ is the expected payoff to the agent, β_p and β_x are the beta of managed and comparison portfolio, respectively. A represents the asset base managed by the fund. $\bar{M}$ is the expected random gross market return. I are the units of nonrandom return associated with the units of information, or expertise, of the agent applied in his investment decisions. Equation 3.1 can be seen to be the sum of two parts. The first part rewards the advisor for bearing

[50]See also Ramakrishnan and Thakor (1984).

[51]I appreciate that there are some differences between the mutual fund industry and the PE industry. For instance, the performance of the PE fund cannot usually be directly compared to a simultaneously observable market return, and hence β_x does not explicitly enter contracts between LPs and GPs. However, when raising a second fund, the GP will compare the returns of the first fund to the then known market returns. So one could argue that implicitly, the PE fund manager is always also compared to the market performance.

systematic risk and thus represents the risk-sharing component: k_b is the fee applied to a return of β_p and k_i is applied to the differences in portfolio beta and market beta, or $(\beta_p - \beta_x)$. The second part is information-based as each fee parameter, k_b and k_i, is applied equally to the same underlying components, A and I. Under a flexible contract, the investor could thus impact the fund manager's activities in particular through the fee components k_b and k_i.

Now consider, however, the empirical finding by Gompers and Lerner (1996) that these provisions are standardized for essentially all contracts for all GPs. Thus we can write $\bar{k}_b$ and $\bar{k}_i$, i.e. they are actually fixed at the 2%/20% level. Devoid of setting incentives, it appears that the only way an LP could then impact the GP's activities is by either adjusting the 'riskiness' (β_p) of the fund's portfolio, or by adjusting the asset base.

Of course, LPs do not 'set' the GP's β_p, but they can instead *choose* funds that fundraise with a proposed specific activity. So a more risk-averse LP may opt for a GP that restricts itself to less risky activities, e.g. buyout funds vs. VC funds.[52]

Interestingly though, this would also imply a reduced payoff, $E(\phi)$, to the GP. In return, for the GP to agree to this limitation, the LP would thus have to increase the asset base, A. Therefore, under this hypothesis, because the LP-GP contract is standardized and because LPs choose GPs with specific activities in mind, they have to compensate the GP for the resulting entrepreneurial limitation by offering the GP a larger asset base. Anecdotal evidence seems to support this notion: In recent years, some 'mega-funds' were raised, and were presumably funded by risk-averse large pension funds.[53]

[52] See, for instance, von Braun and Harhoff (2004) and Weidig and Mathonet (2004).

[53] It is of course open to debate if the 'mega-funds' in recent years were, in hindsight, truly less risky to the LP. However, what matters at this stage is more what the expected, or perceived, riskiness was at the outset. From Kaplan and Schoar (2005) we know that fund returns over fund generations are persistent, concave and correlated with increasing size. Therefore, it seems likely new LPs perceived the large brand-name PE funds as relatively safe choices.

LP-screening hypothesis. The third hypothesis on size bias focuses on the GP. One can argue that GPs themselves have an incentive to limit the total number of LPs to a certain degree. Hagenmüller (2004) analyses how GPs interact with their LPs, i.e. their investor relations. Managing multiple investors at a time is costly as all need to be continuously informed and some may pose special requests. Hence, the GP may prefer fewer LPs that can underwrite comparably larger individual investments. At the same time, the illiquid nature of the investment provides GPs with an incentive to not only limit their LP number, but to also select LPs that are likely to remain solvent throughout the fund lifetime. As Lerner and Schoar (2004) discuss, fund managers in fact seem to screen for deep-pocket investors, i.e. for those who are unlikely to face a sudden liquidity stock. This is not just the case because it is inconvenient for the GP to rely on fewer financial resources. Rather, signaling theory predicts that any new investor, for instance for follow-on funds, will be unable to differentiate whether the reneging LP pulled out because of the GP's poor investment expertise, or for its own reasons. This imposes fundraising costs on the GP that are unrelated to the GP's abilities. Therefore, the combination of limiting investor relations costs today, and lowering fundraising costs for future funds will lead GPs to screen for LPs that can take larger shares in funds. As the size of the GP grows, the larger the LP contribution must therefore be. As a consequence, only large LPs can afford to sign growing commitment-sizes.

In summary, three different arguments, here called the *constrained-attention*, *GP-compensation* and the *LP-screening hypotheses* all point to the same overall hypothesis, **size bias**: That there should be a high correlation between LP size and GP size.

3.3.3 Summary

The review of LPs, interviews and additional theoretical considerations lead me to I identify the following hypotheses for subsequent confirmatory testing.

LP Preference

H 1: ***Fund preference*** – *LPs differ in their general preference for fund types. Buyout funds: Pension funds, insurances, sovereign wealth funds / government* *agencies. VC funds: Endowments, family offices, US and European government agencies. Other LPs, in particular FoFs, have mixed / undetermined preferences.*

H 2: ***Home bias*** – *LP types differ in their degree of home bias: In particular, globally active investment corporations and FoFs are least subject to home bias. For other investors, in particular public pension funds, endowments and family offices, home bias significantly affects their PE allocations.*

H 3: ***Strategy Adjustment*** – *Endowments more quickly adjust their allocation within the PE asset class, especially after 2001.*

LP Sophistication

H 4_a: ***US LP Performance differences: LP expertise*** – *Endowments, FoFs and investment corporations achieve the highest returns within each fund type. Pension funds are among the worst investors within each fund type.*

H 4_b: ***US LP Performance differences: Specific fund expertise*** – *Overall, returns will be driven partly by timing and expertise in a specific fund type and its performance over time. Hence, LPs with an expertise to invest in VC funds will have benefitted most during the nineties, LPs with an expertise to invest in buyout funds most thereafter.*

Note that the two hypotheses contradict each other somewhat: The first is based primarily on findings by Lerner et al. (2007b) and the general notion that some LPs are generally better investors. The second hypothesis, in contrast, implicates that differences in returns depend on the specific fund type. This is also why I denoted them with subscripts.

H 5: ***Experience*** – *The ability to select funds is positively related to investment experience.*

H 6: ***LP size*** – *Smaller LPs have better internal incentive structures and hence achieve higher fund returns than large LPs.*

H 7: ***Global LP Performance*** – *Non-US LPs operate in PE markets that are less developed while LPs themselves are less experienced. Hence, when adjusted for timing and experience, non-US LPs and LPs do not differ significantly.*

H 8: ***Risk-taking*** – *Because of their fund preference and longer investment time-horizon, endowments could afford to achieve higher overall absolute returns by taking risks: In this case, endowments should have invested more often in both well-performing and poorly performing funds. Alternatively, if risk-taking was not important, this pattern should not exist.*

H 9: ***External advisors*** – *Large and/or inexperienced investors employ external advisors. External advisors have a positive performance effect for those LPs. Alternatively, the PE fund market is so mature and transparent that advisors have no identifiable effect.*

H 10: ***Proximity*** – *LPs invest in local VC funds with greater confidence and more often than in funds that are farther away. Hence, returns for LPs are strongly influenced by local VC funds.*

Additional / untested hypotheses

The hypotheses presented above form the basis of the empirical inquiries in the subsequent chapters. However, additional themes emerged that I state as hypotheses here but that I do not test in this research.

H 11: ***Investment Objectives*** – *Some LPs invest according to additional investment objectives. Banks may invest in funds to also generate income from debt and IPO underwriting. Government agencies in the US and Europe invest in VC funds to support nascent industries. Public pension funds may favor investing in funds* *that invest in local companies or firms with a significant number of employees.*

While very interesting, I do not aim to test this hypothesis directly. I would need direct information from the investors, e.g. through surveys etc. if the investment decision was indeed motivated by additional objectives. Rather, I come back to the potential objectives in my discussions as they may help to interpret potential deviations from expected results.

H 12: ***LP Signaling*** – *Some LPs, in particular large and/or inexperienced LPs, are more likely to invest in a fund if other LPs with high reputations decide to (re-) invest.*

This is also an interesting proposition as it would suggest that investors follow the decisions of other investors, as is also observed, for instance, in public equity markets. Again, however, it would be difficult for me to test for this possibility. First, one would need a measure of the reputation and ability of some 'leading LPs'. Second, in most cases I do not know the actual identity of the individual LP as I do not know the actual names. Hence it would be difficult, by name, to identify those 'leading LPs'. Third, one would need to know the timing of a commitment to a given fund to analyze of one LP only invested after it observed others to invest. Still, the role of leading LPs in the decision process of other LPs might be a fascinating motivation for future research endeavors.

H 13: ***Size Bias.*** – *There is a strong correlation between the size of LPs (e.g. in terms of assets under management) and the size of the fund.*

As described, there are three separate arguments for this hypothesis. However, in order to test this proposition, I would need to be able to compare marginal effects of LP size differences on the fund sizes of selected GPs. Ideally, one would also test this by comparing LP types and the effects of increasing size of LPs - size bias should affect all LP types, independent from LP-type specific preferences. Unfortunately, even the largest endowment, for instance, is vastly smaller than the average insurance, and hence marginal effects of LP size differences are hard to compare. For example, one might expect a similar

%-increase in the size of a much larger insurance to have a different effect than for an endowment.[54] From an econometric point of view, this makes a comparison of differences in LP size on the level of individual LP types very difficult. Still, this hypothesis might motivate future research.

[54]Imagine, for example, an insurance with assets under management of $ 500 billion, and endowment with assets under management of $ 10 billion. A 10 % increase in the size of the insurance translates in vastly more investment volume, $ 50 billion, than for the endowment, $ 1 billion.

Chapter 4

Data

This chapter discusses the data and methods used in this research. Section 4.1 describes and acknowledges the source of the data, while section 4.2 describes the preparation of the original data for analysis. Subsequently, section 4.3 describes the key variables presented by GPs, LPs and the investments of LPs in GPs. However, the presentation here is largely descriptive, the interpretation of mean and other descriptive results is left to the respective analytic chapters. The chapter concludes in section 4.4 with a description of the principal methods and employed statistical software tools.

4.1 Source

My primary source of data is PreQin's[1] compilation of LP profiles and their investments in GPs. The data on LPs, their investments and data on the GPs thus stem from one data provider. PreQin is headed by Mark O'Hare, who over the last few years created these databases. To obtain the information, PreQin screens public and financial press releases, systematically reviews webpages and other voluntary disclosures by LPs and GPs, regularly surveys both GPs and LPs, conducts interviews, and exploits for US LP investments provisions of the Freedom of Information Act. However, the last source does not apply for non-US LPs. This may have impacted the data collection process for non-US LPs, as will also be discussed later.

[1] PreQin is found under www.preqin.com.

This dataset has several outstanding features. First, it contains hereto unpublished data on PE funds, their returns, and their LPs from 1969 until early 2007. Second, the data contains not only US observations, but global data. It also comprises a number of non-buyout, non-VC PE funds, as well as thus far rarely analyzed LP types, e.g. PE FoFs, family offices and government agencies. Third, PreQin uses different methods to check their reliability. For instance, PreQin compares the reported IRRs of funds by GPs with the figure provided by the LPs; in addition, PreQin double-checks by calculating the IRR based on funds' cashflows where available. Fourth, the GP data, in particular the performance data, is largely the same used by Lerner, Schoar, and Wongsunwai (2007b) (henceforth also referred to as 'LSW') for their smaller subset. My data set differs, however, in that it covers many more years, and was also complemented by the more extensive LP data.

4.2 Data Preparation

The original data was compiled in a number of spreadsheets: LP characteristics, GP characteristics and LP-GP investments were all contained in separate data-files. Using unique LP and GP identifiers, I subsequently combined the dataset and thus created a set of multiple investments by LPs in multiple GPs. For confidentiality reasons, I was not communicated the exact names and locations of the LPs, except in the case of public pension funds and to some degree also for university endowments. However, I am not allowed to publish any names.

In preparing the dataset, I discarded a number of observations. For instance, in some instances the investor or fund identifier were not unique and were entered twice. Because I do not know the names, i.e. identity, of the LPs, I discarded all LPs with the same identifier and all their investment observations. If fund identifiers were entered in multiplication, I checked if those were actually the same fund (which was simply entered twice, i.e. double of the same), or if they represented two separate funds. In the former case, I deleted all but one entry, in the latter case I deleted all funds with this identifier. I also discarded all LPs with no recorded investments.

In analyzing the dataset, it becomes clear that not all variables are available for all entries. This means there is a problem of missing values. This is not uncommon for empiric data. In principle, the examiner faces two possibilities: Leave it as it is, or impute the missing data. For example, I could have filled the missing data, e.g. using the average entry for that variable. This is a common method, especially for researchers with datasets of limited size. However, it can raise concerns that the imputed values create false results, depending on the method and if there is a fundamental reason for the missing values. In contrast, I did not compute the missing values. In multivariate analysis, in particular, this usually limits the total sample size; i.e. all entries with missing values in any of the used variables are discarded. Therefore, statistical significance in an econometric sense can suffer. However, I reasoned that I had retained enough observations to work with the data at hand and to not impute the missing values. Overall, the resulting dataset contains 19,222 investment observations by 1933 LPs in 3005 PE funds between 1969 and 2007. This is significantly more than that of the largest comparable similar publication by Lerner et al. (2007b), as presented in figure 4.1 as LSW (my dataset: DH). However, in their publication, only investments between 1991 and 1998 were analyzed. Over this time period, my dataset contains a very similar number of observations.

4.3 Descriptives

4.3.1 General Partners

The earliest recorded fund by PreQin was established in 1969, the latest vintages stem from 2007. However, I only focus on a more narrow data universe. To gauge LP preferences, which does not require fund returns, I use data from 1991 until 2005. In order to investigate LP investment success, however, I use a shorter dataset. Therefore, I only include funds with reported return measures up to 2003 to reflect meaningful IRRs. This also excludes a number of funds with vintage 2003 but for which PreQin does not yet calculate a confirmed IRR. Still, this means that for some of the youngest funds I utilize return data that is about 4.5 years old. I appreciate that many funds have a longer time-horizon. However, I defend this choice for four reasons. First, Kaplan and Schoar (2005) show that for funds up to 2001 (the end of their observation

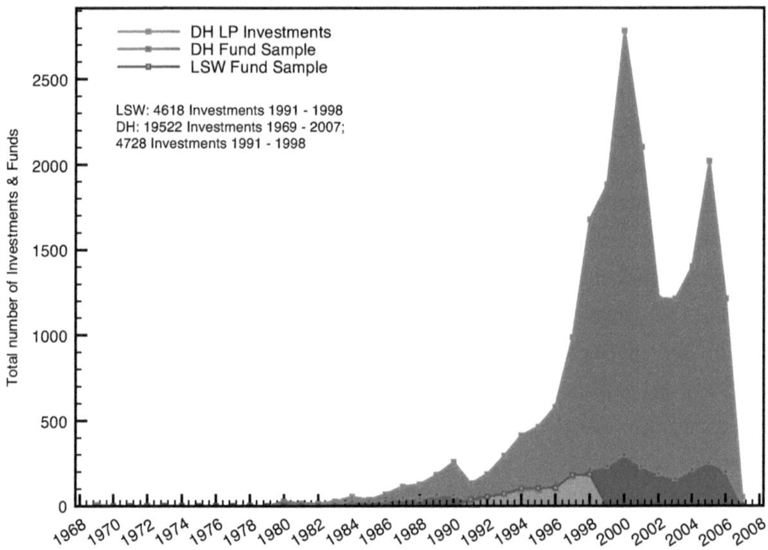

Figure 4.1: Number of Funds and Investments in them by LPs

range), the IRR after five years can be used for performance estimates: "This suggests that calculated performance 5 years out is a strong indication of final or ultimate fund performance."[2] Second, since then, after 2001, the 'quick flip', i.e. the tendency of GPs to quickly sell portfolio companies again, became more commonplace; hence, IRRs even after four years are likely good predictors. Third, I am not directly interested in actual average fund returns. Rather, I am interested in comparative differences across LP types. So even if fund returns for funds from 2003 are possibly biased, this only needs to concern me if this bias affected some LPs more than others. In unreported analysis I repeat major analyses with funds only up to 2002 and find no significant differences in the interpretation. Fourth, PreQin communicated only fund returns to me for funds that they would also publish through their own for-fee consulting and online service. They assured me that it is in their own interest to present fund return data that they feel comfortable with publishing themselves.

[2]Kaplan and Schoar (2005), page 1801.

PreQin uses a number of different fund categories, in addition to buyout and VC funds. For instance, for VC funds PreQin differentiates also between early stage or seed funds. Those were grouped into early VC funds. However, in addition, there are a large number of non-buyout, non-VC funds. I group these under the category 'other', or 'opportunity' funds. They include the following categories: Balanced, co-investment, distressed debt, forestry, general special situations, infrastructure, mezzanine, natural resources, real estate, real estate FoFs, FoFs, secondaries, turnaround, venture debt. While some of these could also be considered 'classic' PE funds (for instance, turnaround funds could be considered buyout funds), I opted to apply fairly strict criteria to maintain the classic PE fund categories found in the literature.

Table 4.1 summarizes the characteristics of the key GP variables employed in this research. The estimates refer, in general, to funds from 1991 – 2005; except for return variables (Net IRR, Multiple, Quartile), for which only funds 1991 – 2003 were considered. Variable *Vintage* indicates the year of closing of 2,444 fundraising funds. The average fund closed late in 1999 and few differences exist for fund types. On average, I compute that 7.1 LPs are recorded as investors per fund. Naturally, the larger buyout funds combine more LPs (11.4) than the other fund types, who record around 5 LPs. In general though, for some funds only one LP is recorded, while for one of the very largest funds 168 LPs are known. The funds are also grouped according to their key continental area of operation.[3] About 76% of funds operate in the US, 17% in Europe and 6% elsewhere; more buyout funds, compared to the average fund, operate outside the US. This probably corresponds to the global PE market, which developed later and is smaller than the US PE market, especially with regard to VC funds.

I now turn to the key **dependent variable**, *Net IRR*. It reflects the GP returns, net of all management fees and carry, expressed as the internal rate of return (IRR). The average fund return is 12.4% IRR. This compares well with figures published elsewhere: It is generally lower than those published by LSW (23.9% IRR), and about the same as that published in a number of

[3]Europe: Euro-denominated markets, UK, the Scandinavian countries and Switzerland. ROW includes all remaining LPs, including also Japanese and Canadian LPs.

other publications.[4] For some funds, a total loss of equity is recorded (-100% IRR), while the best fund return was 515% IRR. Moreover, the returns by fund type are, on average, all relatively close: Only early VC funds had significantly lower returns, on average (6.9% IRR). Yet, again, when comparing the mean fund returns to previously published data, it is particularly noteworthy that VC fund returns in my sample are considerably lower. This is due to the relatively poor performance of these funds since the turn of the millennium. To illustrate this point, table 4.2 and figure 4.2 present the number of funds per vintage, and their average returns, since 1990. It becomes clear that the nineties were a period of unprecedented success for VC funds, while buyout funds outperformed since (I restrict my sample to funds until 2003 to capture meaningful returns; however, in unreported results I estimate that 2004 buyout funds post returns north of 25% IRR on average). Overall, the median return in my sample is 9.4% IRR. This suggests some skewness, but not a very significant one. Still, because this variable serves as the key dependent variable, I present in figure 4.3 distribution plots. As is evident, the return distributions are, even for individual fund types, approximately normal. However, returns for both late and early VC funds appear somewhat skewed, driven by some very positive outliers. This is an important pointer for the empiric analyses, where in robustness tests I exclude the most positive and negative fund returns, where necessary. Those very high returns were achieved by VC funds in particular in the nineties. Hence, in the analyses, I take particular care to respect those time-dependent variations in fund returns.

[4] For instance, see Kaplan and Schoar (2005), who estimate for all funds IRRs before 1996 between 12% and 17% (page 1798). However, as described before, there is a range of publications that all try to use different methods to adjust for risk and illiquidity. Therefore, see also for instance Jones and Rhodes-Kropf (2003), Ljungqvist and Richardson (2003a), Cochrane (2005) or Phalippou and Gottschalg (2007) for further estimates of PE returns.

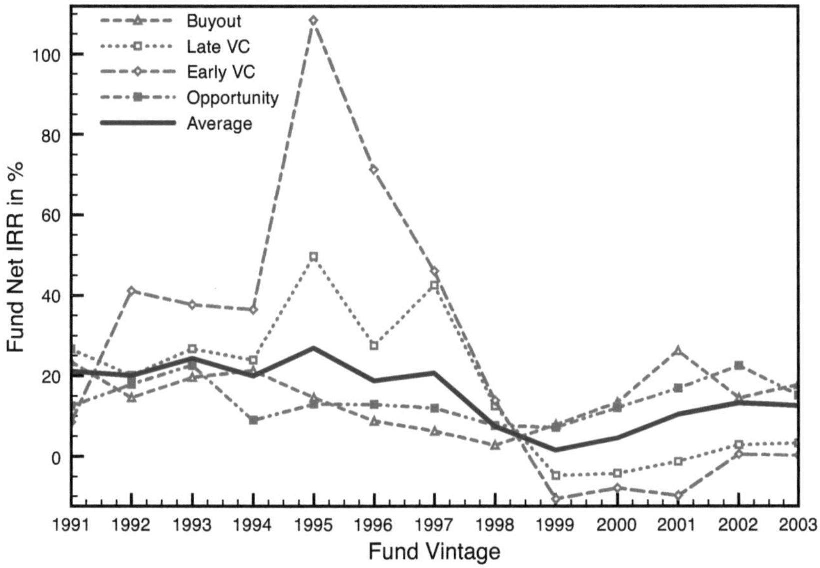

Figure 4.2: IRRs by Fund Type over Time

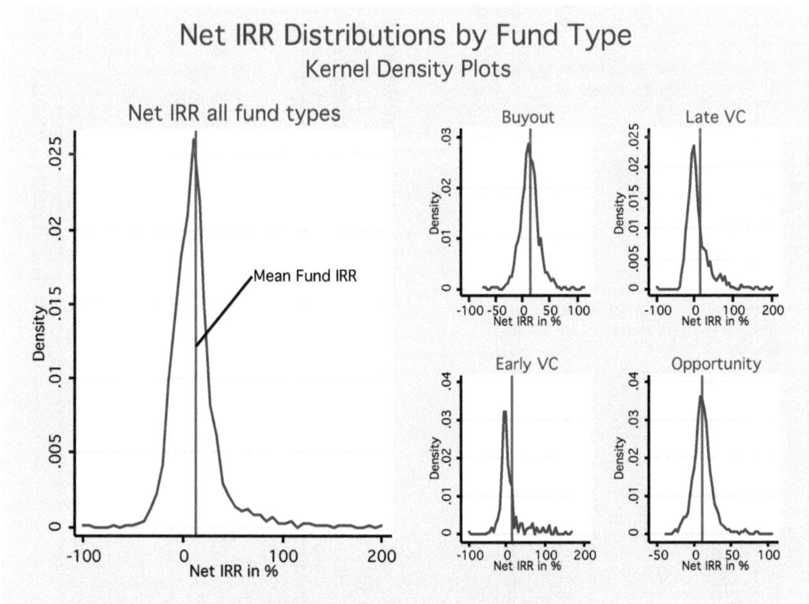

Figure 4.3: Net IRR Distribution

Descriptive Statistics – GP Variables

	All Funds						Buyout		Late VC		Early VC		Opportunity	
GPType	N	Mean	SD	Min	Med	Max	N	Mean	N	Mean	N	Mean	N	Mean
Vintage	2444	1999.7	3.6	1991	2000	2005	697	1999.6	621	1998.9	245	2000.1	881	2000.3
No of LPs per Fund	2444	7.1	12.0	1	4	168	697	11.4	621	5.7	245	5.9	881	5.0
Region														
USA	2441	76%		0%	100%	100%	697	68%	621	74%	245	86%	881	82%
Europe	2441	17%		0%	0%	100%	697	25%	621	18%	245	9%	878	13%
ROW	2441	6%		0%	0%	100%	697	7%	621	8%	245	5%	878	5%
Net IRR	1637	12.4	31.7	-100	9.4	515	488	12.7	445	12.6	156	6.9	548	13.6
Multiple	1866	1.6	2.0	0	1.3	42.5	528	1.5	531	1.7	186	1.7	621	1.5
Quartile	1866	2.4	1.1	1	2	4	528	2.5	531	2.5	186	2.5	621	2.3
Fund Size $ mn	2219	555.2	879.5	1	275	8500	653	920.8	580	245.7	230	202.9	756	584.1

Table 4.1: GP Descriptives

Global Funds and Returns by GP Type and by Vintage

This table shows the number of funds per vintage in the sample and, in italics, the mean IRR of that fund type for the year. Fund returns for funds after 2004 are not included.

	'69 –'90	'91	'92	'93	'94	'95	'96	'97	'98	'99	'00	'01	'02	'03	'04	'05	>'05	Total
Buyout	68	9	14	20	33	36	39	49	70	65	82	43	53	43	53	88	59	824
netirr	*20.0%*	*23.5*	*14.6*	*19.6*	*21.3*	*14.6*	*8.8*	*6.3*	*2.8*	*7.9*	*13.4*	*26.2*	*14.5*	*17.8*	*20.2*			*12.7*
LVC	158	11	21	28	28	29	32	51	50	74	97	58	49	24	33	36	42	821
netirr	*15.2%*	*26.6*	*20.1*	*26.7*	*23.9*	*49.7*	*27.5*	*42.6*	*12.5*	*-4.8*	*-4.3*	*-1.3*	*2.9*	*3.3*	*-4.2*			*12.6*
EVC	42	1	5	6	9	2	9	12	21	26	42	29	24	14	21	24	21	308
netirr	*12.6%*	*8.5*	*41.1*	*37.7*	*36.5*	*108.4*	*71.3*	*46.1*	*13.9*	*-10.6*	*-7.9*	*-9.8*	*0.5*	*0.2*	*-9.6*			*7.0*
Opp.	77	7	19	17	23	24	49	61	74	69	79	102	63	79	107	108	108	1,047
netirr	*10.6%*	*12.5*	*17.9*	*22.6*	*9.0*	*13.0*	*12.9*	*12.0*	*7.7*	*7.2*	*12.1*	*16.9*	*22.5*	*15.2*	*13.3*			*13.6*
Total	345	28	59	71	93	91	129	173	215	234	300	232	189	160	214	256	467	3000
netirr	*15.4%*	*21.1*	*20.1*	*24.4*	*20.0*	*26.9*	*18.8*	*20.7*	*7.5*	*1.6*	*4.6*	*10.4*	*13.3*	*12.6*	*9.9*			*12.4*

Table 4.2: Global Funds and Returns by Vintage and Type

A key concern could be that returns reported by PreQin suffer from (overly positive) reporting bias and survivorship bias.[5] However, I believe that my sample is largely representative. First, as already described, my returns are usually lower or equal than those published in the academic literature elsewhere. Second, as is also shown in table 6.1, I compare the fund returns to that published by 'Cambridge Associates' (CA) and 'Venture Economics' (VE), two commonly used benchmarks. The comparison is mixed: My sample reports higher returns than the VE benchmark, but lower than the CA benchmark.

Another concern could be that there is differential bias among LP classes, i.e. that some LP classes report complete investment data and others only their most successful funds. This could be the case, for instance, if individual investment managers at some LP classes fear to be uncovered as poor investors. However, it should be noted that this incentive is most compelling only for the most recent investment data. This is because those investment managers will most likely fear to be judged for their performance in recent years and not for investments many years ago and that were possibly not even made by them. Since I restrict most analyses to funds raised up to 2003, even though the latest entries stem from 2007, such reporting bias should therefore be less severe. Also, in many cases PreQin obtains the complete LP list for any GP, which includes all LPs that have invested in that fund, including those potential LPs that otherwise would not want to disclose that investment.

A key **covariable** used in the analyses is the *fund size*.[6] A number of reasons motivate the choice of this covariable. First, Kaplan and Schoar (2005) identified a link between the growing size of funds over fund generation and the success of the funds. It is thus a tacit signal of future performance to the LP. Second, there are general differences over time and in different regions. Older funds were smaller, and so are many funds in only nascent PE industries. Therefore, I employ the fund size as a covariable. On average, the 2219 funds for which fund sizes are known in the sample managed about 555 million (mn) USD, but buyout funds were nearly twice the size on average, early VC funds not even half that size. Also, the fund size distribution is skewed.

[5] For a discussion of this problem in the somewhat comparable mutual fund industry, see Carhart et al. (2002).

[6] Figures are given in USD mn. However, I used exchange rates as of September 2007 to translate non-USD figures in USD.

The smallest fund raised only 1 mn USD, the largest 8.5 billion (bn) USD. The median fund size is 275 mn USD and hence about the size of the average late VC fund, the variable is therefore fairly skewed.

I use the natural log of the variable and show the distribution of this transformed variable in figure 4.4: The variable is approximately normally distributed.

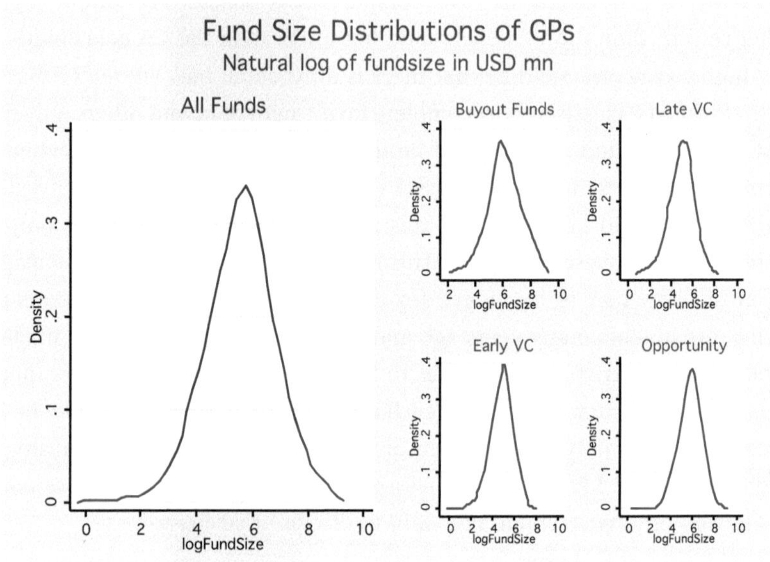

Figure 4.4: Fundsize Distribution

4.3.2 Limited Partners

As for the fund types, PreQin knows a relatively large number of different investor types. Those were grouped by me into nine LP types. The criteria to establish those groups were largely based on Davis and Steil (2001), who clearly differentiate between pension funds and insurances and investment corporations, on the LP types used by Lerner et al. (2007b) and Mayer et al. (2005), as well as on my own web-based criteria. Hence, PE FoF contain, in majority, 'PE FoFs' as well as 'PE fund investor'. Public pension funds also contains Australian 'superannuation schemes', who fulfill a similar role.

'Banks' represent both 'banks' and 'investment banks'. It would be tempting to separate the two. However, for many 'banks' it is from the data not at all clear that those investors do not also have investment banking activities. In particular for European banks, who have less of a tradition of being separated into either retail or investment banks, the situation is less clear. Lerner et al. (2007b) approach this problem by analyzing the revenue streams of their banks. However, since I do not know the exact identify of the LPs in my dataset, I cannot fulfill this check. 'Endowments', 'family offices', 'corporate pension' funds, 'insurances' and 'government agencies' are taken directly from PreQin, no additional investors are grouped into these categories. Finally, the group 'investment corporation' groups all remaining, shareholder-value driven investors: 'Asset manager', 'investment company', 'investment trust', 'corporate investor' and 'real estate investor'. The group also contains two investors that could have been linked to PE FoFs: 'Secondary FoFs' and 'real estate FoFs'. However, these are fewer than 11 investors (out of 1864) and I decided to keep the category PE FoFs as a group of 'classic' direct PE fund investors and therefore did not include those related, yet different LP types.

Table 4.3 presents key variables for the LP types. The average LP in the sample invested in about 10.4 funds (*No of Invest.*). This is predominantly driven by public pension funds, for which more than 34.9 investments are recorded, on average, per public pension fund. The lowest number of average investments is recorded for corporate pension funds, with only 4.1 investments. Moreover, there are a large number of LPs for which only one fund is recorded (min: 1 investment), yet there is even one LP for which 513 investments are known. This indicates that there are many LPs for which only few investments are known. This may be of concern for the analyses regarding LP preferences and will be discussed in the respective chapter.

The average LP has about 2.8 years of investment experience (*Experience at Investment*). This is measured at the time of the individual investment, while some LPs have significantly more experience.[7] In contrast, the *First Year Inv.* variable shows the first recorded investment observation, on average 1998. Both variables indicate, therefore, that the sample contains many relatively

[7]The average experience is measured not based on the first investment since 1991, but based on the entire dataset since 1969.

young LPs: PE as an asset class grew to be larger and more important in the last decade and many new LPs engaged in investing in PE in recent years. In fact only public pension funds entered, on average, the PE market before the average LP. However, the average fund *Vintage*, per investment, is late 2000. This differs from the same variable for GPs. Why? The reason lies in the fact that the more recent funds are larger and have thus more investors; hence, the average vintage per investment can differ from the average fund vintage.

Descriptive Statistics – LP Variables

	All LPs						PE FoF		Public Pension		Banks	
	N	Mean	SD	Min	Med	Max	N	Mean	N	Mean	N	Mean
No of Invest.	1864	10.4	29.8	1	2	513	612	7.0	272	34.9	102	4.5
Experience at Investment	1864	2.8	4.6	0	1	33.5	612	2.2	272	6.1	102	2.0
First Year Invest.	1864	1998.1	5.5	1969	1999	2005	612	1998.7	272	1995.0	102	1998.8
Vintage	1864	2000.8	2.3	1991	2000.631	2005	612	2000.9	272	2001.1	102	2000.9
External Advisor	1550	17.9%		0.0%	0.0%	100.0%	298	4.4%	272	49.6%	102	1.0%
Avg. Allocation in PE	803	23.3%	35.9%	0	5.3%	100%	178	68.6%	191	4.8%	36	13.0%
LP Region												
USA	1864	45.5%		0.0%	0.0%	100.0%	612	22.9%	272	60.7%	102	28.4%
Europe	1864	42.0%		0.0%	0.0%	100.0%	612	71.7%	272	27.2%	102	44.1%
ROW	1864	12.6%		0.0%	0.0%	100.0%	612	5.4%	272	12.1%	102	27.5%
LPAuM mn USD	1252	45,725.9	175,399.8	0	3,000.0	1,982,875.0	235	30,697.2	264	15,890.9	80	280,294.7

	Invest. Corp.		Insurances		Corp. Pension		Endowments		Family Offices		Govt. Agen.	
	N	Mean	N	Mean	N	Mean	N	Mean	N	Mean	N	Mean
No of Invest.	251	4.2	125	5.7	180	4.1	137	9.5	158	8.2	27	5.7
Experience at Investment	251	1.7	125	2.7	180	1.8	137	2.8	158	2.8	27	2.4
First Year Invest.	251	1998.9	125	1998.3	180	1998.8	137	1997.8	158	1998.1	27	1998.7
Vintage	251	2000.6	125	2001.1	180	2000.6	137	2000.6	158	2000.9	27	2001.1
External Advisor	251	1.6%	125	4.8%	180	23.9%	137	34.3%	158	16.5%	27	11.1%
Avg. Allocation in PE	79	27.7%	54	3.1%	106	4.7%	80	10.1%	67	13.0%	12	49.2%
LP Region												
USA	251	37.5%	125	34.4%	180	58.3%	137	92.0%	158	87.3%	27	29.6%
Europe	251	32.7%	125	46.4%	180	30.0%	137	6.6%	158	9.5%	27	22.2%
ROW	251	29.9%	125	19.2%	180	11.7%	137	1.5%	158	3.2%	27	48.1%
LPAuM mn USD	140	91,295.9	98	66,258.9	155	18,178.5	125	2,028.6	135	2,192.9	20	38,703.8

Table 4.3: LP Descriptives

The table also shows the entry on the use of external advisors. When PreQin collects its data, it also asks the LPs if they use external advisors, and who. There are number of possible answers and entries. I count every entry with a clear affirmation as 'Does use an advisor'. This also means that every answer that is either 'No Advisor', 'Use in-house advisor' or blanks (no answer) is counted as 'Does not use an advisor'. Hence, the variable 'External Advisor' takes the value of 1 if the LP clearly *affirms* the use of an external advisor, and 0 otherwise. For global LPs, about 17.9% of LPs affirmed the use of an external advisor, and this is primarily the case for public pension funds (49.6%) and Endowments (34.3%).

In terms of region of operation, the LP sample is more international than the fund sample. 45.5% of LPs are situated in the US, nearly as many (42%) in Europe, the remainder in the rest of the world (ROW).[8] However, European LPs are dominated by PE FoFs, while pension funds, insurances, endowments and family offices are actually a lot more US-based LPs. This may be indication that in Europe, perhaps for historic reasons, institutional investors in general may be less likely to invest in PE funds directly, and instead use FoFs more widely to gain exposure to this asset class. However, banks and insurances are slightly more often found in Europe.

The table also shows the percentage of assets allocated to PE. While this variable is not used in the analyses, they are interesting in their own right. On average, LPs allocate almost a quarter of their assets in PE. However, this is of course driven by FoFs (68.6%) and government agencies (49.2%).[9] More interesting are the measures for the larger, 'average' LPs, e.g. public pension funds (4.8%), insurances (3.1%) and corporate pension funds (4.7%). Those numbers are largely in line with estimates presented in section 3, figure 3.1. However, the numbers for the remaining LPs show how endowments and with them family offices, but also banks, allocate much more to PE.

In most regressions, where indicated, I use two key **covariables**, *LPAuM in mn USD* and *Experience at Investment*. The average LP manages about 53 bn

[8]For the region classifications, I use the same as for the funds, see above.

[9]Note, however, that the entries for government agencies on PE allocation, and also average fund size are driven by the Western LPs, who are charged with investing much in alternative assets, compared to sovereign wealth funds in the Middle East for instance. The measures here are average numbers.

USD. However, this measure is driven primarily by the large banks, for which the total assets (i.e. including private banking / wealth management assets) are also included – this explain the maximal assets of nearly 2 trillion USD for some banks. Instead, on average, the largest investor types, are investment corporations and insurances, who manage a mean 89 bn USD and 65 bn USD, respectively. The data is therefore somewhat skewed.

I transform this variable by taking the natural log. Likewise, I do the same for the already described variable *Experience at Investment*. However, I also first add one year (i.e. I assume at least one year of experience per LP at investment, perhaps to establish a fund investment team) and then also take the natural log. As figure 4.5 shows, both variables are thus transformed into approximately normally distributed variables.[10]

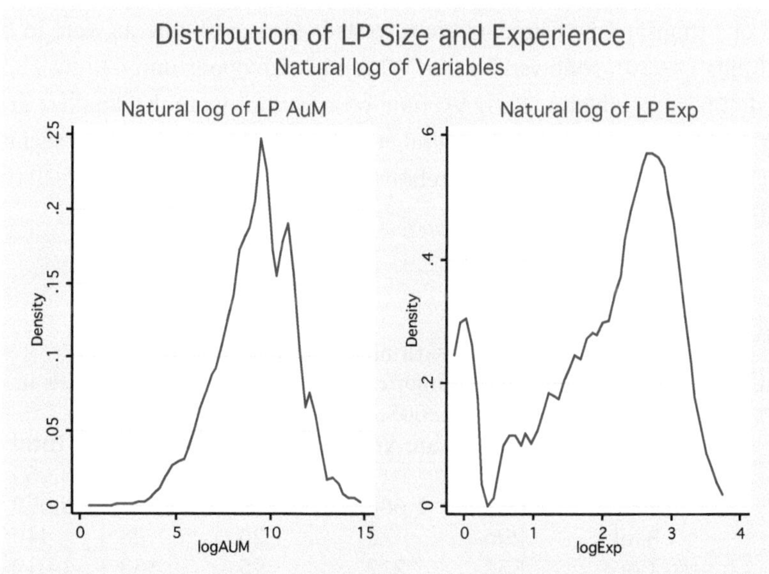

Figure 4.5: Distribution of logAuM and logExp

[10]The large number of zero-values for experience is explained by LPs with only one year of experience. The natural log of 1 is 0.

4.3.3 LP – GP investments

To analyze the data, I treat each investment in a fund as a given observation. In total, the sample records 19,222 observations of LP investments in GPs up to 2007. However, as described, I only use a subset of this universe. Table 4.4 presents the total number investments by LP type in various fund types between 1991 and 2005; 17,345 investments in total. For the smaller sample to calculate LP returns, I base my analysis on only 12,343 fund investments until 2003; however, the distribution among LP types remains largely the same. The largest investors in the table by recorded investments are public pension funds (8,058), followed by PE fund-of-funds (3,965). The endowments in my sample are recorded with 1,174 investments, family offices with a similar number (1,233), while investment corporations enter with 1,012 observations. For corporate pension funds, insurances, banks and government agencies, fewer than one thousand investments are recorded. Most investments were in buyout funds (7,939), followed by late VC funds and 'opportunity' funds (3,552 and 4,406, respectively). Early VC fund observations were the smallest group with 1,448 observations. In general, the distribution in the table seems to match anecdotal evidence on the relative importance of LP types and GP types in the PE industry.

Investment Observations by LP and GP type

This table presents the total number of investments analyzed by LPs in GPs in the entire sample 1991 – 2005.

LP Type	Buyout	Late VC	Early VC	Opport.	Total
PE FoFs	2,181	911	461	412	3,965
Public Pension	3,082	1,686	569	2,721	8,058
Banks	296	76	20	48	440
Invest. Corp.	552	212	95	153	1,012
Insurances	390	106	31	119	646
Corporate Pension	387	102	42	157	688
Endowments	518	216	92	348	1,174
Family Offices	473	207	127	426	1,233
Govt. Agencies	60	36	11	22	129
Total	7,939	3,552	1,448	4,406	17,345

Table 4.4: LP Investments

When I described the key variables, I presented approximately normal distributions of fund returns. A concern could be, however, that return data for the LP types could be subject to reporting bias, for instance. Therefore, figure 4.6 presents the return distribution of the recorded investments. All distributions are approximately normally distributed, by LP type. However, probably because of the lower numbers of investments, the overall distribution is more dispersed for government agencies.

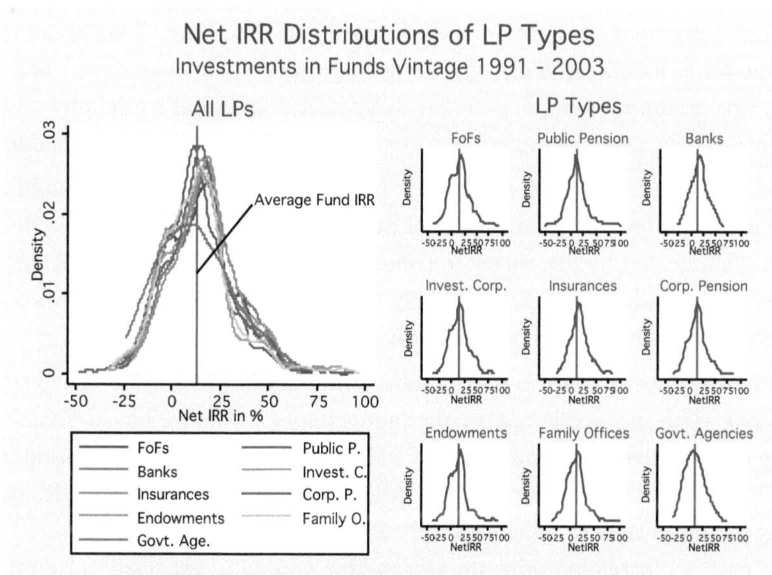

Figure 4.6: Net IRR Distribution by LP Type

4.4 Methods

This research employs a number of multivariate analytic methods to identify and isolate effects of individual variables. The chiefly employed methods are the pooled OLS-regression[11] and logit- or the related multinomial logit regression. In addition, in robustness tests I also use a number of related of methods. In particular, I also use a panel data set with either OLS-regression,

[11]OLS: Ordinary Least Squares.

or combined with a generalized linear model (GLM) to estimate effects for a dependent variable that is a fraction.

Ordinary Least Squares and assumptions. A principal advantage of **OLS-regressions** is the ease of interpreting coefficients as marginal effects. Moreover, if a set assumptions is fulfilled, according to the Gauss-Markov theorem, OLS-regression is the best linear unbiased estimator (BLUE).[12]

The first important assumption is the **linearity in variables**. This implies that the model is based on additively connected independent variables. Technically, this assumption applies to the underlying population model and which is expressed as a theoretical structural, formal model applied to the sample.

A principle assumption is also that of **random sampling**. The examined sample should be a random sample of the population. In empiric work, this is often complicated by the ability to collect data. Moreover, in some instances, the overall population may not actually be exactly defined, which makes comparison of the sample naturally difficult.

The third assumption is that of **zero conditional mean**. This means that the error term, not explained by the independent variables, has an expected value of zero given any values of the independent variables. This essentially also means that there is no omitted variable that is correlated with the used independent variables. However, this does not mean that omitted variables could not be correlated with the dependent variable. Especially in empiric work, it is usually impossible to include all variables that may have an impact on the dependent variable.

Fourth, there is the assumption of **no perfect multicollinearity**. This says that there must not be any perfect, i.e. no direct, linear combination or correlation of the independent variables in the model. If this was the case, the matrix of independent variables would not have full rank and could not be estimated. Note, however, that this does not mean that the independent variables mustn't be correlated at all. In fact, it is one of the strengths of regression analysis to accommodate for this. However, if the correlation is high, estimation of coefficients becomes more difficult, and a larger sample is needed to

[12] See Wooldridge (2003), page 103.

identify statistical significance.[13]

Based on these assumptions, OLS-regressions are considered unbiased. In addition, for OLS to permit statistical inference, the assumption of **homoskedasticity** is important. This implies that the variance of the error term is the same for all combinations of outcomes of the explanatory variables. In other words, the variance of the error term does not depend on the used independent variables. In empiric work the assumption of homoskedasticity cannot always be upheld. In such cases, OLS regression would still produce unbiased estimators of the population parameters. However, the estimates of the variances of the estimates, and hence also the standard errors, would be biased.[14] This means that they can no longer be used for statistical inference, and hence t- and F-statistics, would be invalid. Fortunately, given large samples, so-called heteroskedasticity-robust standard errors can easily be calculated using standard econometric software.[15]

Pooled OLS and panel data. A special case, used widely in chapter 6 to assess LP performance over time, is the **pooled OLS**. It is a commonly used method for time series data with limited time data points.[16] For pooled OLS, a (random) sample is pooled from the population across different points in time. In principal, the same assumptions and methods as for regular OLS apply. However, sampling from the population at different points in time leads to observations that are probably not identically distributed. This is easily accommodated by allowing different intercepts for each period. This can be achieved by adding year-dummies with one year being the 'base' year. In such cases it is then common to estimate the intercept, but to not report it. In my pooled OLS regressions, I follow this convention. The coefficients on the remaining variables can thus be interpreted as estimates independent of timing effects. In addition, pooled OLS datasets have often changing error variances across time, i.e. are heteroskedastic. For this reason, I also usually always

[13] Alternatively, if multicollinearity seems to be a problem, variables can be tested to be jointly significant using F-Tests (also called the Wald Test). See Wooldridge (2003), pages 142 – 148.

[14] See Wooldridge (2003), pages 84 – 103.

[15] See Wooldridge (2003), pages 257 – 264. Named after their inventors, the standard errors are often also called *White-*, *Huber-* or *Eicker-* robust standard errors. For simplicity, I just call them 'robust standard errors'.

[16] For an introduction, see Wooldridge (2003), pages 426 – 438.

calculate robust standard errors. In addition, I also appreciate a special nature of my dataset: Multiple LPs invest in multiple GPs. Therefore, the same GP is represented multiple times. Therefore, I also cluster the regressions on the fund level.

In contrast to a pooled cross-section, the dataset can also have the structure of a **panel**: In this case, a set of specific subjects, e.g. LPs, are analyzed at specific points in time. This means that the observations are not independently distributed across time. This has a particular advantage, as any unobserved factors will likely remain robust across time. Those can then be 'differenced' away over time since they are assumed constant over time. One thus controls for any constant, unobserved heterogeneity. If the time dimension is small compared to the number of analyzed units, it is also common to include year dummies to account for external changes that are not being modeled and that can be captured by time-specific dummies.[17] In this research, I only use a panel method in a robustness test in section 5.1.1, and follow this methodology to test if logit-estimates for the preference of LPs for PE funds are robust if I focus on a subset of LPs. In this particular case, I estimate PE fund portfolio compositions of LPs in a synthetic panel derived from the overall dataset.

Generalized Linear Models. The panel data-structure described in the previous paragraph can be analyzed using OLS. I do so in a robustness test in section 5.1.1. However, in that section I also use a special kind of generalized linear models (GLM) proposed by Papke and Wooldridge (1996) for a special class of dependent variables. As also Kieschnick and McCullough (2003) review, if the range of the dependent variable is bounded on two sides on the interval [0,1], OLS-methods can be inappropriate.[18] In this specific case, the dependent variable is a fraction of a portfolio, e.g. '40% of investments are in buyout funds'. The dependent variable is thus bounded by 0% and 100% portfolio allocation. This introduces two problems. First, OLS could estimate results that lie outside a boundary, even though an estimated portfolio of '110% of investments are in buyout funds' is of course senseless. Second,

[17] See Wooldridge (2003), pages 438 – 453.

[18] Cook et al. (2007) also review existing publications in which proportions or portfolios are estimated; they conclude that a significant number of papers use inappropriate estimation procedures.

the estimates are necessarily heteroskedastic: OLS estimates a single variance for the linear prediction. However, the variance at, say, the midpoint must be necessarily different than near the boundaries 0 or 1. Near the boundaries, the variance must approach zero, or the confidence intervals would lie over or below the boundaries. Hence, while OLS is usually a good estimator, it is technically not consistent, and the usual corrections for robust standard errors do not apply.[19] Fortunately, there is an easily implementable quasi-likelihood estimation method for regressions with fractional dependent variables, first proposed by Papke and Wooldridge (1996). This method can be implemented using STATA® as a generalized linear model (GLM), based on a logit link and the binomial family.[20] Compared to OLS, this estimation is not only more consistent, but also more efficient.[21]

Closely related to this special case of GLM estimation is the more general case of **logit** regression. I employ this method commonly in chapter 5, where I analyze the preferences of LP types for different fund types. Logit is commonly used for cases in which the dependent variable is limited to only two values, generally 0 or 1.[22] In principle, the estimates of the dependent variable is read as probability given the independent variables and calculated as the coefficients on the independent variables. To achieve this estimate, the probability is a function – in this case the logistic distribution – of a linear set of independent variables. The logistic, sigmoid function approaches 1 at large values, and 0 at low values. However, this implies that the model is not estimated linearly. Therefore, OLS estimation is not possible. Instead so-called maximum likelihood estimators (MLE) are used. In principle, the same assumptions as for OLS are required for unbiasedness. However, maximum likelihood estimation is based on a distribution of the dependent variable, given directly by the set of independent variables in the sample. Therefore, as Wooldridge

[19] One may assert that one could use a Tobit regression. However, Tobit only deals with a lower boundary at 0, but not a higher boundary.

[20] See http://www.ats.ucla.edu/stat/Stata/faq/proportion.htm, date of access: July 30, 2008.

[21] Cook et al. (2007) also point to yet another method, based on the Beta distribution (or zero-inflated beta model) known in probability theory and statistics. I do not use this alternative method, but add-ons for STATA® are available.

[22] For a closer discussion of logit and probit models, see Wooldridge (2003), pages 554 – 565.

(2003) points out, "heteroskedasticity is ... automatically accounted for."[23] Fortunately, common econometric software packages commonly estimate logit regressions.

This also applies to the related **multinomial logit** models. In such models, the dependent variable not only takes the values of 0 or 1, but can take multiple categorical values. For instance, a 0 could represent buyout funds, a 1 late VC funds, a 2 early VC funds and a 3 other / opportunity funds. In multinomial logit models, one of the categories is then taken as a 'base' category, and separate regressions are estimated for each of the remaining categories. A key assumption for the multinomial logit model is that the dependent variable categories are not dependently conditional of each other, e.g. a buyout fund is not a buyout fund because it it is a stronger expression of a late VC fund. This assumption is valid on the grounds that fund managers establish a fund of a certain type *ex-ante* based on their own abilities, i.e. the fund type is not established *ex-post* by someone categorizing fund types conditional on some external criteria.[24]

While logit models are commonly used and estimated by econometric software packages, including standard errors and other measures for statistical inference, the non-linear underlying model complicates the interpretation of the coefficients somewhat. The coefficients are estimated as odds-values, not as linear, marginal coefficients as in OLS. Odds-values can be easily transformed given a value of the independent variable. However, a functional add-on for the statistical software package STATA ® can easily be installed that greatly aids in this transformation, also for several variables simultaneously.[25]

Finally, I briefly point to the **instruments** used for the research. The original data was communicated in a Microsoft Excel ® file and subsequently first

[23]Wooldridge (2003), page 557.

[24]In this case, it would be a conditional logit model. This can be used if someone wanted to assess car choices by customers. If the dependent variable represented different car types, like compact car vs. a Sports Utility Vehicle (SUV), it would likely be a multinomial logit model. If, however, the researcher looked a group of cars and then used criteria to classify the cars into 'slow', 'fast' and 'very fast' cars, it would constitute a conditional logit model.

[25]Specifically, I used the *spost9ado* package available from www.indiana.edu/ jslsoc/stata and developed at Indiana University.

viewed in SPSS ®, Version 9. In order to prepare the data, I used mainly SPSS ® and to some extent Excel®, both because of the easier-to-use spreadsheet-based interface. However, all statistical analysis was performed in STATA/IC ® Version 10.1.

Chapter 5

LP Investment Preferences

This chapter tests specific hypotheses with regard to investment preferences of LPs. First, I test if LPs have a stable preference, or bias, for specific fund types. Second, I ask if they are subject to home bias. This research is presented in the first part to the chapter, in section 5.1. The second part of this chapter focuses on a hypothesis specific for endowments: In section 5.2 I test if endowments adjust their portfolio allocation after 2001 more flexibly than other LP types.

This chapter is therefore structured as follows: Section 5.1.1 discusses the *fund preference* hypothesis. Section 5.1.2 presents evidence on the *home bias* hypothesis. Finally, section 5.2 examines if endowments more flexibly adjusted their portfolio allocations after 2001, as posited by the *strategy adjustment* hypothesis. Section 5.3 summarizes and discusses the results.

5.1 LP Preferences

5.1.1 Fund Preferences

In this section I investigate the fund preferences by LPs. In particular, I hypothesized:

H 1: Fund preference – LPs differ in their general preference for fund types. *Buyout funds*: Pension funds, insurances, sovereign wealth funds /

government agencies. *VC funds*: Endowments, family offices, US and European government agencies. Other LPs, in particular FoFs, have mixed / undetermined preferences.

Analysis – Mean results. In figure 5.1 I present a percentage distribution of recorded investments by LP type. Overall, 45.9% of recorded investments were in buyout funds, 20.5% in late VC funds, only 8.3% in early VC funds and more than 25% in opportunity funds. Viewed by LP type, two major themes emerge: First, some LPs are recorded much more frequently to invest buyout funds than others. For instance, for banks, PE FoFs, investment corporations and corporate pension funds more than half of recorded investments were in buyout funds. Second, there seems to be a trade-off in particular between buyout funds and opportunity funds. LPs that invested less often in buyout funds than others seem to have overweighed investments in opportunity funds.

Note that this presentation is not really a portfolio-presentation. Rather, it presents the likelihood of an investment in the dataset being an investment in a specific fund type by a specific LP type. This could be biased, for instance, by timing-issues: If some GP types were more 'popular' at some points, and some LP types started investing in PE funds at other times, then this could skew the results. Moreover, the previous section on size bias highlights of course an additional important caveat: If GP investments are driven by structural LP-characteristics such as LP size, and not the LP preferences, then this univariate presentation may be somewhat misleading.

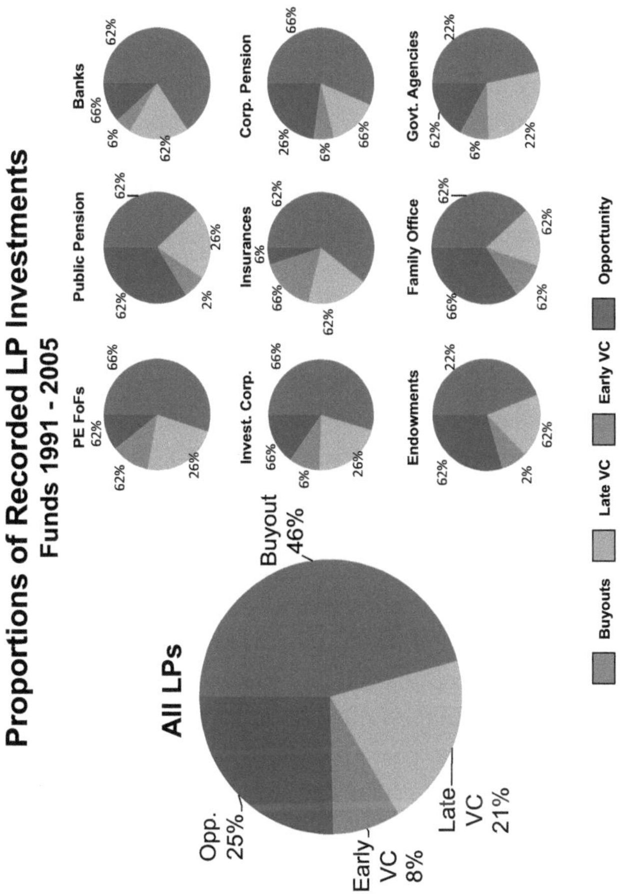

Figure 5.1: Pie Charts: Investments by LP Type

Analysis – Multinomial logit regressions. Those points motivate the multinomial logit regression, presented in table 5.1. This method estimates the odds of an investment being in one of the categories of the dependent variable, GP Type, conditioned on the independent variables. Those also include year fixed effects, and in most cases also region fixed effects; so timing and region-specific results are conditioned for. The dependent variable in this case takes as the comparison category buyout funds. The LP types are compared to the base category PE FoFs.

At this stage, I only look at the signs and the statistical significance of the variables. In table 5.2, further below, I also transform the estimates into predicted probabilities. The coefficients on the LPs show that most LPs invest in buyout funds less often than PE FoFs in buyout funds, and instead in opportunity funds (see, for example, the coefficient of +1.78 for public pension funds). The coefficients on VC funds are less clear, but if significant are negative. This leads to the interpretation of a trade-off between buyout funds and opportunity, while for VC funds the trade-off is less clear. While I discuss this trade-off in more detail at the end of the chapter, it is worth noting here that this likely points to a greater effort by small LPs to diversify within the asset class. The 'alternative', opportunity funds are a collection of unusual funds that offer investment strategies within PE that are in many ways niches and that thus offer attractive risk/return characteristics. The coefficients on all fund types for LP size (logAuM) are negative and significant. The coefficients therefore indicate that the larger the LP, the less likely it invests in funds other than buyout funds. The coefficients on experience, in contrast, are positive and significant. Hence, the more experience the LP has, the more likely it also invests in funds other than buyout funds. This is an interesting finding, as it suggests that a) large LPs prefer buyout funds, and b) the more experienced LPs also consider non-buyout funds. In general, this trade-off is quite pervasive. To illustrate this point better, based on the regression in table 5.1, in figure 5.2 I document the predicted and fitted values within fund types from the multinomial logit regressions. For buyout funds, the larger the investor, the larger the fund; the reverse is true for the other fund types.

Probability of Investing in Fund Types

Multinomial logit Models: This table presents multinomial logit regression to estimate the likelihood of picking a certain fund type by LP type. The comparison category is buyout funds. All estimations include year fixed effects. Funds 1991 – 2005 were included. Significance levels: *** $p<0.01$, ** $p<0.05$, * $p<0.1$. Covariates as shown in the table – commonly used also in subsequent tables. Constant estimated but not reported. All observations were clustered at the fund level, robust standard errors are reported in brackets. Base categories for comparison: Buyout funds for the dependent variable; PE FoFs for the LP dummies.

	Opp.	LVC	EVC
Public Pension	1.78***	0.06	-0.49***
	(0.14)	(0.12)	(0.14)
Banks	0.25	-0.56**	-1.24***
	(0.26)	(0.22)	(0.39)
Invest. Corp.	0.81***	0.04	-0.13
	(0.16)	(0.14)	(0.18)
Insurances	1.17***	-0.22	-0.69***
	(0.17)	(0.18)	(0.26)
Corporate Pension	1.20***	-0.14	-0.35
	(0.17)	(0.16)	(0.24)
Endowments	1.30***	-0.06	-0.41**
	(0.17)	(0.14)	(0.19)
Family Offices	1.58***	-0.04	0.04
	(0.14)	(0.14)	(0.16)
Govt. Agencies	0.69**	0.14	-0.46
	(0.30)	(0.30)	(0.44)
logAUM	-0.15***	-0.06***	-0.06**
	(0.02)	(0.02)	(0.03)
logExp	-0.00	0.17***	0.24***
	(0.04)	(0.05)	(0.08)
logFundSize	-0.68***	-1.44***	-1.78***
	(0.10)	(0.09)	(0.14)
Region Fixed Effects?	Yes	Yes	Yes
Year Fixed Effects	Yes	Yes	Yes
Observations	15305	15305	15305
Log-L.	-14893.2	-14893.2	-14893.2

Table 5.1: Probability of Picking Specific Fund Type

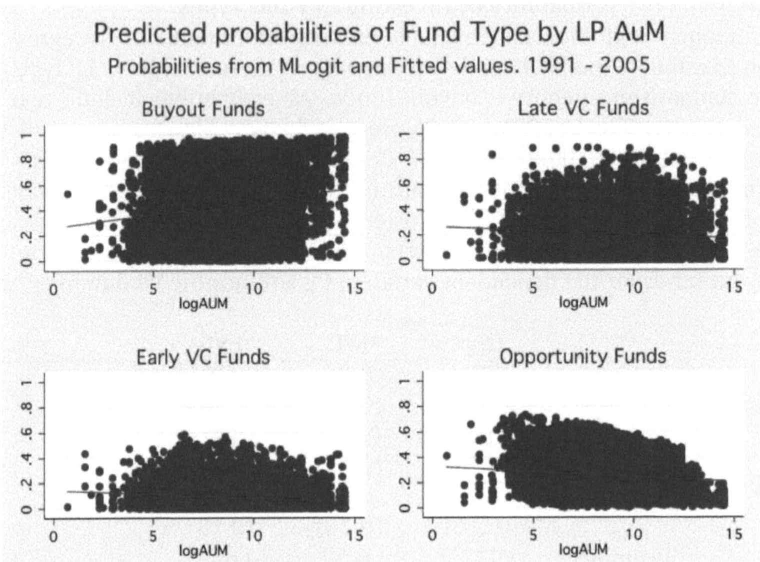

Figure 5.2: Predicted and Fitted Probabilities: Fund Types and logAuM

Analysis – Portfolio estimation. Based on the multinomial logit regressions, I now try to estimate 'portfolios'. A key advantage of the multinomial logit regression is that coefficients are estimated in interdependence with each other. Therefore, when transforming the coefficients into probabilities, they add up to 100%.[1]

The results are shown in table 5.2. Therefore, based on the regression in table 5.1 for individual LP types, I estimate the portfolios by LP type. Note that these estimates are robust to timing and LP region effects, as well as experience and fund size. The table has, for ease of reading, two parts. In the first part, I simply show the predicted allocations by LP type. In the second part, the differences to the average LP are shown, and set in bold where the differences are significant at the 5% level. For instance, banks allocate 66.75% to buyout funds, or 22.33% (in absolute terms) more to buyout funds than the average LP. This representation thus shows a large degree of variation, or heterogene-

[1] Of course, technically these are still not real portfolios, but rather weighted probabilities of picking one fund over the others, depending on the covariables used in the multinomial logit estimations.

ity, across LP types. Banks, PE FoFs, insurances, corporate pension funds and investment corporations allocate more to buyout funds than the average LP, they also allocate less to VC funds (except for investment corporations). Compared to the simple mean records (see table 5.1), the estimated portfolios are relatively close to the original proportions of recorded investments. However, the predicted probabilities to invest in buyout funds are lower for insurances and investment corporations; higher for government agencies. Instead, allocations to opportunity funds are the ones that differ primarily.

Estimated Portfolios by LP types and Size
The table shows predicted portfolio distributions from multinomial logit estimates.

	Buyout	Late VC	Early VC	Opp.
Average	**44.42%**	**20.83%**	**8.18%**	**26.58%**
By LPs				
PE FoFs	55.90%	22.93%	10.31%	10.86%
Public Pension	39.17%	17.15%	4.71%	38.97%
Banks	66.75%	14.80%	3.21%	38.97%
Invest. Corp.	51.04%	20.52%	7.94%	20.50%
Insurances	55.11%	14.79%	4.00%	26.11%
Corp. Pension	53.01%	14.90%	5.24%	26.85%
Endowments	45.76%	18.65%	6.84%	28.74%
Family Offices	38.79%	17.45%	9.65%	34.11%
Govt. Agencies	53.37%	20.77%	4.98%	20.88%
Differences from average predicted LP				
PE FoFs	**11.48%**	2.10%	2.13%	**-15.72%**
Public Pension	**-5.25%**	**-3.68%**	**-3.47%**	**12.39%**
Banks	**22.33%**	**-6.03%**	**-4.97%**	**-11.34%**
Invest. Corp.	**6.62%**	-0.31%	-0.24%	-6.08%
Insurances	**10.69%**	**-6.04%**	**-4.18%**	-0.47%
Corp. Pension	**8.59%**	**-5.93%**	**-2.94%**	0.27%
Endowments	1.34%	-2.18%	-1.34%	2.16%
Family Offices	**-5.63%**	-3.38%	1.47%	**7.53%**
Govt. Agencies	8.95%	-0.06%	**-3.20%**	-5.70%

Bold: Shows allocations that are significantly different from the average predicted allocation at the 5% level

Table 5.2: LP Portfolio Estimates

Hypothesis: Interpretation. The interpretation with regard to the hypothesis is mixed. First, the inquiry showed that there are significant differences in preference for fund types, depending on the LP type. The null hypothesis of no differences between investor types can therefore be rejected. Second, however, the preferences are not exactly as I had predicted. After controlling for fund size and experience, endowments, family offices, insurances and corporate pension funds preferred the fund types that had been hypothesized. In contrast, the allocations of public pension funds and FoFs were not as had been hypothesized. Public pension funds invested much less often in buyout funds than had been expected, while FoFs much more often. I thus conclude that LPs do differ significantly from each other in their preferences. However, the LP differences are not necessarily in the direction that was hypothesized. It will be discussed at the end of the chapter what the differing results could implicate.

Robustness Tests. Naturally, the key concern with this type of investigation is that the results are driven by the nature of the dataset and the employed method. I do not actually investigate portfolios of LPs, but look at the entirety of individual investment observations. This could impact the analysis. For instance, PreQin collects data on all LPs it can. However, this creates also a large number of LP entries for which only a few, serendipitously collected, investments exist, but who otherwise do not disclose their investments. For other LPs, in contrast, PreQin obtains a much larger number of investment observations. So if there are systemic differences for either LP type, the results could be skewed. Ideally, thus, I would obtain original data on actual portfolios: I would then know the percentage of investments, even their size, and could thus better estimate actual predicted portfolios.

Unfortunately, I do not have actual portfolios. Still, to test for the robustness, therefore, I would like to check if the results remain comparable if I a) use a different method and b) use a specific subset of the original dataset. Therefore, I create a *synthetic* panel and hence quasi-portfolios over time. To do so, I focus on funds with vintages 2001 – 2005 (five years) and I discard all LPs with fewer than 10 investments during that period. This reduces the observation universe from about 15,305 to 1,014. I then collapse the investment observations on the level of the individual LP. I thus essentially create, for the investigated time-period, a synthetic, unbalanced panel of LPs with a significant number of investments. I then estimate, on the level of the LP, predicted allocations, in percent, per fund type. The dependent variable is therefore, for instance, 'percentage of investments in buyout funds'.

Unfortunately, this kind of regression has its own pitfalls. Using ordinary least squares (OLS) regressions are inappropriate for dependent variables that are a proportion, or percentage. As Kieschnick and McCullough (2003) describe, this is because the possible range of values is bounded on two sides on the interval [0,1].[2] Therefore, in section 4.4, when describing the research methods, I discussed a Generalized Linear Model (GLM), proposed by Papke and Wooldridge (1996) for dependent variables that are a proportion or fraction. This method is generally more consistent and efficient than OLS. I use this GLM method to predict percentages of portfolios from the quasi-panel that I created. I therefore regress 'percentage of X fund type' on LP dummies and other characteristics. The results are shown in table 5.3. In column (1) I first show a simple OLS. In columns (2) to (5) I show the estimations per individual fund types using GLM. When comparing (1) to (2), the same dependent variable, it becomes clear that for all variables OLS and GLM estimate the same sign and essentially the same statistical significance. Only for corporate pension funds GLM seems more efficient.

Columns (2) to (5), the GLM regressions, are separate regressions – a simultaneous / multinomial GLM estimation procedure akin multinomial logit has not yet been developed. However, in column (6) I add the multinomial logit column for opportunity funds from table 5.1. Compared to column (3), all coefficients are very similar and also similarly significant statistically. The coefficients can be compared well, since the GLM procedure is based on the same logit link function as multinomial logit. However, the high similarity of coefficients and statistical significance does surprise somewhat, given that the overall number of observations was reduced so drastically.[3]

---

[2]Cook et al. (2007) also review existing publications in which proportions or portfolios are estimated; they conclude that a significant number of papers use inappropriate estimation procedures.

[3]Note, however, the significantly weaker Log-Likelihood coefficients of about -400 compared to -14 893 for the multinomial logit estimates.

Robustness: Estimated Allocations of LP Types in Comparison
Panel Estimation Tables: This table presents the quasi-panel estimations of LP type portfolios between 2001 – 2005. Column (1) was estimated by OLS, columns (2) – (5) by GLM using a logit link function as described in the text. In principle, significance levels and directions of the signs in column (2), from the GLM estimation, can thus be compared to column (1) from the OLS. Column (6) is the same as the first column of regression B of the multinomial logit table before and serves to compare the estimates to column (3) of the GLM here. All estimates are after inclusion of Region and Year Fixed Effects. Funds 2001 – 2005 were included, except for column (6), where funds 1991 – 2005 are used. Significance levels: *** p<0.01, ** p<0.05, * p<0.1. Covariates as shown. Constant estimated but not reported. All observations were clustered at the fund level, robust standard errors are reported in brackets.

	OLS		GLM			MLogit
	(1)	(2)	(3)	(4)	(5)	(6)
	Buyout	Buyout	Opp.	LVC	EVC	Opp.
Public Pension	-0.22***	-1.13***	2.18***	-0.47***	-0.97***	1.78***
	(0.03)	(0.13)	(0.19)	(0.16)	(0.16)	(0.14)
Banks	-0.08	-0.13	0.43	-0.17	-2.35**	0.25
	(0.05)	(0.40)	(0.56)	(0.53)	(1.04)	(0.26)
Invest. Corp.	-0.03	-0.14	0.46	-0.10	-0.35	0.81***
	(0.04)	(0.26)	(0.39)	(0.35)	(0.40)	(0.16)
Insurances	-0.15**	-0.78**	2.21***	-0.92**	-2.63***	1.17***
	(0.06)	(0.33)	(0.34)	(0.44)	(0.80)	(0.17)
Corp. Pension	-0.11**	-0.63***	1.67***	-0.87**	-0.70	1.20***
	(0.05)	(0.24)	(0.30)	(0.42)	(0.66)	(0.17)
Endowments	-0.15***	-0.75***	1.88***	-1.11***	-0.62*	1.30***
	(0.04)	(0.20)	(0.24)	(0.27)	(0.32)	(0.17)
Family Offices	-0.21***	-1.05***	1.80***	-0.32	-0.45	1.58***
	(0.04)	(0.18)	(0.22)	(0.26)	(0.32)	(0.14)
Govt. Agencies	0.09	0.43	-1.50	0.72	-1.99*	0.69**
	(0.13)	(0.89)	(1.24)	(0.60)	(1.04)	(0.30)
logAUM	0.03***	0.17***	-0.19***	0.00	0.01	-0.15***
	(0.01)	(0.03)	(0.04)	(0.04)	(0.05)	(0.02)
logExp	-0.02	-0.11	-0.05	0.17*	0.14	-0.00
	(0.014)	(0.07)	(0.09)	(0.10)	(0.12)	(0.04)
logFundSize	0.16***	0.90***	-0.19***	-0.66***	-0.59***	-0.68***
	(0.01)	(0.08)	(0.07)	(0.08)	(0.10)	(0.10)
Region Fixed E.?	Yes	Yes	Yes	Yes	Yes	Yes
Year Fixed E.?	Yes	Yes	Yes	Yes	Yes	Yes ('91 – '05)
Observations	1014	1014	1014	1014	1014	15305
R-squared	0.442					
Log-L.		-450.81	-432.47	-296.94	-192.64	-14893.3

Table 5.3: LP Portfolios – Synthetic Panel

The table thus leads to two interesting interpretations. First, despite focusing on the subset of fewer LPs, overall estimates with regard to opportunity funds, and with them 'buyout' funds, were similar for both the multinomial logit and this quasi-panel approach using a GLM. This suggests that estimated portfolios from multinomial logit were indeed robust and not driven by a large number of LPs with only very few observations. Second, the coefficients on the fund types again suggests the already described trade-off between buyout funds and opportunity funds, the larger the LP.

To underscore this argument once more, figure 5.3 shows the predicted and fitted values per fund type in dependence of LP size, from the independently estimated regressions in columns (2) to (5). The predicted and fitted values show the trade-off within fund types. They also look very similar to the comparable figure 5.2, even though two different estimation methods and a smaller dataset was used. I therefore conclude that the portfolios estimated from multinomial logits are robust.

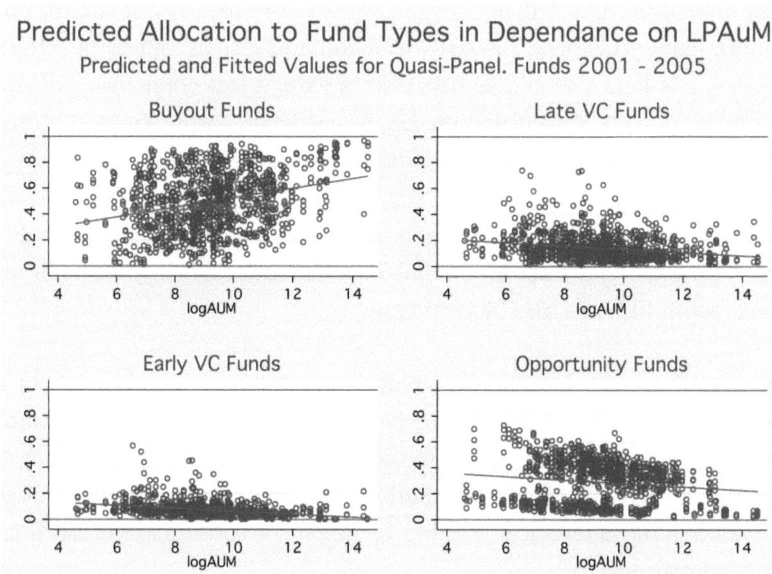

Figure 5.3: Predicted and Fitted Probabilities: Synthetic Panel

5.1.2 Home Bias

As I also use international data, I am able to investigate an additional, important question with regard to international PE investment flows: Is there home bias and to what degree? Specifically, I hypothesized:

H 2: Home bias – LP types differ in their degree of home bias: In particular, globally active investment corporations and FoFs are least subject to home bias. For other investors, in particular public pension funds, endowments and family offices, home bias significantly affects their PE investments.

Because of the difficulties of due diligence in other continents, and indeed to even know about a fund that is raising money, home bias within PE was hypothesized to be significant. In particular, small investors that cannot afford to maintain multiple offices, as well as public pension funds that have no political incentives to settle abroad, can be expected to invest less often abroad than other LPs. Other investors, for instance investment corporations, are more likely to expend the costs of maintaining small offices in different countries, and hence should be expected to exhibit less home bias. Investors in countries outside Europe and the US, in particular sovereign wealth funds, are least likely to suffer from home bias. Likewise, PE FoFs may offer access to other markets and should thus also show little home bias.

If looked at by fund type, the bias should be most severe for difficult-to-assess VC funds, and least for (large) buyout funds. Thus, LPs should also differ in terms of home bias by fund type.

Data specifics. The location, by country, is registered for most LPs in the dataset. However, those are only the headquarters. Subsidiaries, for instance in other countries, are not known to me. Based on the data, I group the LPs in three major groups: 1. USA, 2. Europe, 3. Rest of World (ROW).[4] LPs are thus coded in the categorical variable 'LP Region' according to the location of their headquarters.

[4]Europe is defined as all Euro-denominated markets, UK, the Scandinavian countries and Switzerland. ROW includes all remaining LPs, including also Japanese and Canadian LPs.

With regard to PE funds, the major continental region of activity is entered in the dataset.[5] For instance, a buyout fund region focus may be 'Europe'. In rare cases, specific countries are indicated, these were grouped by continental region. The categorical variable 'GP Region' therefore matches in structure the variable 'LP Region'. Note that coding by region of fund activity in this way can therefore classify two funds of the same PE firm into different regions, if the funds are raised for investments in different continental regions. However, this is uncommon: Only very few, usually the very largest, PE firms raise multiple funds for investments in multiple regions.

Based on the two variables, I generate the variable 'Invest in same area' and code every investment in the same continental area as a '1', others as '0'. Thus, a continental home investment is coded as '1'. I use funds raised from 1991 to 2005.

Analysis – Mean results. Table 5.4 highlights the high degree of home bias in LP–GP investments. The table shows the number of investments by, say, US LPs in European GPs. For example, about 46% of LPs are located in the US. 63% of all recorded investments by all LPs worldwide were on the US continent. In relative terms, however, this means that 86% of US LP investments were in funds in the US. This suggests a significant degree of home bias if one wanted to make sure one also invests in foreign funds for diversification purposes. One may concede, of course, that there are more US funds. However, as the table shows, the 86% are also more than there are funds in the US: 76% of all funds. So even in relative terms there seems to be home bias.

This impression is even more extreme for European and ROW-LPs. For instance, while only 17% of funds are located in Europe, European LPs allocated 57% of their investments in Europe. This is more than 3 times as many as one might have expected based on the fund universe. Similarly, despite the fact that only about 6% of funds are located outside the US or Europe, about 16% of investments by LPs in those regions were in fact in those funds.

Having established that home bias seems significant, I now turn to the question if LP types differ in this respect, and if there are differences by fund type.

[5] This means, of course, that I do not use the country of fund registration.

In table 5.5 I therefore present mean results of home bias by LP type and by GP type. The table is ordered by LPs with highest percentage of home investments. Overall, the three LPs that were expected to exhibit the highest degree of home bias indeed top that list: Endowments, public pension funds and family offices. Financial institutions, with the opportunities to operate multiple offices and to have personnel to focus on other regions, are the least affected. Government agencies are the only LP type that records investments that are more abroad than at home.

Buyout funds are most commonly international in nature, VC fund investors more often invest at home. However, home bias seems even most severe for opportunity funds. This pattern is robust for essentially all LP types: Buyout fund investments are more likely to be also across continents (low home bias) than for all other fund types (higher home bias). One exception, however, are PE FoFs. The results suggest, as was discussed earlier, that FoFs offer international access to markets and are therefore less subject to home bias. Hence, LPs that may have good local access to funds may still also invest in PE FoFs to gain international exposure. However, in contrast to other LPs, FoFs invest more often in local buyout funds than for VC funds.

Analysis – Regression results. Naturally, the mean results could be subject to important biases. For example, the mean results reflect not only the LPs, but also the sizes of the PE markets. The US PE market boasts many more funds. So if there are more LPs of one type in the US than in Europe, for instance, it should not surprise that this LP type also records more mean investments locally than others.[6]

There are also other considerations: The European market developed later than the US market, and PE in emerging markets is still at its early stages. Also, one may expect larger LPs to be able to maintain multiple global offices – even within one LP type. Similarly, experienced LPs may have greater confidence to

[6]To illustrate this, imagine the following: There are 1000 funds in the USA, and only 500 in Europe. If all endowments are found in the USA, and if they invest in proportion to the existing fund universe, endowments will record about 66% of investments in the USA – as a home investment. However, if all endowments were found in Europe, and they invested exactly the same proportion in US and European funds as before, they would still record 66% of investments in the USA – but this would not be scored as a home investment.

Investment Flows by Region

The table shows investments of LPs in GPs by regional flows. For instance, 45.5% of LPs in the data are situated in the US. 63.1% of all recorded investments went from the US to Europe, or 86.6% of all investments by US LPs went to US GPs. However, only 76% of GPs are also located in the US. Therefore, based on the global distribution of GPs, 1.14 times as many investments went to US GPs than would have been predicted. The values in italics under 'Total' (76.5% and 2.38x) indicate average measures of the home-home investments and bias entries. This means that 76.5% is the average of the USA-USA, Europe-Europe and ROW-ROW investments. Similarly, 2.38x is the average of 1.14x, 3.36x and 2.65x

% of LPs	LP–GP by Region	Freq.	Absolute %	Relative %	GP Distr.	x Bias
US LPs:	USA-USA	8,480	63.1%	86.6%	76%	1.14x
45.5%	USA-Eur.	1,109	8.3%	11.3%	17%	0.67x
	USA-ROW	202	1.5%	2.1%	6%	0.34x
Eur. LPs:	Europe-USA	1,167	8.7%	39.4%	76%	0.52x
42.0%	Eur.-Eur.	1,692	12.6%	57.1%	17%	3.36x
	Eur.-ROW	103	0.8%	3.5%	6%	0.58x
ROW LPs:	ROW-USA	332	2.5%	48.0%	76%	0.63x
12.5%	ROW-Eur.	249	1.9%	36.0%	17%	2.12x
	ROW-ROW	110	0.8%	15.9%	6%	2.65x
	Total	13,444	100.0%	*76.5%*		*2.38x*

Table 5.4: International PE Flows

also invest elsewhere.

To accommodate those effects, I perform logit estimates of investing in the same continental area, regressed on LP, fund and region dummies, as well as covariates and year fixed effects. Table 5.6 summarizes the results. In column (1) I first simply regress the dependent variable on fund types, were buyout funds are the base category. For late VC and opportunity funds, the coefficients are significant and large: Home bias is strong for those funds. In column (2) I replicate essentially the results from the mean table. The comparison category are PE FoFs, the presumably most diversified investors, and which came third from the bottom in the ranking of LPs with home bias. The regression confirms the general result: All LPs, except investment corporations and government agencies (who had scored even lower in the mean table), have sig-

Mean Results of LP Home Bias by Fund Type

This table shows the mean, in percent, observations of investments in the same region as the LP. The measure is recorded if the investment was from an LP in one continental region in a GP in the same continental region. Funds 1991–2005 were considered. Standard errors (as percentages) are reported in brackets. The LPs in the table are ordered by the LPs from largest to lowest home bias, based on overall measures.

Key measure: Did the investment take place in the same continental region? Yes= 100%, No= 0%

Overall	Obs.	Overall	Buyout	LVC	EVC	Opp.
Endowments	950	87.6%	79.5%	93.3%	100.0%	94.0%
		(1.1%)	(1.9%)	(1.8%)	(0.0%)	(1.5%)
Public Pension	6399	87.5%	82.9%	92.1%	96.5%	87.8%
		(0.4%)	(0.8%)	(0.7%)	(0.9%)	(0.7%)
Family Offices	1014	87.0%	82.8%	87.6%	89.8%	90.9%
		(1.1%)	(1.9%)	(2.5%)	(3.1%)	(1.6%)
Corp. Pension	538	70.4%	69.1%	74.7%	77.8%	68.8%
		(2.0%)	(2.6%)	(4.8%)	(7.0%)	(4.4%)
Insurances	460	65.4%	60.7%	83.3%	76.9%	59.1%
		(2.2%)	(3.0%)	(4.1%)	(8.4%)	(5.3%)
Banks	312	63.8%	60.5%	78.0%	73.3%	59.3%
		(2.7%)	(3.3%)	(5.9%)	(11.8%)	(9.6%)
PE FoFs	2931	56.0%	61.0%	52.8%	43.0%	50.3%
		(0.9%)	(1.2%)	(1.9%)	(2.7%)	(2.8%)
Invest. Corp.	766	54.8%	54.8%	60.0%	54.3%	47.7%
		(1.8%)	(2.4%)	(3.9%)	(6.0%)	(4.8%)
Govt. Agen.	74	43.2%	19.4%	60.9%	50.0%	64.3%
		(5.8%)	(7.2%)	(10.4%)	(22.4%)	(13.3%)
Total	13444	76.5%	72.3%	79.9%	75.2%	81.9%
		(0.4%)	(0.6%)	(0.7%)	(1.3%)	(0.7%)

Table 5.5: Mean Estimates of Home Bias

nificant and positive coefficients, i.e. are more subject to home bias than PE FoFs. In column (3), however, I now turn to the question of the significance of LP location. I therefore add dummies for LP region to correct for the fact that LPs themselves may be unequally distributed across continental regions. For most LPs, the coefficients remain similar. However, for investment corporations, the coefficient turns from an insignificant one to a significant positive one; for government agencies the significant negative coefficient becomes insignificant. Of particular interest are also banks: From an economically small positive coefficient to a strong and economically more pronounced positive. This suggests that conditioning on the LP Region corrects the coefficients.

Analysis: Predicted values. In fact, in table 5.7 I calculate, from column (3) of the logit estimation, the new predicted 'home bias' proportions. This table reveals some surprising movements: Banks are now among the LPs with highest home bias, and PE FoFs the lowest. Moreover, the average percentages have gone up for the lowest ranked LPs in general: While government agencies were recorded to invest 43.2% locally in the mean table, logit now predicts that they do so now 74.4% at a time. Overall, 81.6% of investments are estimated to be on the same continent. Home bias is thus really quite prevalent.

Finally, in table 5.6, column (4), I also interact LPs with fund types, while still conditioning on the LP Region. Not for all LPs coefficients are significant, but for most the results indicate that VC investments are more affected by home bias. The only exception are PE FoFs (as the base category, the coefficients directly on the VC and opportunity funds are relevant), for which coefficients are negative and significant. For FoFs this means that their home-bias is most prevalent for buyout funds (this was also seen in table 5.5). Also of interest is the fact that the coefficients on opportunity funds are rarely significant, and if, lower than those for late VC funds (exception: Government agencies). Hence, when adjusted for the LP region, investments in opportunity funds are not more likely to be local.

Logit Estimates of Investing in the Same Continental Region. This table shows the logit estimates of investing in the same continental region. The dependent variable 'invest in same area' takes the value of 1 if the investment took place in the same region, 0 otherwise. Funds 1991– 2005 are considered. LP Europe and LP ROW are dummies that take the value of 1 if the LP is located in Europe, or ROW, respectively; USA is the comparison category. Other comparison categories: Buyout Funds, PE FoFs. (1) *Funds* shows estimates simply by fund type. (2) *LPs* introduces LP dummies, (3) *LP Region* also controls for the location of the LP. (4) *Interact* shows interactions of LPs and region dummies (Endowments * EVC is dropped because of insufficient observations outside the same area). Significance levels: *** $p<0.01$, ** $p<0.05$, * $p<0.1$. Covariates as used in previous regressions. Categories for comparison are buyout funds, PE FoFs and USA, where applicable.

Dependent variable: Invest in same area? '1' if yes, '0' otherwise.

	Funds (1)	LPs (2)	LP Region (3)	Interact (4)
Fund Types				
Late VC	0.30**	0.27**	0.28**	-0.41***
	(0.13)	(0.13)	(0.13)	(0.16)
Early VC	0.05	0.07	-0.04	-0.95***
	(0.19)	(0.18)	(0.18)	(0.24)
Opp.	0.42***	0.07	0.11	-0.35
	(0.13)	(0.13)	(0.14)	(0.24)
LPs				
Public Pension		1.67***	1.22***	0.72***
		(0.12)	(0.10)	(0.15)
Banks		0.34**	1.18***	0.95***
		(0.14)	(0.17)	(0.18)
Invest. Corp.		-0.14	0.64***	0.37**
		(0.10)	(0.13)	(0.16)
Insurances		0.40***	0.62***	0.23
		(0.14)	(0.16)	(0.18)
Corporate Pension		0.63***	0.53***	0.32*
		(0.13)	(0.14)	(0.16)
Endowments		1.67***	1.04***	0.34*
		(0.21)	(0.12)	(0.20)
Family Offices		1.71***	1.12***	0.69***

Continued on next page

Table 5.6 – *continued from previous page*

	Funds (1)	LPs (2)	LP Region (3)	Interact (4)
		(0.17)	(0.13)	(0.18)
Govt. Agencies		-0.69**	0.45	-0.96
		(0.28)	(0.39)	(0.74)
LP Region				
LP Europe			-1.02***	-1.00***
			(0.27)	(0.27)
LP ROW			-3.37***	-3.44***
			(0.24)	(0.24)
Interactions				
Public P. * LVC				1.20***
				(0.25)
Public P. * EVC				2.45***
				(0.48)
Public P. * Opp.				0.66*
				(0.37)
Banks* LVC				0.78
				(0.67)
Banks * EVC				0.99*
				(0.57)
Banks * Opp.				-0.40
				(0.60)
Invest. Corp.* LVC				0.92***
				(0.36)
Invest. Corp. * EVC				0.27
				(0.46)
Invest. Corp. * Opp.				0.29
				(0.35)
Insurances * LVC				1.40***
				(0.47)
Insurances * EVC				0.84
				(0.60)
Insurances * Opp.				0.48
				(0.41)

Continued on next page

Table 5.6 – *continued from previous page*

	Funds (1)	LPs (2)	LP Region (3)	Interact (4)
Corporate P. * LVC				0.62
				(0.42)
Corporate P. * EVC				0.62
				(0.44)
Corporate P. * Opp.				0.10
				(0.38)
Endowments * LVC				1.49***
				(0.46)
Endowments * Opp.				1.38**
				(0.53)
Family Offices * LVC				0.65
				(0.42)
Family Offices * EVC				1.30***
				(0.38)
Family Offices * Opp.				0.73
				(0.46)
Govt. Agen. * LVC				1.75*
				(1.02)
Govt. Agen. * EVC				1.23
				(1.11)
Govt. Agen. * Opp.				3.24***
				(1.03)
logFundSize	-0.11**	-0.13**	-0.15***	-0.15***
	(0.05)	(0.05)	(0.05)	(0.05)
logAUM	0.03*	0.02	-0.01	-0.02
	(0.02)	(0.02)	(0.02)	(0.02)
logExp	0.28***	0.04	-0.02	-0.03
	(0.04)	(0.04)	(0.04)	(0.04)
Year Fixed Effects?	Yes	Yes	Yes	Yes
Observations	11902	11902	11902	11837

Table 5.6: Logit Regressions of Home Bias

Hypothesis: Interpretation. The results suggest that the null hypothesis of no home bias can be rejected. Instead, home bias seems prevalent among LPs, between 65% and 86% of investments can be expected to be in the same continental region as the LP, based on logit predictions. Moreover, public pension

Predicted Probabilities of Home Bias

The table shows predicted probabilities of investing in the same continental region, based on the previous logit regression, column (3). LPs are sorted according to the predicted values in ascending order. 95% confidence interval is also shown. The last column, Mean, shows the previously described mean values for comparison.

LP Type	Prediction Logit	95% confidence interval	Mean
Public Pension	86.1%	[84.3% – 87.9%]	87.5%
Banks	85.8%	[81.4% – 90.1%]	63.8%
Family Office	84.9%	[81.7% – 88.0%]	87.0%
Endowments	83.8%	[79.7% – 87.9%]	87.6%
Invest. Corp.	77.7%	[72.6% – 82.8%]	54.8%
Insurances	77.4%	[71.7% – 83.1%]	65.4%
Corporate Pension	75.9%	[70.7% – 81.2%]	70.4%
Govt. Agencies	74.4%	[59.5% – 89.3%]	43.2%
PE FoF	64.9%	[60.5% – 69.3%]	56.0%
Overall	81.6%	[79.9% – 83.7%]	76.5%

Table 5.7: Predicted Probabilities of Home Bias

funds, endowments and family offices are, as was hypothesized, more likely to prefer 'local' funds. In addition, for funds that presumably require the highest amount of due diligence, and probably personal interaction (i.e. VC funds), LPs are less likely to venture abroad. For opportunity funds, one may speculate that the large 'home bias' in the mean results are driven by the fact that most opportunity, alternative strategy, funds are located in the US, and so are most LPs. Therefore, for this fund type, adjusting for the regional distribution eliminates the measured home bias. Finally, the large degree of home bias for banks was unexpected. However, as will be discussed at the end of the chapter, the results are in fact not entirely surprising given what is known about banks from other publications and other asset classes.

The results, of course, should be read with a degree of cautiousness. First, it is likely that many smaller GPs only fundraise in their home country, so home bias may also be a function of the knowledge of fundraising funds. Second, the continental regions may seem somewhat coarse. For instance, within Europe one may be able to find differences among LPs in the UK and Germany. However, the activities of GPs are usually not closer defined as the general continental region, i.e. GPs are not usually restricted to single countries. Therefore, it will be more difficult to drill down on the level of individual countries. Third, because I do not have the actual data on all LP office representations, I can only interpret the results as if some LPs are able to open subsidiaries, while I suspect others are not. I can only assume that family offices only operate with one office, while investment corporations may have subsidiaries, or have other means to bridge information barriers.

Still, overall, the results suggest that the null hypothesis of 'no home bias' can be rejected. Instead, home bias really seems prevalent and particularly so for the LP types that were hypothesized to be most subject to it.

5.2 The Strategy Adjustment Hypothesis

I now turn to a hypothesis that relates to the dynamic development of preferences. There are likely differences across LP types not only in their fund preference, but also in how they react to outside changes. Hence, preference for a fund type will not just be a function of the LP's general preference, but also the LPs' different perception of market trends and risk-factors of GP types that in turn affect adjustments of portfolios. Of the LP types in question, endowments are said to be more sophisticated and to embrace new investment options.[7] Some evidence was already presented here in this paper: On average, endowments are among the more experienced investors and allocate a larger share to alternative investments than others.[8] However, within the asset class, little has been said about the dynamic weighting among fund types. I hypothesized, in principle, that endowments are more flexible allocators of their funds than other LPs in response to market changes. As argued before, the general thrust of this argument is that endowments are smaller with faster reaction times, are more sophisticated and are freer to embrace alternatives than other LPs.

[7] See Lerner et al. (2007a) and Lerner et al. (2007b) for this argument; also Swensen (2000), page 335.

[8] See chapter 4.

Natural Experiment. A simple way of trying to approach this hypothesis could be to look at how, over time, endowments changed their portfolio allocations compared to other LPs. Even if those changes were statistically significant, however, one could not easily identify the causes of the swings. There could be a number of omitted variables, such as unobserved regulatory changes, gradual changes in the sophistication of investors or differences in the activities of endowments that use the receipts of the investments. A stronger test for the ability to react to general market changes would be to look at allocation swings after an event that affected all investors and that, ideally, even came as a surprise so that investors could hardly prepare for it. One can then make the valuable assumption that the unobserved differences between different investor types are stable over time and that changes in the allocation to fund types are really a response to market changes. One can also make the second valuable assumption that short-term changes in the PE fund market, e.g. the number of PE funds, should impact all investors similarly. This then essentially permits a *differences-in-differences* estimation approach.

Naturally, a number of surprising and important events occurred in 2001. While the burst of the internet bubble might have been somewhat predictable for some investors, the terrorist attacks hardly were. The economic future looked uncertain for everyone and long-term investments in PE funds probably appeared particularly challenging. If endowments really differed in the way they take allocation decisions, then one should be able to identify those differences best after those events. Hence, I stated the following hypothesis:

H 3: Strategy Adjustment – Endowments more quickly adjust their allocation within the PE asset class, especially after 2001.

Analysis – Mean results. If endowments did react more quickly, then this change should be expressed most strongly in their allocation to the largest fund type category, **buyout funds**. Specifically, I graph the number of recorded investments in buyout funds, as a percentage of the total number of investments, over time.[9] In figure 5.4 the investments in buyout funds are repre-

[9]Note that this is not a dollar-weighted measure. Investments in buyout funds were, on an individual investment level, likely larger than for other funds. This approach therefore concentrates on the number of investments, not their volume. LPs usually allocate considerably larger amounts to buyout funds than to VC funds. So by way of

sented by the dark blue line. In 2000, prior to the event, 55% of all recorded investments by endowments were in buyout funds. The thinner, dashed blue line represents the same for all other LPs, on average, excluding endowments. In the same year, only 43% of recorded investments by all other LPs were in buyout funds, i.e. approximately 12% less. This is similar for the years before (14% less in 1999, 8% less in 1998).

In 2001, all LPs allocated considerably less to buyout funds, probably in response to the market changes. For endowments, buyout investments dropped to 28%, which is still 6% higher than the average LP with 22%. This suggests that the drop might be a function both of general perception of buyout attractiveness, but also, perhaps, the number of available buyout funds.

After 2001, buyout investments 'rebounded'. The average LP even invested comparably more often in buyout funds than before (46% in 2002 vs. 43% in 2000). This implies that there were plenty of buyout funds to invest in. Endowments, however, did not rebound nearly as sharply. In fact, with 34% of recorded investments in buyout funds in 2002, endowments now invested 12% *less often* in this fund type than other LPs. This suggests a relative change of – 24% compared to pre-2001 levels and the average LP (before 2001: 55% - 43% = + 12%, after: 34%-46% = – 12%). In principle, this is robust for the subsequent years 2003 and 2004.

This 'difference in the differences' in the allocation to buyout funds over time might suffice to argue that endowments reacted differently to the events in 2001. However, I appreciate that the portfolio allocation is also a relative measure: A drop in buyout investments is necessarily accompanied by a rise in investments in other fund types. I there expand the inquiry and ask: Where did endowments invest in instead? Specifically, I present the data on **opportunity fund investments.**[10]

Figure 5.4 therefore also shows the recorded investments in opportunity funds. In 2000, endowments allocated about the same number of investments

illustration, even if only, say, 30% of investments by number are in buyout funds, this translates likely into more of 50% of volume on a portfolio level.

[10] In principle, the comparison of buyout fund allocations before and after 2001 can be thought of as a differences-in-differences estimation. The mean results (with a difference-in-difference of 24%) already suggest a significant change. The *additional* comparison to swings in opportunity fund allocations could also be thought of as a differences-in-differences-in-differences estimation.

to opportunity funds as other LPs (both 18%), in the years before that somewhat *less often* (e.g. 10% vs. 23% for other LPs in 1999). Even in 2001, though all LPs increased their allocation to opportunity funds, the average LP still invested more often in opportunity funds than endowments (34% vs. 29%). Thus, until and including 2001, endowments invested less often in opportunity funds than the average LP – in complete contrast to what was seen for buyout funds. After 2001, however, endowments now strongly increased their allocations to opportunity funds, from 29% to 51%, while other LPs did not (in fact, a drop from 34% to 29% is recorded). In comparative terms, from 2000 to 2002 this represents a change of + 22 % to pre-2001 levels and the average LP (before 2001: 18%-18% = 0%, after 2001: 51%-29% = 22%).[11] The –24% comparative change in allocations to buyout funds is thus nearly matched by a +22% increase in investments in opportunity funds. Moreover, for the years 2003 and 2004, similar calculations yield qualitatively similar results.[12]

[11]The comparison to other LPs is particularly important and a strength of the differences-in-differences approach. Without comparison, one might reason that already after 1999, endowments commenced an upward trend from 10% allocation to eventually 62% in 2004. However, the comparison highlights two important facets. First, until 2002, only the year 2000 is a year where other LPs and endowments might differ somewhat in their allocations (there is a downward trend for all LPs from 1998 to 1999), as both endowments and other LPs increased their allocations again in 2001. Second, up until 2001, endowments always invested less often in opportunity funds. So any increasing previous trend (from 10% to 18% to 29%) might also simply be interpreted as a convergence process to 'average LP' levels. The real strength of the difference-in-difference argument therefore bears out if one appreciates that not only did endowments increase their allocations to opportunity funds after 2001, but even more than the average LP.

[12]The pre-2001 levels obviously remain the same. For 2003, comparative buyout fund allocations were 37% (endowments) -48% (other LPs) = –11%, for opportunity funds 45%-37% = + 8%; for 2004 buyout allocations comparative allocations were 14%-28% = –14%, for opportunity funds 62%-45% = + 17%. Thus, even in those years, changes in the allocations in one fund type were largely accompanied by similar changes in the other fund type.

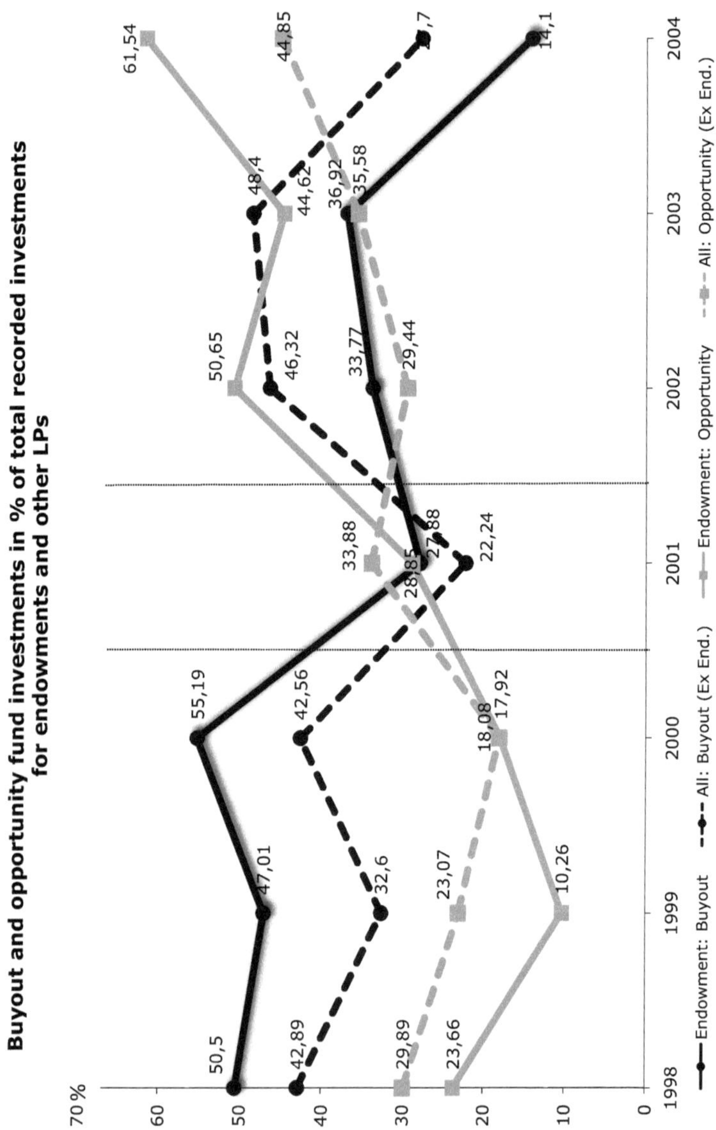

Figure 5.4: Endowment Allocations over Time

Analysis – Multinomial logit regression. While the graphs are informative, I also aimed at testing the conclusions in multivariate analysis. Wooldridge (2003) gives an introduction to an econometric treatment of the difference-in-differences estimation.[13] A convenient way to estimate effects of abrupt changes is the use of a time-dummy variable, interacted with the relevant independent variables in a pooled regression. The coefficient on this *interaction term* then indicates the effect compared to the two time-periods.[14]

In this specific case, I also aim to assess not only the changes in buyout allocations, but also, because the two are naturally interrelated, the simultaneous allocation to opportunity funds. I therefore employ a multinomial logit analysis to assess the *relative probability* of LPs picking a certain fund type, compared to each other, and, by use of a time-dummy, over time. The time-dummy takes a value of 1 if the investment took place after 2001, and 0 otherwise. By using a multinomial logit approach, I can therefore gain a probabilistic measure if endowments, compared to other LPs, preferred opportunity funds over buyout funds after 2001.

In this analysis, I only include US LPs and their US investments. The multinomial logit base category is 'buyout', i.e. the comparative probability of picking one fund type compared to the probability of picking a buyout fund. I report the results in table 5.8. In regression A: Post 2001 I show that for endowments, compared to all other LPs, the likelihood of picking an opportunity fund after 2001 is considerably higher than picking a buyout fund. This is evidenced by the statistically significant coefficients of 1.24 on the interaction term 'Endowment * Post 2001' in column (1) for opportunity funds. Late VC funds (column 2) also had positive, but statistically less significant, signs (0.68). This suggests that some of the reduction in buyout fund allocation also spilled over into higher probabilities of picking late VC funds.

In many descriptions of difference-in-difference estimations, the discussion focuses on the interpretation of this interaction term. However, some

[13] See Wooldridge (2003), pages 432 – 438.

[14] The difference-in-differences estimator is commonly used to assess policy impacts. For example, in an important paper, Ashenfelter (1978) uses this method to assess the effect of training programs for workers on their subsequent earnings. Similarly, Hastings (2004) looks at the changes in gasoline prices in southern California after a local change of the competitive landscape of gas-stations.

argue that an even more stringent test would be to see if the periods preceding the external change did not already exhibit a similar trend. For instance, Wooldridge (2003) does not discuss this additional test,[15] while Hastings (2004) does discuss the preceding development.

I therefore test if endowments had always invested more often in opportunity funds. From the visual inspection of the figure 5.4, this seems highly unlikely (if anything, they invested less often than the average LP in opportunity funds before 2001), but the use of covariables and the focus on US LPs might yield different results.

Naturally, I would be inclined to ask that question for the period until 2001 and prior to 2002. However, I exclude 2001 on the grounds that this was the year of heightened general volatility and turmoil. In other words: the events that may have had an impact on changing LP behavior after 2001 actually occurred in that very year and I would like to avoid it on that grounds alone.[16] So instead I look at the years 1998–2000 and find that prior to 2001, endowments did not significantly deviate from the average LP, i.e. they did not already invest more often in opportunity funds than the average LP (if anything, less often, but the estimates are statistically not significant: -0.78 for instance). This result is shown in regression B, column (4) to (6) of table 5.8; none of the interaction terms are statistically significant. This suggests that indeed endowments invested significantly more often in opportunity funds after 2001 than other LPs, in response to changes at that time.

Hypothesis: Interpretation. Based on the results I conclude that the null hypothesis that endowments do not react more strongly in their strategy definition than other LPs can be rejected. Rather, it looks that after 2001, endowments, who had previously invested more often in buyout funds than the average LP, now invested less often in that fund type. At the same time, endowments weighted, more than any other LP type, opportunity funds. This suggests these LPs not only reacted more sharply to the events, but also invested in funds that seemed less directly correlated with other PE funds, i.e. to diversify more than other LPs within PE.

[15] See Wooldridge (2003), pages 432 – 438.

[16] In this vein it should be noted again that the years are vintages, and an investment could have taken place before September 2001, or after – but both would be reflected in the average measure for this year.

Robustness Tests. There may be two major concerns with the employed strategy. First, perhaps endowments aimed only at opportunity funds because they saw some few exceptional opportunities that were 'too-good-to-miss' and that therefore impacted the overall portfolio allocation even though this had not been planned. I therefore repeat the analysis (and also the subsequent robustness tests) by dropping the top and bottom 1% of funds by net IRR. However, this has no bearing on the results. Second, the results could be an artifact of the very particular years chosen. I therefore test if including more or fewer years impacts the results. First, I examine if the results were any different if I asked not what happened after 2001, but already after 2000. One could argue that during the year 2001, LPs already adjusted their allocations. In this robustness test, the coefficients become smaller, but remain significant. I also repeat the original analysis by including the year 1997; the results remain qualitatively the same. Therefore, the robustness tests do not impact the conclusion: Endowments shifted between buyout funds and opportunity funds more dramatically than all other LPs prior and post 2001, presumably to react to events in and around 2001.

5.3 Summary and Discussion

In this chapter I tested a number of hypotheses regarding the investment preferences of LPs. In principal, I found supporting evidence for the *home bias* and *strategy adjustment* hypotheses. I also showed that LP types differ in their preference for specific fund types. However, I identified portfolio allocations, *fund preferences*, that differed somewhat from what I had predicted.

Before I turn to individual LP types, I reflect on the general findings on **GP fund types**. First, there is a trade-off between allocations by LPs to buyout and opportunity funds. Second, home bias is most severe for VC funds. Perhaps there is an underlying factor to explain this result? From the interviews, it becomes clear that the selection of funds is a particular challenge, and that the difficulties are greatest for non-buyout funds. This would explain home bias and preference for buyout funds by the least sophisticated LPs: Limited investment teams likely contributed to home bias, and GPs probably also prefer fundraising among LPs that are close and do not require trans-Atlantic

Probability of Investing in Fund Types: Differences-in-Differences Estimates
Multinomial logit models: The regressions include US investment observations of LPs in various GP types. The estimates thus indicate the likelihood of an investment observation being an investment in a given fund type. The dependent variable is the categorical variable representing GP types. The omitted variable for comparison is buyout fund. Columns (1) – (6) thus compare investments in the fund type to buyout funds. By use of the endowment dummy, this LP type is compared to all other LPs. Regression A present investments after 2001, i.e. after the collapse of the Internet bubble and 9–11 compared to before. Regression B is a robustness test to see if the results from Regression A had already existed in 1998 and 1999 compared to 2000, i.e. before the collapse of the Internet bubble and 9–11. Robust and clustered (at fund level) standard errors are given in brackets. Post2001 represents the time dummy of investments after 2001 and takes the value of 1 if the investment took place after 2001 and 0 otherwise. In regression B, Pre2000 is a dummy that takes the value of 1 if the investment took place in 2000 and 0 otherwise. Years of observations for the analysis: 1998 – 2004, for the robustness test in regression B 1998 – 2000. Significance levels: *** p<0.01, ** p<0.05, * p<0.1. Covariates as used in previous regressions. Constant estimated but not reported.

	Multinomial logit – Buyout Funds vs. Other Funds					
	A: Post 2001			B: Pre 2000 - Test		
	Opp.	LVC	EVC	Opp.	LVC	EVC
	(1)	(2)	(3)	(4)	(5)	(6)
End.*Post2001	1.24***	0.69*	0.60			
	(0.37)	(0.39)	(0.47)			
End.*Pre2000				-0.78	-0.26	-0.02
				(0.73)	(0.55)	(0.62)
Post2001	0.51*	-0.53*	-0.42			
	(0.28)	(0.31)	(0.37)			
Pre2000				0.02	0.74	0.81
				(0.49)	(0.50)	(0.65)
Endowment	-0.54***	-0.47***	-0.44	-0.40	-0.18	-0.31
	(0.26)	(0.21)	(0.26)	(0.58)	(0.43)	(0.49)
Constant	-0.57***	-0.46**	-1.13***	-0.36	-0.84**	-1.60***
	(0.19)	(0.19)	(0.25)	(0.33)	(0.35)	(0.42)
Covariates	Yes	Yes	Yes	Yes	Yes	Yes
Observations	6125	6125	6125	2159	2159	2159
pseudo R2	0.0177	0.0177	0.0177	0.0154	0.0154	0.0154
LogL.	-7782	-7782	-7782	-2719	-2719	-2719

Table 5.8: Differences-in-Differences – Endowment Allocations

investor relation efforts. This reasoning would also explain the trade-off between buyout and opportunity funds. As some very large, new LPs entered the market, they focused on the easier-to-understand buyout funds. Smaller investors, in contrast, may have tried to avoid this 'herding' behavior and instead opted to diversify. This is an interesting proposition, as those alternative funds likely offered an appealing risk/return profile. For example, 'venture debt' funds or 'secondary' funds would likely flourish during times when the classic VC and buyout funds would struggle somewhat. However, in order to take this investment decision, the LPs would need some sort of additional understanding of the opportunity at hand. The results suggest that larger LPs did not yet consider those alternatives.

This argument leads me to commence the LP-specific discussion with a contrast between **endowments / family offices** to **public pension** funds. Perhaps somewhat surprisingly, I found that all three had similar portfolio allocations, i.e. measured apparent fund preferences. They were also, presumably for similar reasons, comparably affected by home bias, where they were among the most likely to invest in the same continental region. This is an unexpected result, as others, in particular Lerner et al. (2007b), had argued that endowments differed dramatically in their PE investments from public pension funds. Were the small endowments not supposed to be among the most flexible, sophisticated and successful PE investors, very different from public pension funds? I, in contrast, find that in terms of overall preferences they share similarities.

My interpretation is that with regard to inter-continental fund investments, i.e. home bias, endowments, family offices and public pension funds are in fact affected in a similar manner: They have too small a staff and budget to maintain investment teams across the globe. At this point, the dynamic findings on the *strategy adjustment* hypothesis are particularly noteworthy. I find that endowments, and in unreported regression to some extent also family offices, are the only LPs that significantly shift their focus from buyout funds to opportunity funds after 2001. Public pension funds, or other LPs for that matter, did not perform the same shift. Instead of possibly herding into one booming fund class, the LPs endowments considered a more diversified, multi-strategy PE fund allocation.

Unfortunately, I cannot easily estimate if this strategy actually also translated into higher returns. Given some of the very successful buyout funds in recent years, one would expect that not investing in buyout funds as often as other LPs may have depressed endowment returns. At the same time, some may argue that the financial crisis in 2007 / 2008 actually must have hurt buyout fund returns, and played into the hands of the more diversified endowments and who allocated to 'alternative' funds with strategies that should have benefitted during that period. Time will tell if this was indeed the case.

A puzzle is also found for **investment corporations**, **insurances** and **corporate pension funds** on the one hand, and **banks** on the other hand. All of the investors share similar fund preference results. Based on the presumed risk-profile, except perhaps for corporate pension funds, one could have expected that to be the case. However, banks stand out, as they are much more subject to home bias. Interestingly, this adds to the existing body of literature on banking relations and clients. For example, based on Allen and Gale (2000), Allen (1993) and also Lerner et al. (2007b), it can be speculated that banks investing in PE funds may be motivated by the hope to also be employed as the fund's preferred leveraged loan underwriter and / or to benefit from IPO activities. This is similar to the argument brought forward by Hellmann et al. (2008) who also find evidence for banks investing strategically in start-up firms to foster future lending relationships. In a related vein, Petersen and Rajan (2002) discuss how geographic proximity is an important factor in relations with small businesses. This fits both the notion of 'special' relations with PE funds, as well as the finding on home bias for banks. Moreover, my results here seem to be confirmed by Mayer et al. (2005): They found that banks generally prefer larger VC funds and funds that are in the same country (i.e. home bias). I conclude that banks are driven by additional investment objectives in their investments.

I now turn to **PE FoFs**. One could expect FoFs to offer a diversified approach – by fund type, fund size and geographic reach. This is because they are likely intermediaries for investors who seek PE exposure. Yet the results raise questions: They have a particular emphasis on funds abroad. The limited home bias suggests, indeed, that they try to diversify more. It may also be evidence that they offer their clients a more global PE exposure. However, their particular emphasis on buyout funds suggests that perhaps they try to invest in well-established, 'brand-name' buyout funds to attract funds from their own investors. A simple look at advertisements for FoFs indicates that they vie for external funds by claiming access to top-quarter funds – clearly based on past performance. Those funds, as described before, usually raise larger follow-on funds;[17] in recent times also so-called 'mega-funds' with very large assets to invest.

Finally, **government agencies** show the predicted pattern in terms of home and fund preferences. The low degree of measured home bias likely reflects the limited investment opportunities for government agencies in the rest of the world who have to invest in the US or Europe. While the coefficients are estimated with a certain level of statistical significance, one should, however, concede that the limited number of recorded observations also limits the validity to some extent.

There may be a number of **alternative explanations** for differing allocations and preferences for LPs. For instance, there may be a number of political restrictions on investment decisions, in particular for public pension funds. However, neither Lerner et al. (2007b) for the US, nor Nielsen (2005) for Denmark, deem political limitation a likely restriction for pension funds. An alternative explanation could be restricted access to funds. Many GPs aim to maintain their LP base over several fund generations. Therefore, 'late-comers', or LPs with little reputation, may be excluded from the investment. While I cannot test for this hypothesis, I refer again to Lerner et al. (2007b) who argued against the notion that exclusion from funds is significant, even for the most successful funds. Moreover, even if access was an issue, it would likely more affect returns from funds, less so the overall portfolio allocation, as then excluded LPs would presumably simply look for a different fund of the similar type. Another possibility would be that LPs with similar measured preferences all had the same external advisor that advised on a specific portfolio allocation. This is to say that preferences were determined by an external body, not the LP. In section 6.2.2 I examine the effects of external advisors on the returns achieved from PE investments. In unreported analyses I then also looked if LPs with and without advisors had different allocations, and if the LPs with advisors had very similar portfolios. However, I do not find any statistically significant findings on the level of overall portfolio allocation. Lastly, it is possible that the decision making process is not as separate as was presented in

[17] See Kaplan and Schoar (2005).

chapter 2; i.e. that fund selection and opportunity had also an impact on the portfolio allocation. In parts, this may be the case: In section 6.2.3 I document that (some) LPs invest more often locally in VC funds than elsewhere. Perhaps this 'local' VC opportunity then crowds out buyout fund investments? While I cannot fully rule out this possibility, I also look, in unreported analyses, if LPs that do not have that local VC investment opportunity (because they are located farther away) then invest more often in buyout funds instead. I do not find significant evidence for this possibility and conclude that 'opportunity-driven' crowding-out is not a significant factor in the overall allocation.

The results indicate a **role of structural limitations**, impediments, to unconstrained investments in PE funds. Is this unique to this asset class? Unfortunately, there is scant empiric evidence from public equity investments, mostly for data reasons, but this research seems to corroborate other research. For example, there is ample evidence that large institutional investors may be subject to 'irrational', attention-driven investment strategies, see Barber and Odean (2006). This is complemented by research that shows those investors are often focusing on different 'investment styles', and hence diverge from classic diversified portfolio strategies; see for instance Barberis and Shleifer (2003) or Froot and Teo (2004). On the other hand, there is particularly strong evidence that home bias is prevalent, as French and Poterba (1991), Cooper and Kaplanis (1994) and Werner and Tesar (1995) discuss. Explanations for this bias include transaction costs of transacting in foreign assets, taxes, and political risk, as well as other factors such as the failure of purchasing power parity (PPP), information asymmetries, and regulation. This bias is even recorded within domestic markets, i.e. the closer the investment target within a country, the more likely the investor chooses investments in this asset; see Coval and Moskowitz (1999). Similarly, Petersen and Rajan (2002) underscore the role of geographic proximity between banks and target firms – my result on home bias for banks are thus also found outside the PE industry. For PE FoFs the best comparison are mutual funds. I speculate that FoFs look particularly at funds that were successful in the past, perhaps for 'marketing' reasons to attract new money from clients. This focus on past performance is also found for mutual funds, as Grinblatt et al. (1995) discuss. In this research, most mutual funds are 'momentum investors', with a significant tendency for 'herding'.

To conclude, I discussed a number of factors that may impact the investment decisions by LPs. I argue that in addition to possible differences in risk-profiles, *structural reasons* impact allocations to GP funds and lead, for instance, to home bias. Those obviously have important implications for the design and regulation of investors. In particular policy makers interested in the performance of public pension funds may take interest in the notion that some of the world's largest investors may be unable to exploit all investment opportunities because of small investment teams or insufficient global representation. It is questionable that they can thus fully pursue their fiduciary role. Likewise, many are interested in the investment strategies employed by 'sophisticated' endowments. Interestingly, they seem strongly affect by home bias. This is surprising. Beyond this finding, however, endowments seem more flexible, to be less subject to herding (in buyout funds for instance) and to invest also in small VC, as well as opportunity funds. Overall, the results suggest, however, that structural limitations impact fund selections, perhaps more so than ex-ante defined differences in risk-preferences.

The research directions were guided by the original theoretical principal-agent considerations in chapter 2. They covered the section on LP risk-sharing and fund preferences. However, the discussion would not be complete without the second component, the selection of funds from a select pool, after the overall allocation decision. Therefore, the performance of LPs achieved with their fund selections is presented in chapter 6.

Chapter 6

LP Investment Performance

In this chapter, I test LP performance hypotheses. The chapter is organized in two parts. In part one, section 6.1, I first present average returns from PE fund investments by LP type, location, time period and fund type (section 6.1.1). I then probe hypotheses regarding the performance of US (section 6.1.2), as well as global LPs (6.1.3). This research also investigates the role of experience and LP size, in addition to important timing effects.

The second part, section 6.2, tests three hypotheses pertaining to the possible drivers of investment success. Specifically, section 6.2.1 asks if endowments outperformed other LPs because they took greater risks. Section 6.2.2 examines if external advisors to LPs have a positive impact on the returns achieved by LPs. Section 6.2.3 then presents evidence on the role of LP proximity to VC-intense and successful geographic areas. Finally, section 6.3 summarizes and discusses the results.

6.1 LP Returns

6.1.1 Mean LP Investment Performances

In this section, I present average fund returns by LPs. I first discuss general results, before discussing three specific LP types, endowments, FoFs and government agencies. I then turn to the issue of selection bias.

Table 6.1 presents the average fund returns of LP types, including different fund categories.[1] I should note that in the following discussion, I only focus on those estimates for which standard errors suggest a meaningful statistical significance, even though the table provides many more estimates than are discussed.

LPs: General Results. Over the entire sample, most successful investors were insurances (with about 3.4% higher IRRs than the average) and banks (2%). This is surprising, as banks had belonged to the worst investors in the sample of Lerner, Schoar, and Wongsunwai (2007b) (henceforth also referred to as LSW). Endowments, best performers in LSW's sample, outperformed the average only by about 1.2% IRR, and with limited statistical significance. Other LP types did not deviate from the average in a statistically significant manner. Overall, therefore, returns by all LPs seem to be much less heterogeneous and closer to the overall average than reported by LSW.

Three factors can account for the differences. First, my dataset includes also investments after 1999. Second, the investments also include non-US investments. Third, my sample also includes investments in funds other than classic buyout and VC funds. Therefore, I group investments according to a) time-periods, b) regions and c) fund types.

When I look at returns 1991 – 1998 vs. 1999 – 2003, it becomes apparent that returns were a lot more homogenous in recent years. For 1991 – 1998, global endowments outperformed most LPs by an average of 5% IRR, but thereafter endowments actually were only average. Instead, banks, who had belonged to the worst LPs up to 1999, were outperformers after 1998. The reverse seems to hold for public pension funds: Average until 1998, underperforming thereafter. Insurances, in contrast, always picked funds that performed above-average: Up to 1998, funds picked by insurances outperformed by about 4%, and about 3.4% thereafter.

When looking at LPs type by region, more differences become apparent. In general, European LPs invested in funds that had IRRs 2.3% higher than their

[1] For some funds, PreQin did not yet post returns in IRRs because they were not yet meaningful. However, for a few more funds, PreQin did include the multiple of equity returned, a figure that is less sensitive to cashflow-timing than the IRR.

US peers. In particular, US and European banks differ strongly: US banks were among the worst LPs (underperforming other LPs by 3.5% IRR), yet in Europe banks were among the very best (outperforming by nearly 5% IRR). Investors in the rest of the world,[2] were even, on average, better than the West. However, this result is driven primarily by FoFs and government agencies. Interestingly though, family offices, small investors, were among the worst outside the US and Europe. Public pension funds were about average in all three regions.

Apart from regional and timing issues, what else can explain the differences? A likely answer for those average results lies in the **differences LPs achieved by fund types**. In general, buyout funds outperformed VC funds and other funds significantly, by about 14% IRR compared to early VC funds for instance – evidence of the performance of these funds since 2000. And within buyout funds, banks and insurances were among the best selectors. In other fund types, however, the investors did not stand out significantly, or even underperformed like banks in their VC investments. Moreover, banks were also among the worst within the opportunity funds.

In the following, I single out three investors with particularly interesting results: Endowments, FoFs and government agencies.

Endowments. In contrast, to previously published results, endowments stand out only in VC fund investments, and even there with only weak statistical significance (12.7% and 10.3% IRR for VC funds). How can this result be reconciled with the outperformance (16.00% IRR) over the entire sample? Together with the high returns achieved until 1998, it becomes clear that endowments had invested more often in successful (mostly VC) funds during the nineties (when they achieved 24.4% overall), so that the average return is quite high. Yet, within the VC fund types, compared to other LPs, endowments outperform only marginally over the entire sample. Together with the results by LSW, who had already demonstrated that endowments outperformed within VC funds until 1998, this suggests that the 'special VC expertise' for endowments was somewhat constrained to the period until 1999. Thereafter,

[2]Which also includes Canada and Japan; but excluding investors from these countries does not markedly change the results (unreported).

endowments perhaps still had some advantages, but those did not bear out. Alternatively, other LPs learned and leveled the playing field. This is also shown more clearly in figure 6.1. The figure shows the relative outperformance of US endowments over the nineties in their fund returns (both late and early VC are pooled) over the average US LP (excluding endowments). To arrive at this measure, I subtracted the average fund return from the endowment fund return per year per fund type. While each individual year-point estimate has relatively large standard errors, cumulatively during the nineties US endowments, compared to US LPs, achieved special returns (mostly from VC funds) that other LPs did not enjoy: I calculate that US endowments achieved fund returns of 26.2% IRR (standard error: 3.4%), the average US LP (excluding endowments) achieved 19.2% IRR (standard error: 0.8%). Thereafter, however, differences became smaller, even negative, and statistically insignificant.

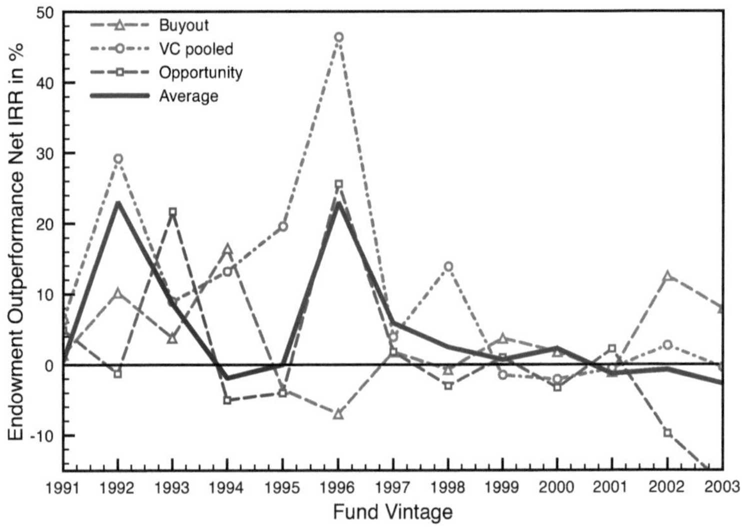

Figure 6.1: Relative Outperformance of Endowments over Time

Fund-of-Funds. A noteworthy result also concerns the general performance of PE FoFs. Any LP naturally faces the question of either investing directly in PE funds, or to entrust a FoF with this task. The presumed advantage is that FoFs should achieve returns that are at least average, as their diversified approach supposedly gives them broad access to funds. Indeed, I find that PE FoFs do achieve fund returns that are fairly close to the average. For instance, for the entire sample, PE FoFs picked funds with average return of 14.6% IRR, the average for all LP types is 14.9% IRR. This is robust when looking at different time periods. The only significant (economically and statistically, considering standard errors) underperformance is found within late VC funds. In general, therefore, PE FoFs did indeed generate average PE fund returns. However, the returns to PE FoFs are obviously not yet net of the fees that the FoF itself charges its own investors.

Government agencies. The sample contains a limited number of observations on governmental agencies. Still, the results suggest a clear separation between possibly sovereign wealth funds, and US/European 'developmentally' motivated agencies. This becomes clear from the returns by region and fund types. Non-western agencies were among the very best (19.4% IRR), and this is likely due to high buyout fund returns (24.1%); US/European agencies, in contrast, were among the very worst (-2.2% / 4.8% IRR), and this is likely driven by particularly poorly performing VC funds (4.7% and -9.9% IRR). Hence, it seems that while sovereign wealth funds invest primarily in buyout funds, US / European agencies might have pursued a mandate to support VC funds for political reasons, irrespective of supposed return expectations.

Selection Bias. I also address the concern that perhaps the data suffers from some sort of over-optimistic reporting bias. For instance, the way PreQin collects the LP investment data, non-US LP investment data may be less representative.[3] In many discussions with LPs, I learned that their own performance was usually assessed by comparison to industry benchmarks, such as that published by Cambridge Associates (CA).[4] Since this advisor publishes only returns by buyout funds or venture funds, I pool my data on late and early VC funds and then compare my sample to that of CA. Specifically, I calculate the difference, or excess, between a fund in my sample and the average return by fund type and vintage reported by CA. As it turns out, essentially all LPs, by

[3]As described, one way for PreQin of obtaining LP investment data from public organizations is via the US Freedom of Information Act.

[4]See www.cambridgeassociates.com

that measure, underperformed the benchmark published by CA. This suggests that my sample also contains a significant number of underperforming funds. However, I then also compare the data to the fund performance benchmarks by Venture Economics (VE) published in 2007.[5] The picture is more mixed: In general, the LP investment data in my dataset seems more available for funds that on average outperformed the overall fund benchmark. In particular, European funds seem to be underreported in my sample. This may be of concern and in later regressions I address it by Heckman regressions. However, under the assumption that the selection bias is on the funds, not the LPs, and since I usually control for LP regions when I include non-US LPs, this issue may be less of a concern than if I attempted to find exact estimates of overall PE fund returns.

In summary, an interesting preliminary story emerges. In principle, buyout funds and VC funds had very different time periods when they were successful, respectively. Moreover, my findings suggest that during the nineties in particular (when VC funds outperformed dramatically), some LPs had a certain expertise in choosing and liking for VC funds – e.g. endowments. Their average outperformance is driven by the returns of these funds. Since then, other LPs, notably investment corporations, banks and insurances, benefitted more than others from their investments in buyout funds, where they seemed to have a persistent comparative advantage. This suggests that LPs differ in their human capital and structural set-ups to benefit differentially when investing in GP types. Moreover, those advantages paid off at different times when the underlying performance of funds fluctuated. Over the entire time-span, therefore, returns balance out to the mean.[6]

[5] In this specific example, I use the capital-weighted measure provided by VC. However, the results are largely the unchanged if I use alternative, non-weighted measures.

[6] One should be careful in the interpretation though: Returns are measured as the average return per fund investment. They do not, therefore, reflect average commitments to funds, or hence portfolio returns. Rather, these measures capture the ability to choose promising funds. However, since the commitments are likely somewhat bigger for the larger buyout funds (even considering the usually larger number of LPs per buyout funds compared to other funds), successful buyout fund-investors since 2000 enjoyed probably even higher overall results, on a portfolio level. Also, in the robustness tests to the later multivariate analysis I aim to address the question by using a simplified portfolio, or weighted IRR, approach.

While very informative, these results may be subject to confounding factors. For instance, the US PE market matured earlier, and more LPs engaged earlier. Hence, timing and region effects should be better accounted for. Also, more generally, there may be obvious institutional differences such as size or experience that should be controlled for. Therefore, I now turn to the specific hypotheses spelled out in section 3.3.3 and test them in multivariate analyses.

Mean Fund Returns by LP Type

The table shows groupings of up to 12,343 investments. IRR's are expressed net of carry and management fees. Mean values given, with standard errors (SE) in brackets. The first group presents mean returns by sample period, where Entire Sample encompasses all funds from 1991 to 2003. By Region presents mean returns by location of the LP.

		Time Periods		By Region 1991 – 2003		
LP Type	**Entire Sample**	**1991-1998**	**1999-2003**	**US**	**Europe**	**ROW**
PE FoFs	14.62%	20.39%	13.00%	13.64%	14.77%	22.39%
	(0.43)	(1.29)	(0.40)	(0.67)	(0.49)	(5.52)
Public Pension	14.55	19.26	10.94	14.27	18.29	17.48
	(0.39)	(0.79)	(0.34)	(0.42)	(1.20)	(1.75)
Banks	16.85	14.38	17.91	10.70	21.97	18.21
	(0.99)	(1.70)	(1.21)	(1.48)	(1.48)	(2.08)
Invest. Corp.	14.96	15.89	14.54	12.72	19.76	13.85
	(0.75)	(1.55)	(0.83)	(1.15)	(1.43)	(1.31)
Insurances	18.26	23.77	15.85	16.38	20.79	17.64
	(1.00)	(2.35)	(0.97)	(1.67)	(1.32)	(2.07)
Corporate Pension	15.05	16.40	14.47	13.29	18.83	13.44
	(0.81)	(1.61)	(0.94)	(1.04)	(1.38)	(3.27)
Endowments	16.00	24.41	12.26	16.01	18.62	8.05
	(1.06)	(2.96)	(0.71)	(1.08)	(1.84)	(9.36)
Family Offices	14.60	19.50	12.49	14.33	20.18	-3.60
	(0.80)	(2.03)	(0.74)	(0.85)	(2.63)	(4.09)
Govt. Agencies	11.80	8.09	14.66	-2.19	4.80	19.36
	(2.36)	(3.67)	(3.05)	(4.03)	(4.66)	(2.73)
Total	14.88%	19.44%	12.46%	14.28%	16.52%	16.68%
Total SE	(0.24)	(0.56)	(0.21)	(0.30)	(0.38)	(1.07)
Observations	12343	4296	8047	9021	2693	629

Continued on next page

Mean Fund Returns by LP Type (*continued from previous page*)

This table continues the previous table on mean fund returns by LP type. Fund Types lists the mean returns by GP tye between 1991 – 2003. Benchmark compares the excess IRR over the capital weighted, yearly, mean benchmarks published by Cambridge Associates (CA) and Venture Economics.

	Fund Types 1991 – 2003				Benchmark: CA		Benchmark: Venture Economics			
LP Type	**Buyout**	**Late VC**	**Early VC**	**Opp.**	**BO US**	**VC US**	**BO US**	**VC US**	**BO EU**	**VC EU**
PE FoFs	20.46%	5.77%	4.05%	15.12%	-1.33%	-3.20%	7.40%	-2.18%	5.43%	9.38%
	(0.40)	(1.25)	(1.35)	(0.83)	(0.37)	(0.53)	(0.37)	(0.64)	(0.38)	(1.59)
Public Pension	15.67	15.37	2.56	15.10	-1.22	-3.64	4.80	-0.56	5.63	10.78
	(0.37)	(1.40)	(1.71)	(0.38)	(0.27)	(0.77)	(0.28)	(0.76)	(0.55)	(1.96)
Banks	22.18	3.26	-3.56	9.01	-1.92	-3.64	9.07	-1.71	5.65	5.48
	(1.05)	(1.97)	(1.53)	(3.26)	(1.08)	(1.27)	(1.03)	(1.18)	(0.80)	(2.89)
Invest. Corp.	20.03	5.03	8.48	14.54	0.03	-3.32	8.22	-1.31	6.00	7.86
	(0.87)	(1.64)	(3.74)	(1.26)	(0.76)	(1.02)	(0.75)	(1.13)	(0.64)	(3.00)
Insurances	22.19	11.88	2.95	17.72	-1.00	-3.43	9.22	-0.80	6.18	15.12
	(0.99)	(3.57)	(4.80)	(1.64)	(1.00)	(1.64)	(0.90)	(2.01)	(0.71)	(5.80)
Corp. Pension	19.45	4.22	5.36	13.74	0.52	-5.34	8.87	-3.57	4.75	2.79
	(0.95)	(1.80)	(4.95)	(1.62)	(0.85)	(1.23)	(0.83)	(1.29)	(0.73)	(2.45)
Endowments	18.76	12.73	10.26	14.98	-0.95	-3.43	6.67	-1.02	5.51	-7.74
	(0.66)	(4.07)	(5.62)	(1.42)	(0.43)	(1.93)	(0.42)	(2.01)	(0.84)	(6.08)
Family Offices	18.36	9.90	6.17	15.17	0.21	-4.00	7.80	-2.23	5.47	9.45
	(0.79)	(3.09)	(3.24)	(1.06)	(0.53)	(1.20)	(0.54)	(1.29)	(0.88)	(3.09)
Govt. Agencies	24.13	4.74	-9.90	8.44	0.07	-16.79	14.49	-15.40	4.98	8.56
	(2.99)	(4.37)	(3.15)	(3.80)	(4.23)	(6.54)	(1.93)	(7.62)	(1.46)	(5.59)
Total	18.34%	11.33%	4.15%	15.03%	-0.93%	-3.57%	6.54%	-1.30%	5.54%	9.13%
Total SE	(0.22)	(0.85)	(0.97)	(0.30)	(0.17)	(0.43)	(0.18)	(0.46)	(0.22)	(0.99)
Observations	5757	2718	989	2879	3658	3034	3658	2849	1937	401

Table 6.1: Mean Returns of LP Investments

6.1.2 US LP Performance

The previous results gave a first indication that LPs differ in their ability to invest in different PE fund types. I also showed that time periods, regions and fund types are important categories that yield different results for LPs. I now turn to the previously stated hypotheses on LP performance differences.

H 4_a: US LP Performance differences: LP expertise – Endowments, FoFs and investment corporations achieve the highest returns within each fund type. Pension funds are among the worst investors within each fund type.

H 4_b: US LP Performance differences: Specific fund expertise – Overall, returns will be driven partly by timing and expertise in a specific fund type and its performance over time. Hence, LPs with an expertise to invest in VC funds will have benefitted most during the nineties, LPs with an expertise to invest in buyout funds most thereafter.

The first hypothesis is largely motivated by the findings of LSW and the general notion that some LPs are generally better or worse than others. The second hypothesis is a result more of the interviews and research and implicates that LPs have different advantages, depending on the fund type. The two hypotheses thus contradict each other somewhat. Note, however, that the first hypothesis deals with specific LPs, the second hypothesis is a more general statement. Generally, the average results presented in the previous section would support the second hypothesis over the first. However, while the mean results are informative, it is likely that other factors, in particular LP experience, the size of the LP or the size of the GP impact LP investment success. In addition, there may be time-related fixed effects that may also be important. In order to test the hypotheses, therefore, I re-examine the data using multivariate analysis. This provides essentially also a robustness test to the mean results.

Analysis – Regressions. In the first set of regressions, as seen in table 6.2, I focus only on US LPs and their US investments. This facilitates comparisons to the results of LSW; it also eliminates, for now, cross-country unobserved effects. I regress 'Net Irr', the IRR per fund net of all fees, on a number of independent variables for LP Types, fund types and covariates.

LP-Returns. In column (1) I report the basic regression using LP dummies, where public pension funds are the base category.[7] After adjusting for time fixed effects, covariables (for LP size, experience and fund size) and fund specific returns, investment corporations, insurances and endowments perform best, government agencies worst. In column (2), however, I investigate how much these results depend on the timing after 1998 (using a dummy, Post 1998, to indicate investments between 1999 and 2003). Indeed, as the descriptive results suggested, before 1999 (LP terms without interaction effects), endowments significantly outperformed other LPs (9.5% IRR in this model), while banks (–10.9%), and investment corporations (–8.7%) were among the worst. This compares well with LSW's results in their analysis of funds between 1991 and 1998: Under similar conditions (i.e. the same comparison categories and with similar fixed effects), LSW find an outperformance of endowments of +11.58%, and an underperformance by banks of –9.1%, compared to public pension funds.[8] However, starting with 1999, as evidenced by the interaction terms, my analysis uncovers differences. Banks and investment corporations were now among the very best, endowments among the worst investors (-8.2% IRR in this model). Over time, their relative return differences thus fluctuated over time.

A word on government agencies. Since in these regressions I only include US LPs in this regression, these government agencies will be essentially only US political entities with some developmental purpose. One would thus expect them to limit themselves in a way that would depress their average returns in VC funds compared to the unrestricted investor. This is what the results suggest, across the board: Government agencies achieved the lowest VC returns in all specifications. Moreover, they underperform in particular before 1999, while thereafter the negative coefficients lose statistical significance.

[7] I choose this base category for two reasons. First, it is the largest. Second, it is also the one used by LSW for their multivariate analyses. Hence, coefficients can be more easily compared.

[8] See Lerner et al. (2007b), pages 746 – 747, column (2) of their regression. They further find a significant underperformance of corporate pension funds (–6.6%), which does *not contradict* my (statistically insignificant) estimates for the same LP type of –5.03%.

Fund-type dependent results. In column (3) I ask if this could perhaps be due to the performance of different fund types. Indeed, the interaction of GP Type and the time-dummy shows that in this fixed effects model, before 1999 buyout funds (the comparison category) significantly underperformed other funds – non-buyout funds have significant positive coefficients of 4.3% – 37.8%. After 1998, non-buyout funds underperformed thereafter: Non-buyout funds had negative coefficients of up to -55.5% in this model. The scale and size of this estimate may sound large, but reflects indeed the large return differences of venture funds compared to buyout funds before and after 1998.[9]

LPs and GPs In table 6.3, Column (1) I investigate if LPs differ specifically by fund type. The coefficients on the interaction terms for VC and opportunity funds, taking buyout funds as the base category, are essentially all negative and statistically significant – i.e. over the entire time span, buyouts outperformed. However, it is noteworthy that the coefficients are again least negative or even insignificant for endowments: 'Only' –8.4% IRR for late VC funds and an insignificant coefficient for early VC funds. Compared to investment corporations, for example, the differences are apparent. Investment corporations had a negative performance of –14.3% in late VC funds, and –13.12% in early VC funds. In fact, most LPs, in particular also banks and FoFs, performed worse than endowments in their (late) VC investments (in the order of –12% to –14% for late VC funds). This again implies that endowments picked better VC funds than other LPs, even though the entire time-span from 1991 to 2003 (and not just up to 1999) is analyzed in this specific regression.

Hypothesis: Interpretation. The results suggest that endowments, FoFs and investment corporations are not always, i.e. at all times and within each fund type, the best investors. Rather, some LP types seem to have specific advantages, depending on the GP Type. Endowments were particularly good at selecting among VC funds; banks, investment corporations, and insurances particularly good at selecting buyout funds. Therefore, I conclude that a) LPs have different comparative advantages, depending on the fund type, and b) that those advantages paid out most when that specific fund type performed

[9]See also figure 2.2 in chapter 2 which shows the vast return differences as recorded by Cambridge Associates.

best. Therefore, I cannot reject the null hypothesis against H 4_a (i.e. the null hypothesis that endowments, FoFs and investment corporations are not better). Instead, based on the results, the interpretation would support H 4_b, i.e. that timing and fund-type specific expertise is significant.

Fund Performance Regressions - Part I

This table reports pooled OLS regressions of net IRR per fund on dummy variables for LP types, fund types and covariates (logAuM, logFundSize and log of LP experience). In this regression, only US LPs and their investments in US-based funds were included. The basic regression specification is found in the text. LP_{norm} is a simple regression using LP dummies with fixed effects and covariates. Columns (2) and (3) also include a variable Post1998 (P98), which indicates if an investment took place after 1998 (1999 – 2003). In column (2) the effect of this timing is shown for interacted LPs (LPs_t), in column (3) for interacted funds ($Funds_t$). Column (4), shows the Heckman regression, comparable to regression (1). Robust standard errors are reported in brackets; all observations were clustered at the fund level. Significance levels: *** p<0.01, ** p<0.05, * p<0.1. Covariates as used in previous regressions. Constant estimated but not reported.

Comparison categories for different dummies, dependent on specification: Public Pension Funds, Buyout Funds

Dep. Variable: Net IRR in %	LP_{norm} (1)	LPs_t (2)	$Funds_t$ (3)	Heckman (4)
LP Types				
PE FoF	2.01	4.37	1.77	2.28
	(1.27)	(4.53)	(1.11)	(2.05)
Banks	1.68	-10.86***	1.80	-0.15
	(1.64)	(4.19)	(1.47)	(5.55)
Invest. Corp.	4.17**	-8.70**	3.76**	5.44
	(1.73)	(4.36)	(1.82)	(4.18)
Insurances	3.19*	5.90	1.77	0.92
	(1.84)	(5.18)	(1.76)	(4.16)
Corp. Pension	2.36	-5.03	-0.31	0.27
	(1.58)	(4.20)	(1.47)	(3.54)
Endowments	3.76**	9.45**	2.90**	3.71*
	(1.52)	(3.99)	(1.35)	(1.99)
Family Offices	2.63*	3.52	2.53*	3.74*
	(1.40)	(3.60)	(1.30)	(2.06)
Govt. Agencies	-10.72**	-15.38**	-10.78	-22.66
	(5.34)	(6.03)	(8.23)	(17.04)
Fund Types				
Opp.	0.73	0.66	4.35**	5.47**
	(1.85)	(1.85)	(2.02)	(2.17)
Late VC	2.18	2.14	36.83***	3.07*

Continued on next page

Table 6.2 – *continued from previous page*

Dep. Variable: Net IRR in %	LP_{norm} (1)	LPs_t (2)	$Funds_t$ (3)	Heckman (4)
	(3.46)	(3.46)	(7.75)	(1.61)
Early VC	-4.02	-4.10	37.80***	2.68
	(3.22)	(3.20)	(8.27)	(3.15)
Timing				
Post 1998		-9.96	10.52	
		(7.89)	(8.35)	
PE FoF * P98		-3.26		
		(4.85)		
Banks * P98		13.90***		
		(4.74)		
Invest. Corp. * P98		14.11***		
		(4.99)		
Insurances * P98		-3.92		
		(5.51)		
Corp. Pension * P98		9.04*		
		(4.77)		
Endowments * P98		-8.27*		
		(4.25)		
Family Offices * P98		-1.67		
		(3.85)		
Govt. Agencies * P98		12.21		
		(9.68)		
Opp. * P98			-4.49	
			(2.88)	
Late VC * P98			-53.09***	
			(8.06)	
Early VC * P98			-55.49***	
			(8.35)	
lambda				-46.46***
				(15.66)
Covariables	Yes	Yes	Yes	Yes
Year Fixed Effects	Yes	Yes	Yes	Yes
Observations	7208	7208	7208	7711
R-squared	0.103	0.105	0.244	

Table 6.2: Fund Performance Regressions - I

Fund Performance Regressions - Part II

This table reports pooled OLS regressions of net IRR per fund on dummy variables for LP types, fund types, as well as covariates. It essentially continues the previous table. Column (1) shows interaction terms for LPs with funds (LPs*GPs). Column (2) shows the effect of the timing on the covariables (Covs.$_{\cdot t}$). Robust standard errors are reported in brackets; all observations were clustered at the fund level. Significance levels: *** $p<0.01$, ** $p<0.05$, * $p<0.1$. Covariates as used in previous regressions. Constant estimated but not reported.
Comparison categories for different dummies, dependent on specification: Public Pension Funds, Buyout Funds

Dep. Variable: Net IRR in %	LPs*GPs (1)	Covs.$_{\cdot t}$ (2)
LP Types		
PE FoF	8.14***	0.93
	(1.65)	(1.29)
Banks	6.81***	-0.43
	(2.26)	(1.60)
Invest. Corp.	10.83***	1.83
	(2.09)	(1.84)
Insurances	6.24***	2.07
	(2.29)	(1.82)
Corp. Pension	8.77***	0.40
	(2.29)	(1.50)
Endowments	7.45***	2.81**
	(1.75)	(1.41)
Family Offices	6.02***	2.52*
	(1.43)	(1.39)
Govt. Agencies	17.36***	-14.14*
	(2.16)	(7.22)
Fund Types		
Opp.	3.07	0.93
	(1.90)	(1.77)
Late VC	6.48	1.19
	(4.04)	(3.35)
Early VC	-2.42	-2.97

Continued on next page

Table 6.3 – *continued from previous page*

Dep. Variable: Net IRR in %	LPs*GPs (1)	Covs.$_{\cdot t}$ (2)
	(3.64)	(3.25)
Timing		
Post 1998	-10.47	-77.80***
	(7.84)	(13.27)
Fund Type Interactions		
PE FoF * Opp.	-10.02***	
	(3.05)	
PE FoF * LVC	-14.50***	
	(4.44)	
PE FoF * EVC	-6.41	
	(4.61)	
Banks * Opp.	-9.79**	
	(4.36)	
Banks * LVC	-12.91**	
	(5.94)	
Banks * EVC	-5.85	
	(4.33)	
Invest. Corp. * Opp.	-9.58**	
	(4.06)	
Invest. Corp. * LVC	-14.33**	
	(6.74)	
Invest. Corp. * EVC	-13.12***	
	(4.04)	
Insurances * Opp.	5.67	
	(5.86)	
Insurances * LVC	-7.11	
	(4.90)	
Insurances * EVC	-7.02*	
	(4.24)	
Corp. Pension * Opp.	-10.44***	
	(3.93)	
Corp. Pension * LVC	-17.98***	
	(4.79)	
Corp. Pension * EVC	-4.25	
	(5.23)	
Endowments * Opp.	-6.92*	

Continued on next page

Table 6.3 – *continued from previous page*

Dep. Variable: Net IRR in %	LPs*GPs (1)	Covs.$_{t}$ (2)
	(3.74)	
Endowments * LVC	-8.42**	
	(3.44)	
Endowments * EVC	1.77	
	(7.41)	
Family Offices * Opp.	-3.62	
	(2.39)	
Family Offices * LVC	-9.37*	
	(5.15)	
Family Offices * EVC	-2.68	
	(4.95)	
Govt. Agencies * Opp.	-26.18***	
	(4.98)	
Govt. Agencies * LVC	-46.36***	
	(9.33)	
Govt. Agencies * EVC	-28.68***	
	(5.29)	
logFundSize	3.05***	-3.45**
	(0.95)	(1.57)
logAUM	-0.13	-1.38**
	(0.23)	(0.60)
logExp	1.43***	5.21***
	(0.54)	(1.51)
logFundSize * P98		10.33***
		(1.82)
logAUM * P98		2.07***
		(0.62)
logExp * P98		-6.36***
		(1.69)
Year Fixed Effects	Yes	Yes
Observations	7208	7208
R-squared	0.110	0.143

Table 6.3: Fund Performance Regressions - II

Experience and Size. Following on from the earlier hypotheses, I now turn to two more hypotheses:

H 5: Experience – The ability to select funds is positively related to investment experience.

H 6: LP size – Smaller LPs have better internal incentive structures and hence achieve higher fund returns than large LPs.

LSW discussed that, in general, experience is positively correlated with fund performance. Since choosing good funds is difficult, this does not surprise. Also, in their assessment, small investors like endowments performed particularly well. It was partly argued that incentive structures and organizational differences would bolster small investor's success. Thus, during the nineties, small LPs with experience, notably endowments, were able to select well-performing (small) VC funds. Correspondingly, in table 6.3, column (2) I also find that experience is positively correlated with fund returns from 1991 – 1998, and investor size and fund size negatively. However, the included covariates also point to interesting period-dependent differences with regard to experience and LP size. The negative coefficient on fund size underlines the relative outperformance of the smaller VC funds during that period. Yet, after 1998, the coefficients reverse: Taken together, this indicates that after 2000, new, large and inexperienced LPs, often large pension funds, entered the PE market. Where would they invest in? Presumably in the large, newly raising buyout funds. However, since these large funds then performed very well, inexperienced, large LPs benefitted more than the experienced, smaller LPs that presumably still also invested in VC funds.

Robustness Tests. I focus on two dimensions of robustness tests for the presented regressions: Selection bias and data-specific tests.

Selection bias. As for selection bias, there could be concern that missing return data may vary systematically. For example, poorly performing or smaller funds might not report their returns. Also, for a few LPs, some covariates were not available and their investments were therefore excluded. A concern could be that there is a systematic reason for this. To ameliorate these issues, I also include a Heckman sample selection regression model in column (4) of table 6.2 with variables directly comparable to column (1).[10] All estimates on the LPs remain economically and statistically very similar, except for investment corporations, where the coefficients become statistically insignificant. This suggests that the constrained dataset used for the normal regression contains less variability in the fund returns for investment corporations. For the GPs, returns for late VC and opportunity funds become stronger and significant. Thus, for opportunity and late VC funds the constrained dataset used in the normal regression may miss out on a few well-performing funds that are captured in the Heckman regression.[11]

Outliers and skewed data. On a different level, a key concern with the existing data is that the results are driven by some few, exceptionally well (or poorly) performing funds. The interpretation is then complicated: Maybe it is exactly the LP's special ability to spot those unique opportunities? Certainly the results by LSW suggests that some university endowments somehow managed to find funds that vastly outperformed. Still, those 'home-runs' may skew the results somewhat. Another concern may be that the average return by fund investment may give a false picture, as it is not really a portfolio approach weighted by actual fund investments. For these reasons, I perform five robustness tests for all my regressions (results not shown): A) Exclusion of top and lowest 1% of funds by IRR. B) Excess (or difference) over the median of

[10] See Carhart et al. (2002) for similar issues regarding the mutual fund industry.

[11] The variables used for the first-stage probit are the LP dummies, fund type dummies and covariates, as well as vintage years and include observations that in normal regressions are dropped because of missing data. Public pension funds and buyout funds served as comparison categories. The coefficients on LPs in the first stage are mixed in dimensions and statistically not significant, indicating that IRR data are not more likely to be available for public pension funds' PE funds. However, coefficients are statistically significantly negative for fund types, indicating that IRR data is more likely available for buyout funds. Coefficients are statistically significantly positive for the covariates, indicating that IRR data were more available for large LPs, large GPs and for LPs with higher experience. Specifically, coefficients were, with standard errors in parenthesis: PE FoFs -0.04 (0.09), banks 0.23 (0.30), investment corporations -0.15 (0.17), insurances 0.33 (0.23), corporate pension funds 0.233 (0.17), endowments 0.01 (0.09), family offices -0.10 (0.08), government agencies 6.09 (0.00), late VC -0.20 (0.08), early VC -0.68 (0.09), opportunity funds -0.56 (0.07), logFundSize 0.15 (0.02), logAUM 0.04 (0.02), logExp 0.05 (0.03).

the fund type by IRR as the return measure. C) Regression of a weighted net IRR. This simulates a portfolio approach. To arrive at the weighted net IRR, I record the average fund size per fund type, divided by the average LP number per fund, in my sample. This produces an estimate of the average commitment per LP per average fund in any given fund type category. I also do the same for all fund types and across the entire fund universe. The ratio of the average commitment per fund type and the overall average commitment results in a weighing factor for my new IRR estimate, weighted IRR.[12] Doing so still results in an average Net IRR of 14.5%, fairly close to the previously reported IRR, but with a much higher weight attached to opportunity and buyout funds, and a lower value to late and in particular early venture funds. D) Regression at the median, using quantile regressions. E) Collapsing the LPs on a fund level. This approach takes the individual fund, not the individual fund investment, and calculates the percentage of individual LP types per fund. This should produce similar results as the approach taken before. However, it is more sensitive to 'extreme' LP compositions: For instance, if no family office invested in a given fund, this will still be recorded as a full zero-value. Since some LP classes are naturally more active as investors in the PE asset class than others, smaller LP classes will still be recorded as 'not having invested'.

I compare the results primarily to column (1) of table 6.2. Based on the tests, my primary results appear fairly robust. However, tests A), B) and D) show that indeed the performance of endowments and family offices seems likely driven by the returns of some spectacular positive funds; their outperforming coefficients drop and lose their statistical significance. This coincides with a drop in the coefficients on late and early venture funds. This result is also found in C): Coefficients on investment corporations, endowments and family offices, as well as venture funds, lose their statistical significance; opportunity funds become much more positive and significant. Finally, collapsing the LP composition, E), leads to much more negative coefficients for government

[12] In doing so, I arrive at average commitment of USD 53 million per fund; USD 50.9 million for buyout funds, USD 32.6 million per late venture funds, USD 26.1 million per early venture funds and USD 101.3 million per opportunity funds. The latter estimate, double that of buyout funds, may either reflect some sort of data bias, or it may reflect the special nature of these 'alternative' PE funds that attract fewer but more solvent LPs.

agencies, and more positive and significant outperformance by family offices. A possible interpretation within the described tests characteristics could be that there are some funds that are primarily funded by either of these two LP types (i.e. only have this one LP type, or only few other LP types as investor). In fact, in personal interviews, investment managers at family offices said that they often try to be dominant LP in a few good funds. If these are indeed above-average, then this could explain the strong outperformance of family offices in this robustness test. The same argument, but in opposite direction could hold for government agencies (namely, being dominant or sole investors in some poorly performing, 'politically' motivated venture funds).

In conclusion, the robustness tests indicate the overall the results are fairly robust. However, some spectacular venture funds in particular impact the average returns by endowments and family offices. This mirrors results discussed above, and also those put forward by LSW.

6.1.3 Global LP Performance

In this section, I focus on regional difference in a multivariate analysis. I hypothesized that the major differences between US LPs and LPs should be primarily timing-related, and possibly due to specifics of the PE market. This, in turn, implies that globally LPs should be largely comparable, if market development and experience is accounted for:

H 7: Global LP Performance – Non-US LPs operate in PE markets that are less developed while LPs themselves are less experienced. Hence, when adjusted for timing and experience, non-US LPs and LPs do not differ significantly.

Analysis – Regressions. I regress the dependent variable 'Net IRR' on variables for LP Types, fund types, as well as region variables and covariables. These include variables for LP size and experience. This regression differs to the one used for table 6.2, in that all global LPs are considered, as well as their global GP investments; in the previous regressions only US LPs with their US GP investments were included. Table 6.4 therefore allows a truly global comparison by region and LP type.

Region-dependent returns. In column (1), basic region regressions are shown. After year fixed effects, and hence adjusting for timing effects, as well as co-variables, there are no significant differences among the regions. The findings therefore differ from the mean results presented in table 6.1. When I look by LP type in column (2), insurances, endowments and family offices outperform the rest. Since this result also considers year fixed and region effects, the interpretation is that these LPs outperform others also on a global level. In column (3) I then interact the LPs with specific regions. PE FoFs in Europe (-3.3%) and family offices in ROW (-15.0% IRR) underperform their peers (for Govt. Agencies, see below). However, other coefficients are insignificant. In contrast, the coefficients on the non-interacted LP types remain largely similar. This shows that the outperformance vis-á-vis the base category US public pension funds is primarily due to US LPs, while non-US LPs do not differ significantly.

According to the regression results, US government agencies invested in funds with the lowest returns (-11.6% IRR). Yet government agencies in the rest of the world (ROW), presumably also including sovereign wealth funds, were among the best LPs in their region (with IRRs of +11.6%). European government agencies do not differ in a statistically significant way from their US counterparts. In unreported analysis I find that the returns of government agencies in ROW seem to be driven primarily by their investments in buyout funds. Large sovereign wealth funds seem to enjoy particularly good fund returns from some of the largest, and since 2001 most promising, buyout funds.

Fund-specific returns. In column (4) I drop the individual LP types and instead look if fund types differed, depending on regions. Investors in late VC funds in Europe (-10.0% IRR) underperformed their US and ROW counterparts by a considerable and significant margin; other coefficients remain insignificant. In contrast, buyout funds in Europe and ROW, the non-interacted terms on the region dummies, are positive (3.2% and 2.7%, respectively): Buyout-funds in those continental regions outperformed their US-peers.

Finally, as before, I report a Heckman sample selection model in column (5), comparable to column (2). Even though this Heckman regression considers data from about 1200 more observations, the coefficients on the LPs remain essentially unchanged. However, the coefficient on late VC funds becomes significant as the standard errors become smaller. Hence, given the additional observations considered in the Heckman regression, late VC funds then also have significant negative coefficients.[13]

Hypothesis: Interpretation. In general, using time fixed effects and covariables, the results do not point to much heterogeneity across LP types across global regions. This is very interesting, since these results come after inclusion of year fixed effects, something that the descriptive mean results did not capture. Indeed, in Europe the PE industry is said to have matured later and LPs engaged in this asset class later. My results therefore suggest that once potential timing issues are controlled for, European and even ROW-LPs do not differ somewhat from their US peers. Exceptions are European FoFs and family offices in the rest of the world, while government agencies in the rest of the world outperform US government agencies. Given this adjustment, I conclude that I do not reject the hypothesis that LPs globally do not differ strongly. However, even when adjusting for timing, European and ROW buyout funds outperformed US buyout funds, while late VC funds in Europe underperformed. This indicates that, perhaps, for those fund types there are some return differences that are not just explained by the later developments of the industries in those regions.

[13]The independent variables used for the first-stage probit are LP type dummies, fund type dummies, global region dummies, covariates and vintages. The comparison categories were public pension funds, buyout funds and the USA as the region. The coefficients in the first stage on the LPs were almost all negative and statistically significant (for PE FoFs, banks, investment corporations and family office), indicating that, compared to opportunity funds, IRR data was more likely available for these LP types. For government agencies, the sign is positive and statistically significant. For the regions, as well as early VC and Other fund types, coefficients were statistically significantly negative: IRR data was thus more likely available for US LPs and buyout funds. Coefficients on covariates were all positive (significant), indicating that data was more likely available for large LPs, large GPs and experienced LPs. Specifically, the coefficients were (standard errors in parenthesis): PE FoFs -0.18 (0.07), banks -0.36 (0.17), investment corporations -0.40 (0.12), insurances 0.07 (0.16), corporate Pension funds -0.02 (0.07), endowments -0.06 (0.07), family offices -0.14 (0.07), government agencies 5.91 (0.30), Europe -0.78 (0.07), ROW -0.54 (0.15), late VC 0.03 (0.05), early VC -0.25 (0.06), opportunity funds -0.20 (0.05), logFundSize 0.25 (0.02), logAUM 0.04 (0.02), logExp 0.07 (0.02).

Robustness Tests. I perform the same robustness tests as in section 6.1.2 (results not shown), namely A) Exclusion of top and lowest 1% of funds by IRR. B) Excess (or difference) over the median of the fund type by IRR. C) Regression of a weighted net IRR / portfolio approach, D) Quantile regression at the median, E) Collapsing LP investment observations at the fund level. I focus in particular on columns (2) – (4) as comparison.

In principle, the results remain robust. However, test A), and to some extent B) and C), affect mostly LPs in late and early VC funds. Hence, the 'outperformance'–coefficients on endowments and family offices in the US are reduced in size, and with them the statistical significance. In contrast, in column (3), PE FoFs in Europe no longer underperform. In column (4), and of particular interest, the negative coefficients on late VC funds in Europe get much closer to zero and are no longer statistically significant. Thus, when conditioning on some spectacular (US) venture funds, LPs in Europe and the US earned the same within that fund type. When I look at the weighted IRRs, there are also no significant changes for the LPs. Similarly, the regression at the median yields little changes on the LPs, even though the significance levels differ. Finally, collapsing the investments on the LP level affects insurances and family offices. In the normal regressions, insurances are found to outperform the rest; in the robustness test this outperformance disappears. However, the coefficients on family offices grow much larger and become significant at the 1% level. This effect is similar as was seen for US LPs only and a possible explanation was that some funds may have only family offices as LPs. If those funds performed better, collapsing the funds attaches a higher weight to family offices in this case.

In conclusion, the robustness tests indicate the same sensitivity as before for LPs to late VC and early VC funds with high returns. However, these do not seem to dramatically impact LPs in different *global regions* differentially. Instead, the overall conclusion seems, when adjusting for timing and outliers, global LPs do not differ in a statistically significant way in their ability to select well performing funds.

Fund Performance Regressions by Global Regions

This table reports the pooled OLS regressions of net IRR per fund on dummy variables for LP types, fund types and region, as well as covariables. In this case, international investments (and not just those in the US) are included. The basic regression specification is found in the text. *LPs* includes LP dummies. *LPs Int.* interacts the LPs with the region dummies. *Fund Int.* interacts region dummies with fund type dummies. *Heckman* shows the Heckman regression, comparable to regression (1). Robust standard errors are reported in brackets; all observations were clustered at the fund level. Significance levels: *** p<0.01, ** p<0.05, * p<0.1. Covariates as shown. Constant estimated but not reported.

Comparison categories for different dummies: USA, public pension funds, buyout funds

Dep. Variable: Net IRR in %	LPs (1)	LPs Int. (2)	Fund Int. (3)	Heckman (4)
Region				
Europe	0.63	1.85	3.28*	0.57
	(1.13)	(1.73)	(1.75)	(1.03)
ROW	1.76	2.56	2.75*	1.72
	(1.52)	(2.20)	(1.41)	(1.41)
LP Type				
PE FoFs	1.09	2.06*		1.09
	(0.93)	(1.13)		(0.82)
Banks	1.13	0.36		1.09
	(1.30)	(1.45)		(1.88)
Invest. Corp.	1.44	2.51*		1.43
	(1.11)	(1.43)		(1.33)
Insurances	3.58***	3.07**		3.57**
	(1.06)	(1.48)		(1.43)
Corporate P.	1.37	1.56		1.38
	(1.08)	(1.30)		(1.36)
Endowments	2.97**	3.12**		2.97***
	(1.30)	(1.34)		(1.03)
Family Offices	2.12*	1.94		2.12**
	(1.20)	(1.27)		(1.03)
Govt. Agen.	-1.84	-11.64**		-1.84
	(2.71)	(4.70)		(3.45)

Continued on next page

Table 6.4 – *continued from previous page*

Dep. Variable: Net IRR in %	LPs (1)	LPs Int. (2)	Fund Int. (3)	Heckman (4)
*LP * Region*				
PE FoFs * Europe		-3.33*		
		(1.79)		
Banks * Europe		2.40		
		(2.77)		
Invest. Corp. * Europe		-0.94		
		(2.27)		
Insurances * Europe		1.30		
		(2.31)		
Corporate P. * Europe		-0.91		
		(2.22)		
Endowments * Europe		-4.11		
		(3.67)		
Family Offices * Europe		3.21		
		(2.76)		
Govt. Agen. * Europe		9.42		
		(6.48)		
PE FoFs * ROW		4.90		
		(5.98)		
Banks * ROW		-1.43		
		(3.57)		
Invest. Corp. * ROW		-3.67		
		(2.67)		
Insurances * ROW		-3.45		
		(3.75)		
Corp. Pen. * ROW		-2.51		
		(3.91)		
Endowments * ROW		-6.77		
		(7.08)		
Family Offices * ROW		-14.95***		
		(4.25)		
Govt. Agen. * ROW		11.60*		
		(6.25)		
Fund Types				
Opportunity	-0.40	-0.32	-0.01	-0.41
	(1.54)	(1.54)	(1.58)	(0.70)
Late VC	-1.24	-1.19	0.50	-1.23*

Continued on next page

Table 6.4 – *continued from previous page*

Dep. Variable: Net IRR in %	LPs (1)	LPs Int. (2)	Fund Int. (3)	Heckman (4)
	(2.78)	(2.79)	(3.23)	(0.74)
Early VC	-5.88**	-5.78**	-5.48*	-5.90***
	(2.86)	(2.86)	(3.06)	(1.10)
*Region * Fund Types*				
Opp. * Europe			-1.63	
			(2.48)	
Late VC * Europe			-10.01***	
			(3.74)	
Early VC * Europe			-1.00	
			(4.30)	
Opp. * ROW			-3.37	
			(2.70)	
Late VC * ROW			0.02	
			(5.45)	
Early VC * ROW			-3.58	
			(3.27)	
logFundSize	3.17***	3.16***	3.20***	3.20***
	(0.75)	(0.75)	(0.75)	(0.41)
logAUM	0.14	0.10	0.02	0.14
	(0.16)	(0.16)	(0.156)	(0.17)
logExp	0.31	0.42	0.01	0.31
	(0.38)	(0.38)	(0.42)	(0.34)
lambda				0.33
				(4.50)
Year Fixed Effects	Yes	Yes	Yes	Yes
Observations	10879	10879	10879	12179
R-squared	0.114	0.115	0.116	

Table 6.4: Performance Regression by Region

6.2 What Drives Investment Success?

I now turn to the question of what factors contribute to the differences in investment success. For instance, what is it that allowed endowments, for instance, to select VC funds in the nineties with returns higher than the average? Did they take more risk on a fund level? Also, what roles do external advisors play for LPs? Do they help selecting better funds? Finally, I also inquire if geographical proximity to VC funds helps selecting good funds.

6.2.1 The Risk-Taking Hypothesis

It was argued that endowments, as long-term financial guardians, have a longer time horizon and can thus take greater risks in investing. For investments in PE funds, especially VC funds, this could be a worthy strategy: In good years, some very successful VC funds return a multiple of invested equity to the LPs. Yet in bad years, even the worst VC funds can 'only' lose their equity once. LPs with a long time horizon, like endowments, could benefit from this most. This led to the following hypothesis:

H 9: Risk-taking – Because of their fund preference and longer investment time-horizon, endowments can afford to achieve higher overall absolute returns by taking risks: Endowments invest more often in both well-performing and poorly-performing funds.

LSW also appreciated this possibility. Therefore, to rule out differences in risk profile, LSW performed a sort of value-at-risk profile which determines the probability of achieving a negative or low return of a given fund. They argue that if endowments invest in more risky funds, then they should not only select more outperforming funds, but also more underperforming funds. Yet in their analysis, they do not find that endowments were also more likely to invest in poorly performing funds.

The problem with this analytic strategy is, however, that the authors looked at all investments by LPs, not by fund type. Considering that endowments at the time may have invested not only in better funds, but also more often in the *generally* better-performing VC funds, it may not surprise that their entire distribution shifted to a higher median, irrespective of the underlying return distribution. When they then compared fund endowments' returns, across all fund types, to those of LPs with more investments in buyout funds during the nineties, it should not have surprised that those latter LPs also recorded more poorly performing funds. In a nutshell, one should look at the distribution within a fund type.

There are, however, a few challenges with this approach. First, presenting somewhat arbitrary quantile cut-off lines does not convey very well the entire return distribution, especially not the returns at the fringes of the distribution. Yet these are of highest interest for the question if endowments took more risk while risking also some very poorly performing funds. Second, the general performance of fund types is obviously volatile, with VC funds returns being strongly depressed after the 2000 vintage years. For these reasons, tables with a few quantile points over the entire sample are not very informative (not shown).

Analysis – Q-Q Plots. Instead of presenting tables for the returns from all fund investments, I concentrate on US LPs and funds for the time 1991 – 1998, the time with greatest variance in VC fund returns, and for which the risk-taking strategy should have paid off most. Also, I present a visual comparison of distributions in the form of quantile-quantile plots. These plots determine the quantiles for all observations of one group, endowments, and compare them to a then calculated equal number of quantiles of the larger, comparison group (all other LPs). Overall, these plots give a limited representation of the mean return, but instead display the comparative return distribution by quantiles much better. What would one expect? If endowments indeed took more risk, then in their VC investments, particularly the early VC investments, they should have more quantiles of return observations that are on the lowest *and* the highest end. Over the more moderate return-span, however, one would expect other LPs to have a larger number of observations.

Figure 6.2 shows that this proposition cannot be justified. To read the plot better, the 45-degree line is a parity line. On the x-axis, returns of endowments are plotted, on the y-axis returns of all other LPs are plotted. Thus, a higher number of observations below the parity line indicates that the in comparison at this IRR quantile the distribution was more skewed in favor of endowments. This is essentially the case across the entire distribution and for all fund types, except buyout funds. However, if endowments were bigger risk-takers, one would expect this to be the case only at the lowest and highest ends of the distribution. Instead, the evidence suggests during the active VC times of the nineties, endowments really were generally better at investing in VC funds.

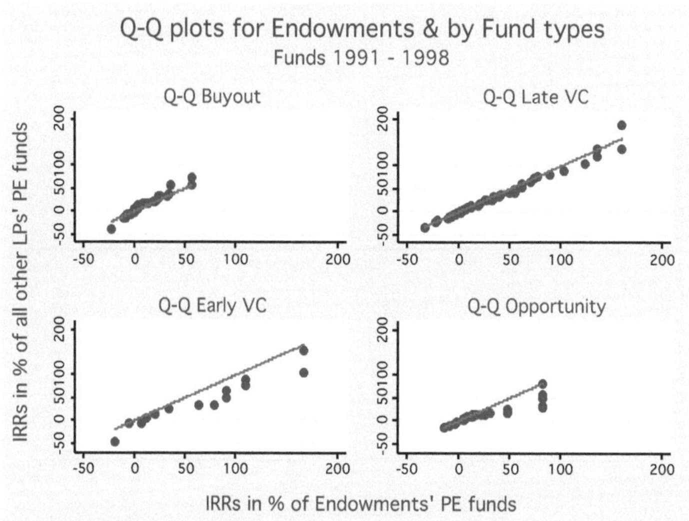

Figure 6.2: Variances of Endowment Returns 1991 – 1998

Hypothesis: Interpretation. In essence, therefore, the Q-Q plots indicate endowments in the nineties did not take excessive risks in selecting funds. This would support the view that the null hypothesis, that endowments were successful risk-takers, can be rejected. Something else, perhaps selection ability, can account for the better performance during the nineties. However, the different variances of fund type returns during the investigated time-periods show once more that if endowments indeed had advantages in selecting VC funds in the nineties, that advantage was not materially relevant anymore since 2000 (see also below): If all VC funds performed badly, a relative advantage in picking them likely did not translate in meaningful return differences.

Robustness Tests. I perform two tests. First, I look at the period after 1998. Figure 6.3 therefore shows the same plots for the time span after 1998, with the same axis-labels. Not surprisingly, returns for VC funds were not only lower, but also considerably more compressed, while buyout and other funds returns retained a similar distribution as before. Second, I drop again the top and bottom 1% of funds by net IRR (not shown). The plots only differ at the margins, without, however, affecting the overall conclusions.

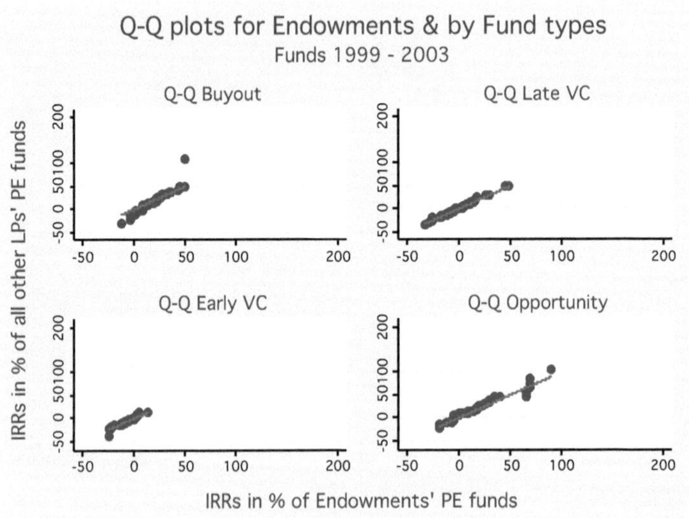

Figure 6.3: Variances of Endowment Returns 1999 – 2003

6.2.2 The External Advisor Hypothesis

There is a significant market for so-called external advisors to LPs that help investors choose PE funds. They were also described in section ??.[14] Since employing external advisors costs fees, it should be expected that they provide a measurable positive effect on the fund selection for LPs. One could note this

[14]They are different, probably, from the LP category 'advisors' described by LSW. In their paper, LSW identify 'advisors' as an actual LP class that invests in PE funds. In fact, they write "Advisors and public pension funds contribute the largest amounts of capital committed to the industry overall". Lerner et al. (2007b), page 741. In contrast, I mean corporations who do not invest in PE funds, but who instead advise actual LPs.

as the key hypothesis for this section:

H 10: External advisors – Large and/or inexperienced investors employ external advisors. External advisors have a positive performance effect for those LPs.

While it remains to be proven who really is 'less sophisticated', a tentative assumption may be that in particular public pension funds should be using external advisors.

Analysis – Mean results. Table 6.5 shows the use and returns by US LP types. Overall, about half indicate the use of an external advisor. However, there are clear differences by LP type: As may have been expected, financial institutions and FoFs all very rarely (if at all) admit employing advisors. Among public pension funds, however, more than 70% indicate using advisors. Somewhat surprising: More than half of endowments also indicate the use of endowments.

In the rest of the table, mean fund returns by use of advisors are indicated. Those are based on *n* observations, as shown in the second column. Overall, there seems to be no difference in fund returns whatsoever, whether advisors are used or not. However, when looking at fund types, a surprising result emerges: LPs that use advisors actually invested in more poorly performing buyout funds than LPs that did not have an advisor (18.3% IRR without advisors vs. 14.4% IRR with advisors). However, the result is not significant at the level of any individual LP type. For VC investments, in particular late VC funds, the result is reverted: Overall, LPs with advisors picked funds that outperformed those picked by LPs without advisors (15.1% IRR with advisors vs. 9.3% IRR without advisors for late VC funds, 4.0% vs. 2.9% for early VC funds). That difference is statistically significant. For opportunity funds, no significant difference is measurable.

Analysis – Regressions. The separation between buyout fund and VC fund returns might surprise in this case. Therefore, before interpreting the results, I check their robustness in a multivariate analysis. Table 6.6 presents the results. In this case I use PE FoF as the base LP category as they record returns that are close to average anyway and because I am primarily interested in the effect of advisors on those LPs that actually use them often: For instance public pension funds. In column (1), the overall effect, conditioned on fund types, is shown: Overall, external advisors seem to have a negative effect. However, the coefficient disappears under inclusion of LP types, in column (2); so across all fund types, the effects of external advisors are insignificant. However, the mean results suggested that differences depend on the fund types. Therefore, in column (3), specific effects are measured on the fund type level, compared to buyout funds as the base category. For non-buyout funds, the use of external advisors appear positive (even for opportunity funds, see coefficients of 3.1%, 7.9% and 4.4%), for buyout funds negative (-3.5% as the base category). Column (4), however, also shows that the effects are not strong enough to be measured on an individual LP type level.

Use and Effects of External Advisor by LP and Fund Type

This table shows mean fund returns by US LPs from funds 1991 – 2003 by the use of External Advisors. Standard errors in brackets. % External Advisor shows the number of LPs, per LP type, that indicate the use of a specific external advisor. This is not a measure on the investment observation level, but of the LPs in the data set. *n* indicates the number of total number of investment observations for which the use of external advisors is indicated.

	Use of Advisor	n	IRR Mean	Overall Advisor? No	Overall Advisor? Yes	Buyout Advisor? No	Buyout Advisor? Yes	Late VC Advisor? No	Late VC Advisor? Yes	Early VC Advisor? No	Early VC Advisor? Yes	Opportunity Advisor? No	Opportunity Advisor? Yes
PE FoFs	0.0%	*1083*	13.64%	13.64%	na	19.99%	na	4.88%	na	3.82%	na	12.87%	na
			(0.67)	(0.67)	na	(0.60)	na	(1.74)	na	(2.12)	na	(1.87)	na
Public Pension	58.22	*5795*	14.27	14.84	14.06	16.02	14.95	15.36	15.20	-0.43	3.42	15.97	14.65
			(0.42)	(0.84)	(0.48)	(0.79)	(0.45)	(3.09)	(1.70)	(3.48)	(1.99)	(0.72)	(0.47)
Banks	0.00	*124*	10.70	10.70	na	17.50	na	1.47	na	-3.40	na	4.11	na
			(1.48)	(1.48)	na	(1.71)	na	(3.22)	na	(1.88)	na	(2.91)	na
Invest. Corp.	1.23	*327*	12.72	12.85	7.37	18.42	16.08	2.21	-4.23	1.10	na	11.31	na
			(1.15)	(1.17)	(5.10)	(1.28)	(5.60)	(2.35)	(1.28)	(5.66)	na	(2.43)	na
Insurances	7.50	*222*	16.38	16.58	8.08	20.42	6.60	12.52	4.60	-2.71	-5.30	23.27	17.25
			(1.67)	(1.71)	(4.37)	(1.57)	na	(5.03)	na	(2.51)	.	(4.39)	(3.25)
Corp. Pension	23.16	*337*	13.29	11.62	16.40	16.97	19.14	1.64	9.76	-2.16	11.32	10.17	16.57
			(1.04)	(1.17)	(1.99)	(1.61)	(2.07)	(2.16)	(5.23)	(4.05)	(10.57)	(1.93)	(4.77)
Endowments	37.82	*933*	16.01	15.32	16.57	19.32	17.87	-1.60	18.65	14.76	7.54	15.17	14.95
			(1.08)	(1.00)	(1.78)	(0.83)	(1.12)	(1.72)	(5.63)	(9.20)	(7.30)	(2.39)	(1.80)
Family Offices	17.60	*971*	14.33	14.93	11.94	17.70	18.44	12.05	4.37	5.89	3.61	15.57	12.49
			(0.85)	(0.97)	(1.69)	(0.91)	(1.95)	(4.05)	(5.06)	(4.22)	(5.24)	(1.16)	(2.64)
Govt. Agencies	28.57	*11*	-2.19	-5.13	9.55	na	9.55	-8.80	na	-7.63	na	-0.17	na
			(4.03)	(3.21)	(16.45)	na	(16.45)	(7.30)	na	(2.97)	na	(7.05)	na
Total	23.59%	*9803*	14.28%	14.28%	14.27%	18.26%	15.47%	9.29%	15.09%	2.79%	4.04%	15.23%	14.62%
			(0.30)	(0.39)	(0.45)	(0.35)	(0.40)	(1.38)	(1.57)	(1.50)	(1.81)	(0.54)	(0.45)

Table 6.5: Mean Advisor Effects

Hypothesis: Interpretation. Based on the results, it seems that within the fund type that likely requires the largest amount of fund selection sophistication, VC funds, the use of external advisors has a positive impact on fund selection. This would confirm the key hypothesis. However, for buyout funds, the effect seems reversed. The results do not give direct indications why this would be the case; therefore, the results are discussed again at the end of the chapter. In summary, the results suggest that a) external advisors aid LPs in their VC investments, but appear to have a negative effect in their buyout fund investments, b) timing is not relevant, c) not (statistically) significantly different by LP type. The null hypothesis of no effects of external advisors should thus be rejected.

Robustness. The results are tested by dropping positive or negative funds. There are no changes in the returns on the level of the LP types, which had not been significant anyway. Overall, dropping some very positive fund outliers reduces the difference for VC funds, but not in a significant degree. I also point to an important robustness test for previous results. It could be argue that the regressions in presented before are significantly biased because the use of the advisor variable impacted the returns of the LPs. Hence, in unreported regressions, I check if the original regressions are still valid and find that inclusion of the external advisor variable does not significantly impact any of the original results.

Regressions: External Advisors Effects on LP Returns in Net IRR

Pooled OLS regressions of 'Net Irr' on dummies for LPs, GPs and external advisor. External Advisor takes the value of 1 if the LP indicated the use of an external advisor. Regression (1) *Advisor* shows the return effects given fund types and covariables. (2) *LPs* introduces LP dummies. (3) *Fund Int.* interacts the funds with External Advisor. (4) *LP Int.* interacts the LPs with External Advisor. Robust standard errors are reported in brackets, observations were clustered at the fund level. Interaction terms in column (4) are dropped for space reasons for banks, investment corporations and insurances as no external advisor has been recorded. US LPs & funds 1991–2003 are considered. Significance levels: *** p<0.01, ** p<0.05, * p<0.1. Covariates as used in previous regressions. Constant estimated but not reported.

Dep. Variable: Net IRR	Advisor	LPs	Fund Int.	LP Int.
	(1)	(2)	(3)	(4)
External Advisor	-4.47***	-0.57	-3.55***	2.91
	(0.72)	(0.51)	(0.80)	(3.47)
Public Pension		-2.21*	-2.05*	-2.32*
		(1.16)	(1.14)	(1.28)
Banks		-1.21	-1.42	-1.21
		(1.40)	(1.35)	(1.40)
Invest. Corp.		0.96	0.77	0.96
		(1.38)	(1.37)	(1.38)
Insurances		1.12	1.27	1.05
		(1.65)	(1.65)	(1.68)
Corporate P.		0.10	0.15	-0.37
		(1.32)	(1.32)	(1.48)
Endowments		1.05	0.81	0.88
		(1.32)	(1.23)	(1.23)
Family Office		-0.36	-0.37	0.16
		(1.27)	(1.28)	(1.43)
Govt. Agencies		-14.47***	-13.41***	-16.28***
		(4.78)	(4.70)	(4.15)
Opportunity	-1.89	0.35	-1.33	0.34
	(1.79)	(1.60)	(1.81)	(1.61)
Late VC	-3.58	0.90	-3.44	0.92
	(2.90)	(3.23)	(2.92)	(3.22)
Early VC	-7.40**	-5.04	-7.33**	-5.02
	(3.22)	(3.09)	(3.22)	(3.09)
Public P. * Ext. Adv.				-3.29
				(3.52)
Corporate P. * Ext. Adv.				-2.32
				(4.01)
Endow. * Ext. Adv.				-3.19
				(3.66)
Family O. * Ext. Adv.				-6.08
				(4.04)
Govt. Age. * Ext. Adv.				4.53
				(15.50)
Opp. * Ext. Adv.	3.65***		3.11***	
	(1.18)		(1.18)	
Late VC * Ext. Adv.	8.17***		7.87***	
	(1.97)		(1.97)	
Early VC * Ext. Adv.	4.59*		4.36*	
	(2.46)		(2.45)	
Covariates	Yes	Yes	Yes	Yes
Year fixed effects?	Yes	Yes	Yes	Yes
Observations	8315	8315	8315	8315
R-squared	0.107	0.106	0.108	0.106

Table 6.6: External Advisor – Regressions

6.2.3 The LP Proximity Hypothesis

I now turn to the question if LP proximity matters when investing in VC funds. The activities of VC funds differ markedly from those of buyout funds. VC fund managers must often combine technological expertise in newly emerging technologies with the ability to judge young, untested entrepreneurs, in addition to being savvy financial engineers. While this is a particular challenge to VC funds, it poses also a challenge to the LP. The investment managers at LPs not only need to assess the expertise of the VC fund manager – something that is likely harder than for buyout fund investment managers. They must also, since VC funds are usually focused on specific industries, take a certain bet on the prospects of that specific industry. Ideally, the LP would like to invest in VC funds just when a technological revolution commences, such as the internet boom at Silicon Valley. However, being too late can cost dearly: As shown earlier, returns for VC funds dropped sharply after 1998. LPs that only then invested probably suffered losses from their late investments.

In numerous discussions with industry practitioners, LPs said that in order to do well in VC fund investments, one must really understand the VC manager and should have a good understanding of the target industry. In fact, one investor said that he would like to be as close as possible to the VC funds to conduct better due diligence, have a feel for their target firms and to learn from their activities to assess future re-investment possibilities. Simply put, "you need to know what is going on."[15] In addition, fundraising VC funds may first approach close LPs before contacting LPs farther away. I therefore hypothesize, that, figuratively speaking, investing 'across the street' should yield measurable benefits.[16]

This notion can thus be encapsulated in the following hypothesis:

H 11: Proximity – LPs invest in local VC funds with greater confidence and more often than in funds that are farther away. Hence, returns for

[15] This is a quote from my personal interviews with industry practitioners.

[16] One may suspect that differential access to funds, i.e. exclusion of LPs that would like to invest but are not permitted because of oversubscription, may also be an issue. However, LSW demonstrate that this kind of access to VC funds cannot explain return differences among LPs.

LPs are strongly influenced by local VC funds.

While this is an interesting hypothesis, testing it is subject to an endogeneity problem: Location of LPs is conceivably a choice-variable. Most investors can simply open an office near hubs of heightened economic activity. In fact, LPs confirmed that this was the reason why many of them maintained offices in the Bay Area or Boston. Since my data only contains the headquarters of LPs, I would not be able to correct for this behavior. However, I reason that there is one large and important LP class that is very unlikely to open offices away from their headquarters: Public pension funds. Created for a local political constituency, these investors are usually confined to their city of origin. For instance, the Teacher Retirement System of Austin, Texas, is unlikely to maintain offices in Boston to better invest in VC firms. Moreover, these investors also represent mostly the 'average' investor with no other additional potential expertise.[17] I therefore argue that public pension funds provide a good natural experiment for the impact of geographic proximity.[18]

Analysis – Mean results and a Geographic Map. To identify the impact of geographic proximity to VC funds on public pension fund returns, I use the following strategy. First, I look at the cities / areas that received the most VC funding in 1998. According to Venture Economics, the following 15 cities / areas received the majority of VC funding in 1998 (in alphabetic order): Atlanta, Bay Area, Boston, Chicago, Dallas, Denver, Los Angeles, New York, Philadelphia, Saint Louis, San Antonio, San Diego, Seattle and Washington, DC. I then plot public pension funds and VC firms on a geographic map of the USA, figure 6.4.[19] The majority of VC firms are located in or near those 15

[17]For instance, one could argue that banks could have special expertise from their lending activities, or that university endowments could benefit from close ties to their Alma Mater and hence contacts to alumni working for VC funds.

[18]One may perhaps argue that public pension funds may feel a political obligation to invest more 'locally'. However, that proposition has been refuted on empiric grounds by LSW; Nielsen (2005) also report similar findings for Danish pension funds. Also, in personal discussions with public pension fund managers I learned that this practice was not common, if it existed at all: "We have a fiduciary role to our pensioners, and we take it very seriously."

[19]Not shown: Alaska and Hawaii.

cities / areas, visible as rectangles.[20] In Boston and San Jose, the stars of the pension funds overlap the symbols for the VC funds; I therefore present in figure 6.5 two little focuses of those areas alone without pension funds to show that there are indeed a large number, a majority, of VC firms located in those areas.[21] Figure 6.4, the large geographic map, thus shows how distributed public pension funds, denoted with stars, are across the country. It also shows the close proximity of most VC firms to their target portfolio companies.[22]

Second, I calculate the average return of the VC funds active in those areas, or within a perimeter of 50 miles. Based thereon, I regroup all VC funds into four major groups: 1 – 3 in order of average returns, and one area for VC funds not found in any of these areas.[23] I call them, for simplicity, "VC area classes". Having reclassified VC funds by one of these VC area classes, I calculate the average fund returns per VC area class. Table 6.7 first shows the total number of VC funds per area (column 1), and then the mean returns per area (2). The difference in returns across VC area classes is large: VC funds in the 'best' group achieved IRRs of 60.28%, on average, between 1991 and 1998 (area 2: 22.09% IRR, area 3: 12.34%). This is in stark contrast to funds that were not in that area, or indeed in any such area at all: VC funds outside any major VC area classes achieved an IRR of only 4.09%, on average.

Third, I then proceed to group the pension funds located in or near those same areas, using the same approach. Note that I *first* create groups based on the VC fund returns, *then* I group pension funds based on those classifications. In other words, I do not group, or select, the pension funds based on their own outcome. Column (3) of table 6.7 shows the number of public pension funds per VC area class. I then determine the number of investments conducted by public pension funds in each VC area class in all fund types, including buyout

[20] I do not include buyout firms in this analysis, as these firms are mostly located in NY and/or Delaware, their funds are registered mostly in tax-havens and because their general activities are much less of a 'local' business than investments in start-ups.

[21] From the city and the state I determined the exact latitudinal and longitudinal coordinates of VC firms and LPs.

[22] This does not surprise, as VC firms naturally choose to be close to their potential targets and their existing portfolio companies. See Lerner (1995) and Kaplan and Stromberg (2001) for the activities of venture capitalists as investors in portfolio companies.

[23] I do so by 'eye', but I also used average-linkage, complete-linkage and Ward's Method clustering. Doing so actually always creates one extra subgroup just for Dallas, but I decided to group this into the top performing group.

funds, anywhere in the US, column (4). Column (5) then presents the average returns of funds of those investments. Public pension funds located in VC area class 1 invested in funds, on average, with the highest returns, and average returns follow the hierarchy determined by the VC area classes (26.90%, 24.80% and 15.11% for the three areas, respectively). However, returns for LPs not in any VC area class were pretty much average (22.85% IRR, the average is 23.43%). When I focus solely on the VC investments, the differences are much more pronounced, with public pension funds located in VC area classes 1 investing in funds with 61.48% IRR on average, see column (7). This is similar to the average return of VC funds located in that area. In correlation with returns by VC area classes, public pension funds located in other areas also had lower average returns (area 2: 48.97%, area 3: 29.68%). However, the correlation is not perfect as the returns are generally higher than their own region; also, again, LPs not in any VC area class achieved 'average' returns (41.42% vs. 45.95% on average). This leads to three natural conclusions: First, LPs close to a VC area often invest locally, and their returns are thus significantly determined by the local entrepreneurial activity. Second, LPs also invest outside their areas, and therefore also generate returns from elsewhere. Third, in synthesis, the investment behavior is a function of first a) local investment opportunities, and then of b) investment opportunities elsewhere.

A specific point merits discussion: One may argue that the location of VC funds may not be fixed. Indeed, while most VC firms will operate from only one operative office, some of the very successful, larger VC firms may maintain representative offices in several locations. Because of my data structure, I am not able to accommodate for this possibility. However, how would this VC mobility affect the results? It would be natural to assume that the returns of the fund managed by the firm would then be a composite, or average, of the investment opportunities in the different locations. Hence, the returns to the LP that invested in that fund would be more of an average too. Therefore, VC fund mobility would more likely result in more average returns to the LPs and therefore should in fact reduce the measured effects in the analysis presented here. In other words, without this possible endogeneity, the results presented here should be even more pronounced.

Mean Net Irr by VC-intense areas and Public Pension Funds in those Areas
The table shows the number of VC funds located in different VC-intense areas (1) and their average IRRs (2), as well as the number of public pension (PP) funds that are located in those areas (3). It then shows the number of total investments by public pension funds in those areas (4), and their average returns for all investments, including buyout funds, (5). The same is shown also just for VC investments, (6) and (7). Standard errors are reported in brackets. *Not in Area* indicates VC funds and LPs that are not located in any of the VC area classes. Only funds with vintage 1991 – 1998 were included.

				All funds		VC only	
Area class	No. of VC funds (1)	Mean GP netirr (2)	No. of PP funds (3)	No. of Invest. (4)	Mean netirr (5)	No. of Invest. (6)	Mean netirr (7)
1	407	60.28%	39	358	26.90%	94	61.48%
					(2.19)		(6.56)
2	171	22.09	14	153	24.80	46	48.97
					(2.74)		(7.28)
3	9	12.24	14	112	15.11	23	29.68
					(1.82)		(6.48)
No Area	33	4.09	63	888	22.85	270	41.42
					(1.16)		(3.18)
Total	620	46.07	130	1511	23.43	433	45.95
					(0.91)		(2.61)

VC Areas: 1 – Bay Area (San Jose), Boston, Dallas, Los Angeles. 2 – Washington DC, San Antonio, Seattle, Philadelphia, Chicago. 3 – New York, Denver, San Diego. Not included (no investment observation during period) Atlanta, Saint Louis.

Table 6.7: Average Fund Returns by VC Area

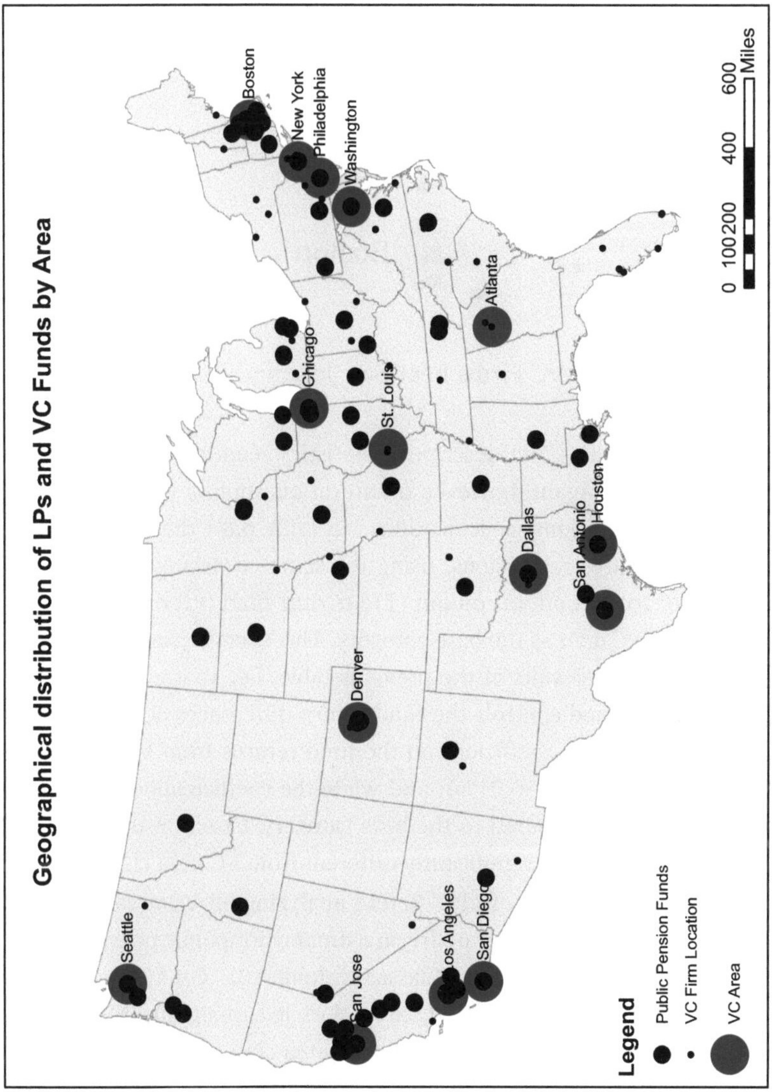

Figure 6.4: Public Pension Funds and VC Areas (not shown: Alaska, Hawaii)

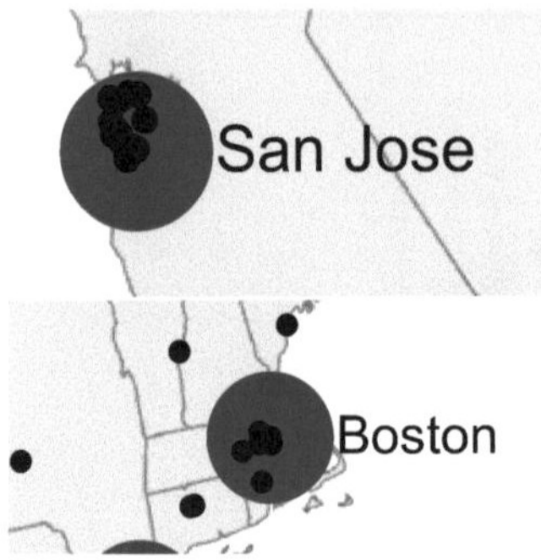

Figure 6.5: VC Firms near San Jose and Boston

Analysis – Regressions. The descriptive statistics seem to confirm the LP proximity hypothesis. Again, however, a natural question is whether the results are robust to additional specifications. In table 6.8 I therefore present the results of respective regressions, using the same covariates as in the regressions before. To start off, in column (1) I regress fund IRR on the VC area class, using *Not in VC area* as the base category. This exercise serves simply to confirm the descriptive results of the previous table, i.e. that even considering year fixed effects and controls the fund return differences across VC area classes remain large. The coefficient on the fund returns from VC area class 1 are large and significant (56.01%), and while the coefficients on the other areas are insignificant compared to the base category, based on the standard errors VC area class 3 is still significantly different from VC area class 1.

I then turn to the returns of LPs. Before analyzing all VC area classes, I first present a simple regression of netirr on a dummy for public pension funds located in any of the three VC Area Classes, column (2). On average, being a public pension fund in the 'best' VC area class led to significantly higher returns than that of LPs that are not in any VC area class at all (17.00% over the comparison category).

One conclusion from the descriptive results was, however, that the outperformance is primarily due to local investments. In column (3) I therefore add a covariable 'Invest in Same Area' that takes the value of 1 if the investment was local, 0 otherwise. While the coefficient (-7.38%) itself is insignificant, the inclusion of this variable enhances the coefficients on the LPs in VC Areas (e.g. the coefficient on LPs in VC area class 1 turn from 17.00% to 21.32%).

I therefore reason that the effect was dependent on the specific LP VC Area Class.[24] Therefore, in column (4) I interacted this variable with the LP VC Area classes. The results show that for all LP VC Area classes, the coefficients were positive, even though only one (LP in Area Class 1 with a coefficient of +70.12%) was also significant. Based in the standard errors, however, the interaction term is still statistically significantly different from the same term on 'LP in Area 3 * Same Area'. Therefore, for LPs in VC area class 1, investing locally was obviously beneficial. The base outcome, 'Invest in Same Area' was statistically significantly negative (-33.76%). This means that if you are an LP that is *not located* in any VC Area, randomly investing in VC funds that are *not located* in a significant VC Area yields comparatively negative returns. Another result is that, once interacted, the original, non-interacted coefficients on the LPs became insignificant. Thus, indeed very much of differences in investment success seems to be driven by the ability to invest in *local*, well-performing funds. In other words, the outperformance of LPs in VC area class is not due to seeking successful funds outside your local area. Hence, much of the outperformance of the LPs in area 1 must be due simply to the geographic, historic accident of being serendipitously located in those areas.

Analysis – Logit regressions. So far, the interpretation that the investment success was due to local funds rested primarily on the correlation of returns. I now also investigate if the probability of a local investment was indeed high. I therefore conduct logit regressions, where the dependent variable takes the value of 1 if the investment by the public pension fund was local, 0 otherwise. This regression is shown in table 6.9, panel A. The coefficients on LPs in VC Area 1 and 3 are significant. This indicates, compared to the base category, that those LPs invested significantly more often in 'their' area than LPs that were not in any VC area class (who, if the variable takes the value of 1, invested also in VC funds that are not in any VC area classes). To make the results easier to understand, I then use the logit regression in column (2) to predict, in percentage terms, the likelihood of investing locally. This is shown in Panel B: LPs in VC area class 1 had a predicted probability of more than

[24] One must also take a bit of caution in interpreting this variable for LPs not in any VC area. Specifically, the 'Invest in Same Area' variable also takes the value of 1 if an LP that is not in any VC Area Class made in an investment in a VC fund that is not in any VC Area Class.

Location Regressions for Public Pension Funds 1991 – 1998

This table reports the pooled OLS regressions of net IRR per VC funds on dummy variables between 1991 and 1998. Regression (1) confirms the average fund performances of funds in respective areas, clustered by area. Regression (2) tests for public pension funds located within 50 miles of the three VC area classes. (3) introduces 'Invest in same area', a dummy that captures if an investment took place in the same VC area class; (4) then also interacts that dummy with the LP VC area class variables. Regressions (5) and (6) are robstness tests that expand the original areas of 50 miles to 75 and 100 miles, respectively. Areas are defined by the the largest amounts of VC funding received in 1998, as defined in the previous table. Only VC funds are considered. Robust standard errors are reported in brackets; observations were clustered at the fund level. Comparison categories: Not in VC area classes, late VC funds, not invested in same area. Significance levels: *** $p<0.01$, ** $p<0.05$, * $p<0.1$. Covariates as used in previous regressions. Constant estimated but not reported.

Dependent variable: Net IRR

			50 Miles		75 Miles	100 Miles
Dep. Variable	VC Area	Normal	Same Area	Interact	Interact	Interact
Net IRR in %	(1)	(2)	(3)	(4)	(5)	(6)
VC area						
VC Area 1	56.02***					
	(10.57)					
VC Area 2	15.49*					
	(8.07)					
VC Area 3	9.86					
	(13.87)					
LP Location						
LPs in Area 1		17.00**	21.32**	-11.64	-15.86	-24.70***
		(6.77)	(8.32)	(10.97)	(10.06)	(8.53)
LPs in Area 2		0.88	2.82	7.71	12.34**	0.20
		(6.72)	(7.09)	(7.97)	(6.13)	(5.44)
LPs in Area 3		-10.91	-10.04	-7.87	-9.31	-8.24
		(7.85)	(7.64)	(8.68)	(8.88)	(6.47)
Invest in 'Same Area'			-7.38	-33.76***	-38.91***	-45.28***
			(7.95)	(11.82)	(12.70)	(13.77)
LPs Area 1*'Same Area'				70.12***	72.86***	70.90***
				(21.21)	(20.70)	(19.79)
LPs Area 2*'Same Area'				9.05	13.56	3.08
				(18.36)	(18.72)	(17.02)
LPs Area 3*'Same Area'				3.24	0.22	17.55
				(16.21)	(14.85)	(16.95)
Dummy early VC		25.74***	25.30***	20.49**	20.61**	20.75**
		(9.43)	(9.46)	(9.54)	(9.51)	(9.66)
LPs	none	Only Public Pension Funds				
Covariables	Yes	Yes	Yes	Yes	Yes	Yes
Year Fixed Effects	Yes	Yes	Yes	Yes	Yes	Yes
Observations	620	409	409	409	409	404
R-squared	0.131	0.208	0.211	0.257	0.256	0.262

Table 6.8: Performance Regressions by VC Area

70% to invest also locally, while all other LPs were more inclined to invest outside their local area. The table also contains the number of VC funds, in percent, of all funds that actually entered the analysis. Based on the confidence intervals for the predicted probabilities, it is not possible to say that LPs in VC area classes 1 and 2 invested more often or less often locally than one may have expected from the percentage of local VC funds. However, LPs in VC area class 3 did invest more often, also in a statistically significant way, in their local area: 39.0% of investments are predicted to be local, but only 1.5% of all VC funds are in fact in those areas. I can therefore conclude that the logit regression does not run counter the interpretation that LPs tend to invest locally and for LPs in area class 3 the results seem to confirm this interpretation. Hence, the results indicate, as hypothesized, that being close to the 'best' VC area class may lead LPs to also invest in successful, local VC funds. LPs elsewhere will be driven by their local investment opportunities – and thus local fund returns – while still trying to some extent to diversify geographically.

Hypothesis: Interpretation. The regressions, which control for year fixed effects, the GP fund size, LP size and the experience of the LP still confirm the univariate results: For the 'average' investor, with no additional expertise, being close to a successful VC-intense area helps investing in good funds. The LP gains particular exposure to that area and also invests more often in local funds than LPs elsewhere. LPs that are in other areas will partly invest locally, while also investing in some funds farther away. Their returns will thus be a mixture. LPs not located in any special area diversify across the nation and therefore generate approximately average, national returns. What is significant, however, is that LPs that are in the very good areas *do not* have average returns, but 'local' returns, i.e. they did not diversify outside their local area and instead benefitted from their historically fortunate proximity to the successful VC funds. In conclusion, therefore, the null hypothesis that LP proximity does not matter can be rejected. Instead, LP proximity does seem to matter.

Robustness Tests. I employ two types of robustness tests. First, I test if the results are robust to a different radius, or distance. Second, I use different regression estimation procedures and drop potential outliers.

Logit and Predicted Probabilities of Investments in the Same Area.
In this table, a logit regression was used to predict the probability of an LP situated in one VC area class to invest in the same VC area class. The dependent variable 'In same area' takes the value of 1 if the investment was in the same area, 0 otherwise. Panel A shows the logit estimates, using year fixed effects, as well as covariables for LP size, LP experience and fund size. Note that the comparison category is 'LPs not in any VC Area'. Based on this regression, predicted probabilities of investing locally were estimated.*

Panel A – Logit regressions of LPs investing in same area.
Dependent Variable: 'Invest in same area', Yes=1, No=0
Comparison category: LPs not in any VC area class at all.

	Logit
LPs in VC Area 1	3.13***
	(0.53)
LPs in VC Area 2	0.87
	(0.81)
LPs in VC Area 3	1.81***
	-(0.60)
logFundSize	-0.58***
	(0.20)
Constant	1.95
	(1.28)
Covariables	Yes
Observations	409
Log-L.	-173.38

Panel B – Predicted Probabilities of investing in same area

	Prob.	95% confidence interval	% Funds
LP in VC Area 1	70.5%	[57.6% – 83.3%]	65.6%
LP in VC Area 2	19.9%	[0.0% – 43.3%]	27.6%
LP in VC Area 3	39.0%	[18.3% – 59.8%]	1.5%
LP not in VC Area	9.4 %	[2.8% – 16.1%]	5.3%

* Estimates in Panel B for 'LPs not in VC area' classes need to be interpreted with care: For these LPs, 'Invest in same area' corresponds to investments in VC funds that are also not in any VC area class themselves. In other words, about 90.6% (1-9.4%) of investments by those LPs were in VC funds that were in fact located in one of the three defined VC area classes.

Table 6.9: Probabilities of Investing Locally

Different radii. To test for the impact of different radii, in table 6.8 I add in columns (5) and (6) the results if I use LPs in different radii from the center of the respective VC area classes. Instead of using a 50 mile radius, I expand the radius to 75 or 100 miles. None of the previous conclusions are negatively impacted. Two coefficients are changed. For LPs in VC area class 2, in column, the coefficient is statistically significant and positive (12.34%). This would indicate that those LPs did not outperform the base category 'Not in any VC area class' with their 'local' investments, but rather with their non-local (i.e. non-interacted) investments – probably by investing in VC funds in area 1. In column (6), where the radius is 100 miles, the coefficient LPs in VC area class 1 becomes statistically significant and negative (-24.70%). This would indicate that not only do these LPs benefit from their 'local' investments (the interacted terms are still 70.90%), but also suffered from investing non-locally.[25] I conclude that given those robustness tests, the essential interpretation is not impacted.

Outliers and skewed data. Second, I again employ the range of additional regression tests that I also used for the previous performance tests in this chapter (results not shown). I compared the results to those in column (3) of table 6.8. The results are robust to dropping outliers and the basic conclusions remain the same. However, the coefficient on the fund fixed variable 'Dummy early VC' becomes smaller and hence loses also statistical significance. The results also remain the same if I use regressions of the excess IRR (over the median), or a capital-weighted IRR (the portfolio approach) as the dependent variable. However, using quantile regression at the median, the results compared to column (3) are interesting: The coefficients on the LPs in VC Areas now all become statistically significant (LPs in VC Area 1 +16.61%***, in Area 2 +9.05%***, in Area 3 7.41%*, compared to 21.32%**, 2.81% and -10.04% in the original regression, respectively); the coefficient on the non-interacted variable 'Invest in Same Area' also becomes significant (-14.09*** compared to -7.38%). This means if only median results are considered, and 'local investments' are conditioned for, LPs generally outperform LPs not in any VC

[25] However, note that at 100 miles and more, the radii start to overlap, which forces me to drop observations. At 25 miles (not shown), the radius is drawn too closely so that very many LPs are in fact identified as 'not in any VC area class'.

area class. The negative coefficient on 'Invest in Same Area' primarily reflects the fact that LPs not in any VC area class would achieve poor returns when investing also in VC funds that are not in any VC area class. It likely also means that for most LPs – except those in area 1 and perhaps in area 2 – local investments would actually lead to sub-average returns. Hence, when this effect is taken into consideration, LPs benefit from investments in the successful VC area classes. Thus, this test not only supports the robustness of the conclusion, it even enhances the interpretation of the effects as it underscores the significance of a few geographically defined areas for LPs.

6.3 Summary and Discussion

In this chapter, I document systematic differences in returns achieved by different investors in PE funds. The results must be seen against the background that buyout and VC funds had different time periods during which either performed particularly well. As I had hypothesized, I found evidence that the returns by different LPs are dependent on the specific fund type: Some LPs achieve above-average returns in one fund type, but not in others. Moreover, also as hypothesized, the overall returns are largely driven by the returns of those fund types over time – so some LPs with an advantage in VC funds benefitted during the nineties, some LPs when buyout funds performed well. This also led me to reject the alternative hypothesis that stated that some LPs, in particular endowments, always outperformed other LPs. Lerner et al. (2007b), stated, in particular for endowments: "Overall, these results suggest that LPs differ in their ability to evaluate the quality of funds and to invest based on this information, that is, in their level of sophistication."[26] I, and somewhat in contrast, conclude that LPs have *differing comparative advantages* in *different fund types*. The dependance on timing also impacts the results on experience and LP size: During the nineties, as was hypothesized, small LPs with experience outperformed other LPs, notably in the VC fund investments. Thereafter, however, it was inexperienced, large LPs, with their large buyout-fund investments, who outperformed others.

With respect to international differences, I find evidence for the hypothesis that, when adjusted for timing and experience, most LPs do not differ interna-

[26] Lerner et al. (2007b), page 733.

tionally in the returns. Only European PE FoFs and family offices in the rest of the world underperformed, while non-US government agencies outperformed peers. As for PE funds, only late VC funds in Europe underperformed US late VC funds significantly. However, in robustness tests I find that this result is primarily driven by some very successful US funds.

I then turn to possible explanations for investment returns. I show that, even when adjusting for the specific fund types, endowments – whose investment success had received particular attention – did not achieve higher fund returns by taking particularly large risks in their fund investments. I therefore reject the *risk-taking hypothesis*. In a different line of inquiry, however, I find evidence for the *external advisor hypothesis*: LPs with advisors achieved higher VC fund returns than those without. Finally, I find support for the *LP proximity hypothesis*: Using US public pension funds as a natural experiment, I show that those LPs who are geographically close to successful VC-intense areas, e.g. Boston or Silicon Valley, achieved significantly higher fund returns and also invested more often locally than LPs located outside such areas.

I now turn to individual LP types. I focus primarily on results for US LPs, since international differences are negligible after adjusting for timing. **Public pension funds** are the largest LP group by number of investments and presumably assets invested. As had been suspected, they truly were among the LPs with the lowest returns. However, it is interesting to note that if I look at individual time-periods, 1991 – 1998 vs. 1999 – 2003, they never underperformed distinctively. At the same time, they never had a period of significant outperformance. In general, therefore, public pension funds always seem to perform a little worse than other LPs. They do not seem to have any special expertise per fund type; they indeed seem to be the slightly 'unsophisticated, large investor' that anecdotal evidence has it. This also underscores the external validity of the findings on the *LP proximity Hypothesis*: While I focus on public pension funds, the results are therefore applicable for any 'average' LP without additional expertise or objective. At this stage one may interject that pension funds may also have an 'obligation' to invest locally. However, that proposition has been refuted on empiric grounds by Lerner et al. (2007b) for US pension funds; Nielsen (2005) also reject this notion for Danish pension funds. In addition, in personal discussions with public pension fund managers

I learned that this practice was not common, if it existed at all: "We have a fiduciary role to our pensioners, and we take it very seriously." Therefore, I reason that the results on LP proximity are valid also for LPs other than public pension funds.

In contrast, **endowments** outperform the average investor in particular because of the VC funds. This result is robust in multivariate analysis. The results are in line, albeit weaker, with the findings by Lerner et al. (2007b) for their time-period. In testing the *Risk-Taking Hypothesis* I also demonstrate, however, that this special expertise in VC funds is likely not a result of a different risk-function: Endowments did not take higher risks when investing in VC funds than other LPs. Compared to endowments, it is interesting that **family offices** are somewhat similar in their average returns, if less pronounced. Family offices also had their strongest period before the turn of the millennium, and achieved also only average buyout fund returns. Like endowments, family offices also outperformed the average LP in their early VC - investments. However, while the coefficients point in the same directions, in multivariate analysis, the similarities lose their statistical significance. This suggests that some of the factors specific for endowments – e.g. small investor size and with it more progressively set incentives – might also be applicable to family offices who are of similar size and possibly have similar time-horizons.

Investment corporations, banks and to some degree also **corporate pension funds** show similar return patterns. They all achieved below-par VC fund returns, but flourished during times when buyout funds excelled. As is the case for endowments with their VC fund investments, this is robust even when conditioning also on the average buyout fund return – these LPs thus have some expertise that allows them to invest in buyout funds that outperform not only the average PE fund, but also the average buyout fund. However, **banks** are particularly poor VC investors. As I had already discussed in section 5.3, there are number of arguments why banks may invest also strategically in VC funds. This would suggest that banks also limit themselves somewhat in their selection. This limitation, in turn, should lead to poorer-than-average returns. Hence, the underperformance for banks in VC funds may indeed be evidence for additional investment objectives for banks.[27]

Insurances are also strong performers. In the mean results they are even the best performers, but multivariate analysis reduces that relative outperformance somewhat. Insurances not only perform well in buyout funds, but also in VC and opportunity funds. Curiously though, when I look at US-only institutions, in neither time-period (before or after the turn of the millennium) do insurances outperform even public pension funds with statistical significance in the multivariate analysis. Yet overall, their performance beats other LPs. In many ways, therefore, insurances are similar to public pension funds, but with a higher 'base' selection performance. This is an interesting notion, if perhaps surprising. However, insurances combine many facets of pension funds – large asset base, fiduciary investment decisions – with experience in investing akin to many 'Wall Street' investors. Perhaps then, for insurances, the combination of similar risk-preference as public pension funds on the one hand, and public scrutiny on the other hand results in investment structures that are favorable to succeed in PE fund investments.

Returns by **PE FoFs** are in almost every dimension 'average'. In neither the mean results, nor the multivariate analysis does this LP type achieve returns that are significantly different from either the average or even public pension funds. The mean results show that they outperformed public pension funds since 2000. However, this is not statistically significant when controlling for covariates in the multivariate analysis. Is this surprising? While FoFs market their selection process, they are also primarily concerned with attracting new funds. This is more easily done by achieving a stable average PE return, and by investing in established 'blue chip' funds, than by investing in unknown, possibly above-average, but also possibly below-average, funds. However, once more one should note that the returns are of course only registered on the level of returns of funds. This does not yet reflect the costs charged by FoFs to their own investors.

Finally, **US government agencies** underperformed all other LPs, and in par-

[27] Again, as in section 5.3, I refer to Allen and Gale (2000), Allen (1993), Mayer et al. (2005), as well as Hellmann et al. (2008).

ticular so in their VC investments. For example, the mean results suggest that this LP selected early VC funds with returns that were nearly more than 14% lower than the average early VC fund. This is not a surprise. As political entities, they are often established for the purpose of supporting nascent industries, in this case indirectly through VC fund investments, and irrespective of returns generated therefrom. The regressions show that this is primarily due to returns from the last century. For non-US / non-European government agencies, e.g. sovereign wealth funds, returns suggest that those investors invested primarily in large and successful buyout funds.

What drives investment performances? I probed three hypotheses: The *risk-taking*, *external advisor* and the *LP proximity* hypotheses. I discussed how the returns achieved by endowments are likely not due to their taking excessive risks. However, what does that implicate? It suggests that endowments were able to minimize risks by screening and selecting good funds better than other LPs. Lerner et al. (2007b) looked at the re-investment decisions and found that endowments are better than other investors at predicting the return of follow-on funds. In fact, in unreported analyses, I also find this pattern for endowments. This suggests that endowments were in much closer interrelation with their funds. Investment managers at endowments may interact more closely with the GP managers, and use this knowledge also to decide on re-investment managers. This requires, among many things, personal incentives that are geared to long-term return bonuses, as well as a low turn-over of staff. Those abilities are particularly important for VC fund investments.

Interestingly, viewed from this perspective, the results of the external advisor hypothesis fit the picture: If larger LPs cannot perform the function of interacting closely with VC funds, then perhaps external advisors can? In parts, therefore, external advisors can offer, in principle, a fund 'coverage' that one might suspect for endowments. For buyout fund investments, this expertise seems less important. Accordingly, neither endowments, nor LPs with external advisors, outperform in their buyout fund investments. The relation of performance of endowments and LPs with advisors is an intriguing proposition. However, one should take care when interpreting the results on external advisors: The data does not directly indicate if an external advisor was used for any given investment observation or when exactly that LP started using advisors, only if, in general, that LP has used advisors.

Of particular interest in this vein are also the findings on the *LP proximity hypothesis*. The results on this hypothesis also point to *personal interaction* as an essential element in VC fund investing. In turn, this means that opening representative offices near such hubs might be a lucrative strategy. Moreover, the results presented before suggest that much of this is due to personal interaction.

Before I turn to research from related fields, I first discuss some **alternative explanations**. One possibility for the differences is that GPs, in particular buyout funds, screen for their own LPs. This is likely the case for many of the very successful buyout funds. Lerner and Schoar (2004) document that GPs have an incentive to screen for liquid LPs, while Kaplan and Schoar (2005) report that the best funds apparently limit their fund size, even though they could attract more funds. The findings here, including also the underperformance by LPs with external advisors, might suggest that this may be one reason why some LP types outperform within buyout funds, but not VC funds: LP reputation may count. This may also be relevant for VC funds, which could first approach 'local' LPs. Another possible explanation could be differences in taxation or other regulatory restrictions. This could be important in two dimensions. First, there could be differences by LP type. Second, there could be differences by country. With regard to the former, those were partly already described in section 3 when I introduced LPs in more detail. However, that discussion did not uncover very stringent limitations, at least not in the US, for any LP type; Lerner et al. (2007b) also do not identify this to be a problem. With regard to the latter dimension, cross-border differences probably do exist and further research into this possibility is warranted. However, at least on the level of continental differences, the regression results for global LPs did not uncover significant differences that could be easily attributed to cross-country regulatory specificities. Finally, it may be the case that preference may drive investment performance: LPs with a certain fund preference may also be better at selecting among those. This is a proposition that will be discussed again in the final conclusion of this research, in chapter 7, where I draw together findings from both preference and performance. However, it is clear that this connection is likely not mediated simply through the additional experience generated by investing more often: The coefficients on LP experience in this chapter are largely insignificant for investments in this millennium.

How do the findings fit in with **related research**? Within research on the PE industry, only Lerner et al. (2007b) are directly comparable, if one looks only at the time period that they investigated, up to 1999. They, too, find particular success of endowments in VC funds, if much stronger so than I do. They also find that public pension funds generally underperform other LPs, and results on corporate pension funds are similarly comparable. However, I find a stronger performance for insurances. In addition, the relative underperformance of banks in VC funds is also identified.[28] Therefore, when looking just at that time-period, in principle, the results are not in serious violation. However, the results after 1998 led me to alternative interpretations, as described.

Outside the PE industry, there are few items that directly point at investment return differences across specific investor types. However, a series of papers, for instance, scrutinize the investment decisions by managers at public pension funds in the UK, see Clark (2004), Clark et al. (2006) and Clark et al. (2007). The general thrust of those papers is that investment managers at those institutions are poorly equipped with skills required to make good investment decisions. The below-average returns found here for PE may be evidence thereof.

The investigation into risk-taking looks at one possible investment 'style'. In public markets, there are a number of different 'styles', as Froot and Teo (2004) describe. However, due to their illiquid and special nature, it is questionable whether PE investment strategies would be as amenable to the same range of investment styles as public equities are.

The special role of LP location and proximity to VC funds should raise eyebrows, however. Of course, home bias, as also described in chapter 5.1.2 has been identified for public markets. Coval and Moskowitz (1999) also document this for domestic, or even locally headquartered companies. Preference

[28]In unreported analysis I also find some evidence for more recent findings by Lerner, Schoar, and Wang (2007): University endowments that belong to the 'Ivy Plus' group outperformed public universities in particular after 2000. However, for lack of additional information I do not investigate this issue further and simply note that I find some evidence that further corroborates the findings be these authors.

for locally active VC funds thus fits this finding. However, the findings are also a particularly interesting extension of the innovation literature. For instance on a portfolio company level, Zucker et al. (1998) documented how for the biotech industry geographic concentration of 'star scientists' was a key factor in nurturing nascent and booming industries; their map of 'ever active stars'/'New Biotech enterprises' and my map of LPs/VCs share many similarities.[29] On the VC level, Lerner (1995) showed, also for the biotech industry, that VC firms are often co-located with their portfolio firms for better oversight. My results now complement this 'financing innovation chain': LPs also invest more often in and benefit from VC firms in their proximity. This result is clearly important for industry practitioners. The result also, however, runs counter to 'efficient' market assumptions, as otherwise one would not expect location to matter in the investment decision. Clearly, PE is far from being 'efficient' in this sense. The result also has important political ramifications, as it suggest that local presence of financial intermediaries, outside banking hubs of the likes of New York or London, could remain a politically viable prerogative. In the same token, however, if location really impacts providers of VC fund funding, country- or region-specific tax and regulatory burdens on the level of the LP might more directly impact financing of start-ups than was previously thought.

To conclude, I presented LP investment returns from 1991 – 2003, for US and global LPs. I argued that LPs have a comparative advantage in investing within specific fund types. Those also drove outperformance of the respective LPs, depending on the underlying fund performance. In parts, the differences can be attributed to the presumed structure and objective of the LP type, or they are attributed to more poorly set incentives within the LPs. Unfortunately, empirical research based solely on returns cannot easily identify just what separates 'good' from 'poor' LPs. However, while taking risks is likely not one of them, employing advisors and being physically close to well-performing VC funds are likely two options investors can pursue to enhance their returns from VC funds.

[29] Zucker et al. (1998), page 295. However, for some smaller national markets, geographic proximity may be less important; see Fritsch and Schilder (2006a) and Fritsch and Schilder (2006b).

The research directions in this chapter were based in hypotheses derived from the discussion of principal-agent arguments in chapter 2. They covered the section on LP fund selection and performances. However, the final step is to draw the results on LP preferences and LP performances together and to conclude the research. This is presented in chapter 7.

type using multinomial logit regressions and therefore conditioned on LP location, LP experience, LP size and timing effects. I estimated the average predicted allocation by fund type as: 45.8% buyout funds, 20.5% late VC funds, 8.3% early VC funds and 25.4% opportunity funds (e.g. venture debt, secondary funds, infrastructure etc.). Investment corporations, insurances, fund-of-funds, banks and corporate pension funds invest more often in buyout funds than the average LP. Endowments, family offices, public pension funds and (US) government agencies do not overweigh buyout funds and instead focus more often on opportunity funds. In my interpretation, the null hypothesis of no differences between investor types can be rejected. This seems to confirm the view that indeed LPs differ in their fund preferences.

H 2: Home Bias. I argued that there is a significant amount of home bias: Based on predicted results from logit estimates, there is a 81.6% chance the average LP invests within the same continental area. Also, home bias is stronger for VC funds than for buyout funds. For public pension funds (86.1%), banks (85.8%) and family offices (84.9%) home bias is strongest, for FoFs lowest (64.9%). I conclude that the null hypothesis of no home bias can be rejected. In contrast, the results would support the theoretical argument that home bias might be high in this asset class, and LP types even differ in their degree of home bias.

H 3: Strategy Adjustment. After 2001, endowments seem to have invested relatively much more often in opportunity funds than other LPs, possibly in response to the economic changes that happened at that time. I therefore reject the null hypothesis that endowments did not react quicker to significant market changes than other LP types. Instead, the evidence would suggest that endowments act faster and stronger in response to market changes than other LPs.

H 4_a and H 4_b: US LP performance by LP type. I stated two somewhat competing hypotheses with respect to the performance of US LPs. Based on the literature review and interviews, H 4_a stated that endowments, FoFs and possibly investment corporations should be best equipped to invest in successful funds. H 4_b instead stated that returns should be dependent on timing and that LPs differ in their ability to pick different fund types. Based on the enquiries, I found evidence that much of the success of endowments in PE rests on their ability to pick good VC funds, in particular during the nineties. Thereafter, they did not outperform. FoFs did not, in general, outperform other LPs. Investment corporations showed an opposite pattern to endowments: Underperforming during the nineties, but better thereafter. I conclude that H 4_a cannot be supported. Instead I do find performance differences that depend on timing and fund types. Therefore, I reject the null hypothesis of general LP differences independent of timing and fund types. Instead, this would support the view of H 4_b that LP returns do depend on timing and the specific fund type that is picked.

H 5 and H 6: LP performance is negatively related to LP size and positively related to experience. In separate regressions I looked at the effect of LP size and experience at investment. I find that during the nineties, the smaller and experienced the LP, the better the returns. This would confirm also results by Lerner et al. (2007b). However, thereafter also large and inexperienced LPs had access to successful funds. Therefore, the null hypothesis of no relation between LP size & experience to returns cannot be rejected. Instead, a potential view would be that LP performance is not dependent on LP size and experience, given timing effects and fund type performance.

H 7: No return differences across global LPs. When conditioning for timing effects & experience, I hypothesized that LPs should not differ significantly in their returns. This is somewhat in contradiction with Lerner et al. (2007b) who had identified strong differences, without, however, conditioning for timing and experience in the same way as I did. In my analyses, I do not find strong return differences, except for FoFs in Europe and family offices outside the US or Europe, who both underperformed. Government agencies outside the US or Europe outperformed. Naturally, one could argue that my test to identify difference was not strong enough. Alternatively, the conditioning on additional effects may lead to the conclusion that there are no differences. I conclude that the null hypothesis of LP differences, based on Lerner et al. (2007b), should be rejected. Instead, the results indicate that internationally, across time and considering experience, LP differences are insignificant.

H 8: Risk-taking. If endowments had achieved above-average returns by taking large risks, i.e. by betting on spectacular fund returns while also potentially absorbing losses, then their return distribution might have shown this. However, I do not find a pattern whereby endowments had more 'home-runs' *and* large fund losses (but where the returns of the home-runs outweighed the losses). Instead, it seems that endowments during the nineties really did pick better VC funds, on average, than other LPs. Based on the results, the null hypothesis that endowments are risk-takers should be rejected. A possible interpretation would be that endowments achieved their returns without taking high risks.

H 9: External advisors. Since external advisors cost money, one might expect them to offer a positive impact in the selection of good funds. I find that, in general, LPs with advisors did indeed pick better VC funds. For buyout funds, however, the reverse is true, i.e. LPs with advisors picked worse funds. For VC funds, where selection expertise might matter most, advisors do seem to offer valuable help. In contrast, for buyout funds I suspected that access and LP reputation might also be important and that LPs that afford advisors might in fact be those with no exceptional reputation or access. I conclude, because of the results for the VC fund investments, that the null hypothesis of no effect of external advisors can be rejected. Instead, the results suggest LPs with advisors achieve higher (VC fund) returns but I also note that the effects are possibly fund type dependent.

H 10: LP proximity. I hypothesized that LPs that were geographically close to the most successful VC funds of the nineties were more likely to invest in the funds and thus also benefit from the returns. As the natural experiment with public pension funds suggests, this notion can be supported. For instance, public pension funds in or near Boston or San Jose vastly outperformed public pension funds elsewhere. I conclude the null hypothesis of no differences based on LP proximity can be rejected. Instead, the interpretation would be that geographic proximity does matter.

Finally, I was not able to test hypotheses on **investment objectives**, **LP signaling** and **size bias** by LP type, given the dataset.

Hypotheses: Overview of Conclusions

This table gives a summary of the tested hypotheses and the conclusions drawn from the empiric inquiries. A (+) marks the rejection of the null hypothesis, i.e. the interpretation is that the stated alternative hypothesis might be valid. A – means the null hypothesis could not be rejected, i.e. that the stated alternative hypothesis should be rejected. The results are also discussed in the text.

Preferences	H 1	Fund Preferences: LP types differ in their fund preferences	(+)
	H 2	Home Bias: There is a significant degree of home bias	(+)
	H 3	Strategy Adjustment: Endowments adjusted their allocation after 2001	(+)
Performances	H 4_a	US LPs: Endowments, FoFs and investment corporations are the best investors	–
	H 4_b	US LPs: Returns by LP type are dependent on timing and fund type	(+)
	H 5	LP Size: Smaller LPs generally invest in better performing funds	–
	H 6	Experience: Fund selection ability is generally related to LP experience	–
	H 7	Global LPs: There are no significant differences across global LPs	(+)
	H 8	Risk-Taking: Endowments did not achieve high returns by taking risks than other LPs	(+)
	H 9	External Advisors: External advisors have a positive impact on LP returns	(+)
	H 10	Proximity: LPs close to successful VC funds achieve higher returns	(+)
Untested	H 11	Investment Objectives: Some LPs pursue specific investment objectives	not tested
	H 12	LP Signaling: Some LPs are guided by the investment decisions of other LPs	not tested
	H 13	Size Bias: There is a correlation between the LP size and the fund size	not tested

Table 7.1: Hypotheses: Overview of Conclusions

I now turn to a comparison of the results on preferences and performance. While the hypotheses imply interesting results in their own right, a side by side comparison of the results may uncover more. Therefore, in table 7.2 I summarize and compare the results. It should be noted that because of the many different analyses here I only present the most general results. Specific results that compare only US LP returns, for instance, are found in respective chapters. In the table, generally, results for all LPs from 1991 to 2003 and from the US, Europe and the rest of the world are presented. Moreover, the 'base' for comparison is the somewhat hypothetical average LP. The signs indicate deviations from the average LP, where applicable based on the 95% confidence interval of specific estimates.

Panel A of table 7.2 shows results across all LPs, i.e. average results. When putting the overall allocation and overall returns side by side, it is interesting to note that there appears to be a relation between the relative fund type performance and the average portfolio allocation. For instance, buyout funds performed best, and also constituted the largest part in the estimated portfolios of the analyzed LPs. This correlation between returns and weighting is robust also for the other fund types. In this vein it also interesting to note that home bias is strongest for VC funds, i.e. if LPs do expend the effort to invest in this fund type, then they prefer to invest in funds in their own geographic region. However, it should be noted that performance differences are timing and region dependent, while the portfolio allocation is a an average across time.

In **panel B**, the table shows significant deviations from the average by LP type. When viewed by individual LP types, it again seems that the LPs that overweighed buyout funds, for instance, also picked the best funds in this category. Those include PE FoFs, banks, investment corporations, insurances and corporate pension funds. For insurances, the average returns of the buyout funds also elevated this LP class to the top performer overall, as indicated by the + under the 'All' column. Only public pension funds and family offices underweighted buyout funds in a statistically significant degree. The LPs that underweighted VC funds also underperformed in this fund type, in particular when compared to endowments. In terms of home bias, FoFs seem least affected, while public pension funds, banks and family offices were particularly susceptible to the bias.

Comparison of Results

The table summarizes key results from this research. Panel A: The rows show general estimates for average LPs. Global (i.e. not just US) estimates were used. + indicates a stronger / larger estimated effect than average, – weaker / smaller estimates. For performances by fund type, two signs are used to show significant deviations. Panel B shows estimates for LP types, in deviation from the mean, i.e. if estimates differ in a statistically significant way. This is based on the 95% confidence interval of the LP estimates compared to the average LP. In this panel, only single signs are used.

	Preference					Performance				
A	**Portfolio Allocation**				**Home Bias**	**Relative Performance**				
	BO	LVC	EVC	Opp.		All	BO	LVC	EVC	Opp.
	46%	21%	8%	25%	+		++	–	– –	+
					VC>BO	Timing / Region Dependent				
B	**Across all LPs**					**Across all LPs**				
PE FoFs	+			–	–		+	–		
Public P.	–	–	–	+	+		–			
Banks	+	–	–	–	+		+	–	–	
Invest. Corp.	+						+	–	–	
Insurances	+	–	–			+	+			
Corp. P.	+	–	–					–		
Endowments									+	
Family O.	–			+	+					
Govt. Age.			–			–			–	–

Table 7.2: Comparison of Results

In summary, the side-by-side comparison suggests that **weighing among fund types and performance** therein might be correlated, even on the level of the individual LP type. In principle, two major factors can account for this. First, LPs who know they have a particular expertise in selecting a certain fund type also adjust their overall portfolio allocation. Second, because the LPs over-weigh a fund type, compared to the average, they also gain more experience in this fund type, and hence become better selectors. I would reason that both are possibilities and probably both apply to a degree. However, I would argue that the first argument is more valid. This is because in the analyses I usually also condition for LP experience, in years of investing, and LP size. Under the assumption that larger and older LPs also invested in more PE funds, both are also a measure of relative experience. Moreover, it is not uncommon for investors to be driven by assets they seem to know better. Indeed, many LPs who overweigh buyout funds are likely also investors who have had more experience in the 'classic' public equity markets – and the activities of buyout funds are more closely related to 'classic' public equity investors than the activities performed by VC funds. In other words, I reason that someone who has less experience in illiquid asset classes is more likely to prefer buyout investments over VC investments.[1]

Overall, therefore, the results all point to a clear demarcation between the **skills required to invest in buyout compared to VC funds**. Most results presented here, taken together, further corroborate this notion: Home bias is stronger for VC funds, experience and size mattered more for VC funds during the nineties, external advisors aid in VC investments, endowments did not achieve higher returns through risk-taking in VC funds and LPs close to well-performing VC funds outperformed their peers. All those results, in addition to the already described research by others on LP performance during the nineties and the criteria of selecting VC funds,[2] point to a separation in skills needed for buyout fund investments compared to other fund investments. It is likely that LPs interested in VC funds should really expend additional resources to build that expertise, hire managers with industry experience and maintain offices close to active VC funds.

7.2 Theory: Conclusion

Having reviewed the key results, I now turn to the theoretical framework that motivated the structure of the research. In chapter 2 I theorized the following:

LP-specific adverse selection and risk-sharing problems are solved through differential GP-selection.

Specifically, *differential GP selection* was further specified:

- **Adverse selection** problems are solved through extensive due diligence

[1] Interestingly, a similar result is found on the level of VC firms investing in portfolio companies, where VC fund managers prefer target management teams that are similar to themselves in terms of experience and training (see Franke et al. (2006)).

[2] In particular, see Tausend (2005) and Lerner et al. (2007b).

of agents in the selection process, while

- **Risk-sharing** preferences are expressed by investing in funds that match the intended risk-profile.

Overall, my results are an indication that indeed, LPs differ in a statistically significant way: First, they exhibit statistically significant differences in their fund preferences. This might reflect differences in risk-profiles. Second, they differ in their ability to invest in good funds. This might reflect differences in their ability to overcome adverse selection problems. Therefore, based on the results, the hypotheses and with them the theory cannot be rejected. This indicates that the PE market encompasses participants with different abilities, risk profiles and that PE is indeed an interesting testbed to comparatively analyze the behavior of different investor types.

7.3 Outlook

The results on preferences, performances and the synthesis thereof **significantly extend previous findings** on LP investments. In particular, the analysis of both LP preferences and performances over such a time-span is new. Moreover, it is the first time that global LP investments, not just that of LPs from a few countries, have been analyzed. In addition, it presents additional insights into the possible reasons behind LP investment success. The detailed discussion at the end of the respective chapters also showed that many of the results match research results on investor behavior in asset classes other than private equity. This suggests that many results, by extension, are also applicable to investor behavior in general.

The theoretical and empirical results, however, also show the **limits of the research**. I base the analyses on a large number of recorded investments by LPs in GPs. While this yields some exciting results, the methodologies also have some shortcomings. Most significantly, I can only examine if an investment took place, but not the investments that did not take place, and for what reason. This issue is particularly important for the question of LP preferences – which is why I tried to use a synthetic panel with different methods. Still, ideally, a true panel dataset, one that can also correct better for time-series correlations, should be used. Also, I can only conjecture about preference and selection ability from the *ex-post* recorded investments and results. However, I cannot look 'inside' LPs. Unfortunately, directly examining the investment decision process will be difficult, and only a combination of methods will shed light. For instance, Tausend (2005) uses a number of methods, including surveys and conjoint-analysis, to assess selection criteria used by FoFs in their selection of VC funds. While very instructive, such methods alone also suffer from shortcomings. Only 'ideal' preferences and criteria can be measured. However, additional factors, such as the subjective 'feeling' by the investor, or the reputation of the LP that drives the GP's fundraising effort, cannot easily be identified. Moreover, the *ex-ante* defined selection criteria must then still be linked to actually realized returns. One such recent effort is partly presented by Kaplan et al. (2007) on the level of GPs and their portfolio companies: They analyze 'soft' criteria of new CEOs that are installed by PE firms after acquisition of the portfolio firm, and link those criteria to the success of the firms thereafter. Likewise, a large-scale assessment of fund preferences and fund selection criteria used by LPs, linked to the actually realized returns of funds selected by the LPs, would shed more light on why LP types differ in their success as investors.

Still, already in this research I offered a range of pointers for **future research** and question marks for practitioners. For example, I touched on the role of *other LPs* in the investment decision, as well as *investment objectives*. In addition, some LPs indicated that their size might be an impacting factor on the investment decision. In fact, as outlined then outlined in greater detail, there might indeed be a correlation, even within the single LP type, between the increasing size of the LP and the choice of the fund. I called this *size bias*. Unfortunately, neither of these could be tested using the data at hand. Instead, future researchers might attempt to approach LPs directly, for instance through surveys and / or methods such as conjoint-analysis. Interestingly, I also highlighted correlations of the results between preferences and performances. This may point to a certain *simultaneity in the decision process* – future research might thus employ simultaneous equation models to identify marginal effects of perceived performance potential on the general fund preference.

This research also leads to a number of **follow-on questions** for further research. First, the apparent division between 'good' buyout and VC investors, underscored by the role of LP proximity, has important implications for the 'financing innovation chain'. In many instances, VC funds are seen as important catalysts for the emergence of innovative start-ups. This could be an extension of the innovation triad of universities, start-ups and VC firms – by investors that provide VC funds their finances. An interesting and fascinating research area would therefore be to further explore the exact nature of the interaction between LP and PE (VC) funds. This would also have important policy implications: National, or even regional, differences in tax or regulatory burdens might impact the ultimate providers of VC funding more than is currently thought. Second, the division of buyout- and VC investment skills also has important ramifications for industry practitioners. The results question if LPs without special VC expertise and who are not located close to booming start-up areas still invest in VC funds. Instead, many LPs should possibly instead employ external advisors, open offices in those areas and hire experienced VC fund investors. Additional research would highlight if investors should indeed expend those additional costs. Third, it should be an interesting question to explore if indeed and how structural implications lead to the identified home bias. One could investigate if the home bias is due to limited personnel and geographic focus of the LPs. If so, policy makers, for instance, may wonder how public pension funds can fulfill their fiduciary role when investing in PE funds. Last, more generally, additional research is warranted into how the PE fund investment market functions on a practical level. Little is known, from an academic point of view, how LPs 'learn' about fundraising funds and what factors are significant in this respect. For instance, LP reputation likely plays a significant role – both for fundraising GPs, as well as for less informed LPs who might try to copy the investment strategy of LPs with high reputations. Detailed analyses of all these questions would enhance the general functioning, or efficiency, of the PE market.

Bibliography

Allen, F., 1993. Stock markets and resource allocation. In: Mayer, C., Vives, X. (Eds.), Capital Markets and Financial Intermediation. Cambridge University Press, Cambridge, Massachusetts, 81–107.

Allen, F., Gale, D., 2000. Comparing Financial Systems. MIT Press, Cambridge, Massachusetts.

Ashenfelter, O., 1978. Estimating the effect of training programs on earnings. The Review of Economics and Statistics 60 (1), 47–57.

Atteslander, P., 2000. Methoden der empirischen Sozialforschung. Vol. 9. de Gruyter, Berlin, New York.

Atteslander, P., Kopp, M., 1995. Befragung. In: Roth, E., Heidenreich, K. (Eds.), Sozialwissenschaftliche Methoden, 4th Edition. Oldenburg Verlag München Wien, 146–174.

Barber, B. M., Odean, T., 2006. All that glitters: The effect of attention and news on the buying behavior of individual and institutional investors. EFA 2005 Moscow Meetings Paper and SSRN Working Paper 460660.

Barberis, N., Shleifer, A., May 2003. Style investing. Journal of Financial Economics 68 (2), 161–199.

Carhart, M. M., Carpenter, J. N., Lynch, A. W., Musto, D. K., 2002. Mutual fund survivorship. The Review of Financial Studies 15 (5), 1439–1463.

CGFS, February 2007. Institutional investors, global savings and asset allocation. Committe on the Global Financial System Papers, Bank for International Settlements 27.

Clark, G. L., 2004. Pension fund governance: expertise and organizational form. Journal of Pension Economics and Finance 3 (02), 233–253.

Clark, G. L., Caerlewy-Smith, E., Marshall, J. C., 2006. Pension fund trustee competence: decision making in problems relevant to investment practice. Journal of Pension Economics and Finance 5 (01), 91–110.

Clark, G. L., Caerlewy-Smith, E., Marshall, J. C., 2007. The consistency of UK pension fund trustee decision-making. Journal of Pension Economics and Finance 6 (01), 67–86.

Cochrane, J. H., Jan 2005. The risk and return of venture capital. Journal of Financial Economics 75 (1), 3–52.

Cook, D. O., Kieschnick, R. L., McCullough, B. D., 2007. Regression analysis of proportions in finance with self selection. SSRN Working Paper 1070261.

Cooper, I. A., Kaplanis, E., 1994. Home bias in equity portfolios, inflation hedging, and international capital market equilibrium. Review of Financial Studies 7, 45–60.

Coval, J. D., Moskowitz, T. J., 1999. Home bias at home: Local equity preference in domestic portfolios. The Journal of Finance 54 (6), 2045–2073.

Covitz, D., Liang, N., 2002. Recent developments in the private equity market and the role of preferred returns. Division of Research and Statistics Board of Governors of the Federal Reserve System, Washington, D.C.

Davis, E. P., Steil, B., 2001. Institutional investors. MIT Press, Cambridge, Massachusetts.

Davis, S. J., Haltiwanger, J., Jarmin, R., Lerner, J., Miranda, J., 2008. Private equity and employment. In: The Global Economic Impact of Private Equity Report 2008. The World Economic Forum 2008.

Diller, C., Kaserer, C., February 2008. What drives private equity returns? Fund inflows, skilled GPs, and/or risk? European Financial Management 14 (Published Online).

Eisenhardt, K. M., Jan 1989. Agency theory: An assessment and review. The Academy of Management Review 14 (1), 57–74.

EVCA, June 2006a. EVCA reporting guidelines. European Venture Capital Association.

EVCA, October 2006b. International private equity and venture capital valuation guidelines. European Venture Capital Association.

Fenn, G. W., Liang, N., Prowse, S., 1995. The economics of the private equity market. Board of Governors of the Federal Reserve System, Washington, DC.

Franke, N., Gruber, M., Harhoff, D., Henkel, J., Nov 2006. What you are is what you like - similarity biases in venture capitalists' evaluations of start-up teams. Journal of Business Venturing 21 (6), 802–826.

Franke, N., Gruber, M., Henkel, J., Hoisl, K., 2004. Die Bewertung von Gründerteams durch Venture-Capital-Geber. Eine empirische Analyse. Die Betriebswirtschaft 64 (6), 651–670.

French, K. R., Poterba, J. M., 1991. Investor diversification and international equity markets. American Economic Review 81, 222–226.

Fried, V. H., Hisrich, R. D., 1994. Toward a model of venture capital investment decision making. Financial Management 23 (3), 28–37.

Fritsch, M., Schilder, D., 2006a. Does venture capital investment really require spatial proximity? An empirical investigation. Discussion Papers on Entrepreneurship, Growth and Public Policy (14). Max Planck Institute of Economics.

Fritsch, M., Schilder, D., 2006b. Is venture capital a regional business? - The role of syndication. Discussion Papers on Entrepreneurship, Growth and Public Policy (25). Max Planck Institute of Economics.

Frommann, H., Dahmann, A., 2003. Zur volkswirtschaftlichen Bedeutung von Private Equity und Venture Capital. Bundesverband Deutscher Kapitalbeteiligungsgesellschaften. Berlin.

Froot, K., Teo, M., 2004. Equity style returns and institutional investor flows. NBER Working Paper W10355.

Golec, J. H., 1992. Empirical tests of principal-agent model of the investor-investment advisor relationship. Journal of Financial and Quantitative Analysis 27, 81–96.

Gompers, P. A., 1995. Optimal investment, monitoring, and the staging of venture capital. Journal of Finance 50 (5), 1461–1489.

Gompers, P. A., 1996. Grandstanding in the venture capital industry. Journal of Financial Economics 42 (1), 133–156.

Gompers, P. A., Lerner, J., 1996. The use of covenant: An empirical analysis of venture partnership agreements. Journal of Law and Economics 39, 463–498.

Gompers, P. A., Lerner, J., 1998. What drives venture capital fundraising. Brookings papers on economic activity, 149–204.

Gompers, P. A., Lerner, J., 1999. An analysis of compensation in the U.S. venture capital partnership. Journal of Financial Economics 51 (1), 3–44.

Gompers, P. A., Lerner, J., Feb 2000. Money chasing deals? The impact of fund inflows on private equity valuations. Journal of Financial Economics 55 (2), 281–325.

Gompers, P. A., Lerner, J., Spr 2001. The Venture Capital Revolution. Journal of Economic Perspectives 15 (2), 145–168.

Gompers, P. A., Metrick, A., Feb 2001. Institutional investors and equity prices. Quarterly Journal of Economics 116 (1), 229–259.

Grinblatt, M., Titman, S., Wermers, R., 1995. Momentum investment strategies, portfolio performance, and herding: A study of mutual fund behavior. American Economic Review 85 (5), 1088–1105.

Hagenmüller, M., 2004. Investor Relations von Private-Equity-Partnerships. Ph.D. thesis, Technische Universität München.

Hastings, J. S., 2004. Vertical relationships and competition in retail gasoline markets: Empirical evidence from contract changes in southern California. The American Economic Review 94 (1), 317–328.

Hege, U., Palomino, F., Schwienbacher, A., 2003. Determinants of venture capital performance: Europe and United States. HEC School of Management.

Hellmann, T., Lindsey, L., Puri, M., 2008. Building relationships early: Banks in venture capital. Review of Financial Studies 21 (2), 513.

IFSL, September 2007. Fund management 2007. International Financial Services London Research.

IMF, April 2007. Global financial stability report. International Monetary Fund.

Jones, C. M., Rhodes-Kropf, M., 2003. The price of diversifiable risk in venture capital and private equity. AFA 2003 Washington, DC Meetings. SSRN Working Paper 342841.

Kaplan, S. N., Klebanov, M. M., Sorensen, M., 2007. Which CEO characteristics and abilities matter? NBER Working Paper W14195.

Kaplan, S. N., Schoar, A., Aug 2005. Private equity performance: Returns, persistence, and capital flows. Journal of Finance 60 (4), 1791–1823.

Kaplan, S. N., Stromberg, P., May 2001. Venture capitalists as principals: Contracting, screening, and monitoring. American Economic Review 91 (2), 426–430.

Kaplan, S. N., Stromberg, P., Apr 2003. Financial contracting theory meets the real world: An empirical analysis of venture capital contracts. Review of Economic Studies 70 (2), 281–315.

Kaserer, C., Diller, C., 2004. European private equity funds - A cash flow based performance analysis. SSRN Working Paper 547142.

Kieschnick, R., McCullough, B. D., 2003. Regression analysis of variates observed on (0, 1): Percentages, proportions and fractions. Statistical Modelling: An International Journal 3 (3), 193 – 213.

Kortum, S., Lerner, J., Win 2000. Assessing the contribution of venture capital to innovation. Rand Journal of Economics 31 (4), 674–692.

Kortum, S. S., Lerner, J., 1998. Does venture capital spur innovation? SSRN Working Paper 227614.

Lakonishok, J., Shleifer, A., Vishny, R., 1992. The structure and performance of the money management industry. Brookings Papers: Microeconomics 1992, 339–379.

Lerner, J., 1994. The syndication of venture capital investments. Financial Management 23 (3), 16–27.

Lerner, J., 1995. Venture capitalists and the oversight of private firms. The Journal of Finance 50 (1), 301–318.

Lerner, J., Schoar, A., Apr 2004. The illiquidity puzzle: Theory and evidence from private equity. Journal of Financial Economics 72 (1), 3–40.

Lerner, J., Schoar, A., Wang, J., 2007a. Secrets of the academy: The drivers of university endowment success. Harvard Business School Finance Working Paper No. 07-066 and SSRN Working Paper 1027450.

Lerner, J., Schoar, A., Wongsunwai, W., April 2007b. Smart institutions, foolish choices: The limited partner performance puzzle. The Journal of Finance 62 (2), 731–764.

Lerner, J., Sorensen, M., Stromberg, P., 2008. Private equity and long-run investments: The case of innovation. In: The Global Economic Impact of Private Equity Report 2008. The World Economic Forum 2008.

Ljungqvist, A., Richardson, M. P., 2003a. The cash flow, return and risk characteristics of private equity. NYU, Finance Working Paper and SSRN Working Paper 369600.

Ljungqvist, A., Richardson, M. P., 2003b. The investment behavior of private equity fund managers. SSRN Working Paper 482546.

Lossen, U., 2006. The performance of private equity funds: Does diversification matter? Munich Business Research Working Paper Series No. 2006-14 and SSRN Working Paper 9167702.

MacMillan, I. C., Kulow, D. M., Khoylian, R., 1989. Venture Capitalists' involvement in their investments: Extent and performance. Journal of Business Venturing 4 (1), 27–47.

MacMillan, I. C., Siegel, R., Subbanarasimha, P. N., 1985. Criteria used by venture capitalists to evaluate new venture proposals. Journal of Business Venturing 1 (1), 119–128.

Manyem, S., 2002. Effect of investment focus and manager selection in private equity returns. University of Chicago, Graduate School of Business.

Mayer, C., Schoors, K. J., Yafeh, Y., 2005. Sources of funds and investment activities of venture capital funds: Evidence from Germany, Israel, Japan and the UK. Journal of Corporate Finance 11 (3), 586–608.

Merton, R. K., Kendall, P. L., 1993. Das fokussierte Interview. In: Hopf, C., Weingarten, E. (Eds.), Qualitative Sozialforschung. Klett-Cotta, Stuttgart, 171–203.

Meuleman, M., Wright, M., 2006. Industry concentration, syndication networks and competition in the U.K. private equity market for management buy-outs. SSRN Working Paper 960420.

Neher, D. V., 1999. Staged Financing: An Agency Perspective. The Review of Economic Studies 66 (2), 255–274.

Nielsen, K. M., 2005. The return to pension funds' private equity investments: Another piece to the private equity premium puzzle? Financial Management Association 2006 Salt Lake City Meetings.

Papke, L. E., Wooldridge, J. M., 1996. Econometric methods for fractional response variables with an application to 401 (k) plan participation rates. Journal of Applied Econometrics 11 (6), 619–632.

Petersen, M. A., Rajan, R. G., 2002. Does distance still matter? The information revolution in small business lending. The Journal of Finance 57 (6), 2533–2570.

Phalippou, L., Gottschalg, O., 2007. Performance of private equity funds. SSRN Working Paper 473221.

Ramakrishnan, R. T. S., Thakor, A. V., Mar. 1984. The valuation of assets under moral hazard. The Journal of Finance 39 (1), 229–238.

Riquelme, H., Rickards, T., 1992. Hybrid conjoint analysis: An estimation probe in new venture decisions. Journal of Business Venturing 7 (6), 505–518.

Romain, A., van Pottelsberghe, B., 2004. The economic impact of venture capital. Discussion Paper. Series 1: Studies of the Economic Research Centre, No. 18 / 2004. Deutsche Bundesbank.

Rudolph, B., 2001. Venture Capital und Private Equity als Finanzierungs - und Anlageinstrumente. In: Hummel, D., Breuer, R.-E. (Eds.), Handbuch Europäischer Kapitalmarkt. Gabler Verlag, Wiesbaden, 502–515.

Rudolph, B., 2003. Theorie und Empirie der Asset Allocation. In: Dichtl, H., Kleeberg, J. M., Schlenger, C. (Eds.), Handbuch Asset Allocation - Innovative Konzepte zur systematischen Portfolioplanung. Uhlenbruch Verlag, Bad Soden, 3–26.

Sahlman, W. A., 1990. The structure and governance of venture-capital organizations. Journal of Financial Economics 27, 473–521.

Sapienza, H. J., 1992. When do venture capitalists add value? Journal of Business Venturing 7 (1), 9–27.

Sapienza, H. J., Timmons, J. A., 1989. The roles of venture capitalists in new ventures: what determines their importance. Academy of Management Best Paper Proceedings, 74–78.

Shleifer, A., Vishny, R., 1997. The Limits of Arbitrage. The Journal of Finance 52, 35–55.

Steiner, M., Bruns, C., 2000. Wertpapiermanagement. Vol. 7. Schäffer-Poeschel, Stuttgart.

Swensen, D. F., 2000. Pioneering portfolio management: An unconventional approach to institutional investment. Free Press, New York.

Tausend, C., 2005. Selektion von Venture Capital-Fonds durch institutionelle Investoren. Ph.D. thesis, Ludwig-Maximilians-Universität München.

Tyebjee, T. T., Bruno, A. V., 1984. A model of venture capitalist investment activity. Management Science 30 (9), 1051–1066.

von Braun, E., Harhoff, D., 2004. Risiko und Renditen von Private-Equity-Investitionen, unpublished working paper, Ludwig-Maximilians-Universität München.

Weidig, T., Mathonet, P.-Y., 2004. The risk profile of private equity. SSRN Working Paper 495482.

Werner, I. M., Tesar, L. L., August 1995. Home bias and high turnover. Journal of International Money and Finance 14 (4), 467–492.

Wooldridge, J. M., 2003. Introductory econometrics: A modern approach, 2nd Edition. South-Western / Thomson, Australia.

Zucker, L. G., Darby, M. R., Brewer, M. B., 1998. Intellectual human capital and the birth of U.S. biotechnology enterprises. The American Economic Review 88 (1), 290–306.

MIX
Papier aus verantwortungsvollen Quellen
Paper from responsible sources
FSC® C105338

FSC
www.fsc.org

If you have any concerns about our products,
you can contact us on
ProductSafety@springernature.com

In case Publisher is established outside the EU,
the EU authorized representative is:
Springer Nature Customer Service Center GmbH
Europaplatz 3, 69115 Heidelberg, Germany

Printed by Libri Plureos GmbH
in Hamburg, Germany